Crisis Communications

Crisis Communications

What Every Executive Needs to Know

DEVON DOUGHERTY

Walker and Company
New York

First published in the United States of America in 1992
by Walker Publishing Company, Inc.

Published simultaneously in Canada by Thomas Allen & Son
Canada, Limited, Markham, Ontario

Library of Congress Cataloging-in-Publication Data
Dougherty, Devon.
   Crisis communications : what every executive needs to know / Devon
Dougherty.
      p.   cm.
   ISBN 0-8027-1195-2
   1. Crisis management.   2. Communication in organizations.
3. Strategic planning.   I. Title.
HD49.D68   1992
658.4—dc20   92-15292
                                                                CIP

Book design by Susan Phillips

Printed in the United States of America

10   9   8   7   6   5   4   3   2   1

Dedicated to
Kelsey Lauren Dougherty,
who blessed us with her arrival during the writing of this book

Contents

Part V: SAMPLE PLANS

Part VI: ADDENDA

Acknowledgments

To Kim Schwartz of the American Red Cross, who originally agreed to write the foreword and then became so enthusiastic about the need for this book that she offered great support and insight in the areas of press relations and the specific communication needs in times of disaster.

The American Red Cross for its support and appreciation of the importance of crisis communications.

Diane Thomas, APR of the Santa Ana Unified School District, who gave excellent insight into the communications needs of public school administrators.

Nick Sylvester, veteran public relations practitioner in health care, for taking the time to talk about his experiences and offering his support and a case study from Alvarado Hospital Medical Center in San Diego.

Di Saggau of Westside Community Schools; Maria Greene of Duke Power Company; Catherine Boire of Marriott Hotels, Resorts, and Suites; Mark Davis of Union Pacific Railroad; and Diane Reesman of the City of Los Angeles Department of Airports for their help in supplying cases and sample plans to make this a practical and useful guidebook.

Deborah Stein and Heather MacLellan for research and other support.

Special thanks to fellow practitioners who have been supportive in my professional development, especially Laer Pearce, APR, David Pincus, APR, and Joan Gladstone, APR.

Above all, thanks to my parents and best friend, who gave me moral support, and my wife, Jolene, whose skills and tireless efforts were crucial in the completion of this book.

Foreword

When I was approached to write the foreword as part of the development of this book, I not only jumped at the opportunity, but also offered to assist with my knowledge on media relations and to provide a case study of the American Red Cross and the San Francisco earthquake.

There is not enough information out there to help communicators in crisis, nor does a current textbook outline the crisis expertise of the American Red Cross, the only agency in the United States mandated by Congress to assist disaster victims.

The American Red Cross realized the importance of crisis communications, and during the writing of this book I was on a national committee to prepare a complete crisis communication plan and notebook for our organization. The recent disasters of Hurricane Hugo and the San Francisco earthquake really pointed out the need for the Red Cross to be able not only to communicate its expertise as a disaster relief organization, but to be able to handle crisis communications, too.

I have learned over the years that handling the relief efforts is just one part of the overall crisis and that communicating during the disaster is equally important.

As we became aware of communication problems during some recent disasters it became apparent that we as a major disaster relief organization would also have to have a communications plan. Our plan is now developed and being distributed nationwide to our various chapters. This plan will surely assist in our efforts to get our message across during a disaster and communicate all the critical information during a crisis.

I am pleased to have been asked to contribute to this crisis communications manual as it is something we as practitioners desperately need. With a theoretical examination of the steps to build a plan, combined with sample cases and examples of other organizations' communications plans, I feel that this will be an invaluable tool for all of us.

The importance of communicating effectively during a crisis cannot be overstated and with the experience I have gained through the American Red Cross and the contacts I've made with key individuals, such as David Giroux, Peggy McGinley, Henry Tuttle, Hope Tuttle, Bud Good, and my husband, Stan Schwartz, I know that I have benefited from the study of this very important and specialized area of public relations and I feel that practitioners are daily gaining new understanding and appreciation of this field.

—Kimberly Schwartz, Director, Marketing/Communications,
American Red Cross, Greater Long Beach Chapter

Preface

When I was preparing to teach a course on crisis communications at a local university, I found there were no textbooks on the subject. True, I had read articles in the *PR Journal* and had attended seminars and luncheons where the topic was discussed. By drawing from personal experience, articles, and some chapters of various books on communications, public relations, or crisis management, I was able to put together a "hands-on" class for students studying crisis communications for the first time.

What this book on crisis communications seeks to accomplish, then, is to pull together all these diverse resources into one easy-to-use manual not only for students learning the subject for the first time, but for practitioners with a need for quick reference in times of crisis, or a guideline to developing a plan by using the forms contained in these pages.

This handbook follows a pattern used in classroom learning by going chronologically step by step from preparation to crisis to aftermath. The cases that follow are used to illustrate various aspects of crisis communications and are designed to foster analysis and discussion.

None of the citations are presented to point fingers in a malicious manner. Rather, any company that made a "mistake" in crisis communications has greatly furthered the study of this all-important and rather new area of communications. From these mistakes we can all learn and benefit. We are therefore indebted to those who ventured first into these uncharted waters and showed us where the challenges were in crisis communications.

As you read and use this book, I hope you will see a few very important themes ringing clearly through: planning, managing, evaluating, and "having your house in order." Practitioners point to the importance of planning and preparation in addition to being able to manage and control the crisis communications so that the problem can be contained and not spread into a far greater crisis. An important part, too, of any public relations function, especially a crisis, involves evaluation after the crisis has passed—although we will note that evaluating during the crisis to ensure that you are staying on target is critical, too.

But so many crises can be averted in the first place by simply having your house in order. This theme is one of the most important, as it simply equates to good business. No amount of preplanned messages would have helped a communicator standing on the deck of the *Titanic*—what was needed was planning and exacting safety procedures to avert the disaster in the first place— getting the house in order.

You will see cases throughout this book that indicate a company was setting itself up for a crisis. And when a crisis can be avoided in the first place by simply operating on sound business principles, it should. Anything else is simply tragic and no amount of good communications will save a company from the rightful wrath of the press and the company's various publics.

Finally, I hope this book will also bring forth the point that no company is exempt from a crisis, and waiting until one occurs before you begin the planning process will have disastrous consequences.

Introduction

One recent Wednesday evening, I turned on the television to see the "top of the news" and get caught up on the day's activities. Now, there was nothing special about this day—really no different from any other day. As usual it was another typically uplifting newscast: A bus crashed on a mountain road outside Palm Springs, California, killing seven Girl Scouts and their leaders; an Amtrak train derailed in South Carolina killing seven; a crash two days earlier involving a Southern Pacific train, which dumped toxic material next to a freeway, was still causing the closure of a major interstate highway in California; and a little girl was killed in a crosswalk by a bus.

I am not trying to be morbid. Rather, I want to emphasize the point that on any given day disaster could befall your organization. The disaster may be anticipated, but it usually is not and occurs in a manner one would not suspect. Borrowing from the Boy Scouts of America, one phrase becomes clearly important: Are you prepared?

If you were the bus company that supplied the vehicle to the Girl Scouts, would you be ready to take action to handle the immediate needs, determine the cause of the accident, communicate your prior safety record, and inform your board of directors and current customers about what happened? If you were the Girl Scout council, how would you communicate with the families of those involved, answer media inquiries, and communicate about the countless trips and activities that occur every day and help innumerable numbers of young people?

If you were with Amtrak or Southern Pacific, how would you answer questions about the toxic chemicals that spilled and closed the freeway, or why the passenger train jumped the track? Would you be prepared to show a sterling safety record or a history of problems? Would you be able to communicate with the correct publics in a timely manner so that passenger travel would not dip, negatively affecting revenue? Would you be able to contact key decision makers who influence legislation for the railroad industry and stave off a backlash of regulatory measures?

The scenarios are endless—and yet so real. They happen every day to some company. Handled incorrectly, a crisis can put you out of business. Handled correctly, you will, at the very least, return to normal quickly with minimal impact; and, at best, you may find your image enhanced.

That is what this book is about—preparing for and handling crises in a step-by-step format. Throughout the book we will discuss theories and provide actual cases to examine. Most importantly, there will be study guides, exercises, and checklists that you may use to become involved in the process of developing your own crisis communications plan.

There is no time like the present to begin preparing, because your company's turn at being on the "top of the news" may be next.

Part I

Before the Crisis

1

Know the Organization: or Finding the Skeletons

Of key importance before developing a crisis communications plan is first understanding your organization. Who are you, why do you exist, what product(s) do you provide, who are your customers, what is your mission? All these questions need to be asked and answered before you can begin the process of developing your plan. Why? Because unless you truly understand your organization, you won't know whom you'll need to address in a crisis, what message you will want to communicate, nor will you be able to assess the impact of a crisis on your organization.

When we speak of knowing your organization, we mean understanding your various departments, the products produced, where your satellite offices are, your key managers and directors, and the myriad other details about your company. If you are a nonprofit organization or service provider you should know how and why your services are rendered, who donates, your board of directors, and your governing bylaws and rules and regulations.

The best place to begin with understanding your company or organization is the mission statement. The importance of this statement, or credo, is best illuminated by David R. Clare, Johnson & Johnson president and executive committee chairman, when he noted the riveting effect of their credo after the Tylenol tampering crisis. He commented that the sound business management philosophy embodied in the company's credo enabled him to make the decisions that led to the survival of Tylenol. Following is that credo written by Robert Wood Johnson:

> We believe our first responsibility is to the doctors, nurses and patients, to others and all others who use our products and services. In meeting their needs everything we do must be of high quality. We must constantly strive to reduce our costs in order to maintain reasonable prices. Customers' orders must be serviced promptly and accurately. Our suppliers and distributors must have an opportunity to make a fair profit.
>
> We are responsible to our employees, the men and women who work with us throughout the world. Everyone must be considered as an individual. We must respect their dignity and recognize their merit. They must have a sense of security in their jobs. Compensation must be fair and adequate, and working conditions clean, orderly and safe. Employees must feel free to make suggestions and complaints. There must be equal opportunity for employment, development and advancement for those qualified. We must provide competent management, and their actions must be just and ethical.
>
> We are responsible to the communities in which we live and work and to the world community as well. We must be good citizens—support good works and charities and bear our fair share of taxes. We must encourage civic improvements and better health and education. We must maintain in good order the property we are privileged to use, protecting the environment and natural resources.
>
> Our final responsibility is to our stockholders. Business must make a sound profit. We must experiment with new ideas. Research must be carried on, innovative programs developed and mistakes paid for. New equipment must be purchased, new facilities provided and new products launched. Reserves must be created to provide for adverse times. When we operate according to these principles, the stockholders should realize a fair return.[1]

Does your organization have a mission statement? Is it accessible, known, and understood by all members? If not, now is a good time to take it off the shelf, dust it off, and make it a useful, dynamic credo that should underpin all your organization does. If you don't have one, now is the time to develop one. There are many good references and business support guides on the subject.

Besides knowing the business, through understanding the goals, mission, products, personnel structure, history, and the like, one almost needs to be an investigator searching for the "skeletons," or areas of vulnerability in one's own company. If they do exist, and chances are no organization is without them, it is just a matter of time before one rears its ugly head. A prepared crisis communications coordinator will seek out these skeletons, understand them, and either work to have them corrected or be prepared to communicate when the inevitable and ensuing crisis occurs.

Conducting an audit may be another way of looking at this form of preparation. Are there some weak links in your structure, product, or service? Are you vulnerable to some new legislation or community opinion? Knowing your weaknesses allows you to prepare for communications should a crisis occur.

In learning about your organization everything can be summed up in the business expression "management by walking around" or learning about your organization to note potential problems. Here is a brief checklist of activities you can complete to conduct your audit and to learn about your organization:

- Review the files in your office to gain historical perspective on activities that have occurred in your organization.
- If your public relations department has kept information on news conferences, review these transcripts and notes.
- Look at news clips and previous news releases.
- Examine memos that have been distributed in the organization.
- Look at the annual report and minutes of board meetings.
- Review any publications and printed materials your organization has distributed.
- Review notebooks that have been put together on various subjects including personnel manuals.
- Spend some time interviewing key managers and board members if possible.
- If you are part of an agency, interview your clients and visit their place of business.
- Spend some time talking with outside consultants about your organization and experts in the area of production, legal, personnel, community relations, government affairs, sales and marketing, physical plant operations, and other specific areas.
- Examine trade journals to learn what is going on in the industry.
- Get on the mailing list of other companies and organizations to track what is going on elsewhere.
- Review your bylaws, rules, and regulations.
- Examine your mission statement.
- Spend time on a daily basis reading newspapers and publications from areas in which your organization operates to learn about community trends and concerns.
- Spend time within your professional organizations to speak with other practitioners and learn of their concerns. Develop lines of communication with fellow practitioners.

At the heart of all this is the simple concept of truly wanting to know and understand your organization. Walk around, talk to people, attend the board meetings, ensure that you are a part of the management team, and listen to what is going on. Read all materials your company produces and study the industry you operate in by reading the trade journals and keeping abreast of business trends. Understand your relative strengths and weaknesses.

After you have spent the necessary time researching and understanding your organization you will need to begin specifically seeking out and labeling those areas in which your organization could be vulnerable to a crisis.

There are two categories of these potential crises, the first being those that can be averted, and the second, those crises that cannot be averted. An example of the former would be a bus company not checking the brakes of its buses and yet letting these vehicles continue to carry people. If the brakes were ever to fail and an accident occurred, the bus company would have a crisis on its hands, and it would be a crisis that could have been avoided if they had proactively worked to ensure all vehicles were safe through regular brake checks.

An example of the latter would be a youth organization planning an activity that involved some form of transportation such as buses. Just as there are risks involved in life, there are risks involved in traveling the highways, and an accident can and sometimes does occur ending in severe injury or death. While the organization will take every opportunity to ensure the safety of its participants, that is all that can be done. So a crisis may still occur even when all the necessary precautions have been taken.

You need to spend the time seeking out those vulnerable areas within your company where you can prevent a crisis and should immediately begin to correct the problem. You should then begin to research those areas where a crisis could occur yet may not be preventable. This is where a crisis communication plan comes into play. You note potential problems, you anticipate that they may occur even after taking every precaution to avoid them, and then label a set of steps to take place to handle the situation and communicate during the crisis. A matrix is included to assist you in this process. It is divided into two key areas: 1) simply noting the crisis and 2) finding out or determining the ways in which the crisis will appear. In my classes I use this opportunity to have individuals discuss their companies and jointly come up with vulnerable points for each organization. Through the discussion process, individuals can list their weak areas and more importantly can talk about how a problem can occur. This speeds them on the way to developing a plan to communicate in the event of a crisis.

There is also a spot on the matrix to note those problems that are avoidable, such as safety issues, having resource manuals in place, and the like. It is a good idea to have background papers put together ahead of time on subjects of importance within your organization.

It is important for the practitioner to begin to analyze and to ask questions regarding the areas of vulnerability and the ramifications should a crisis occur. Here is a list of questions to guide you through this process:

- What is the main issue of the potential crisis, and which departments would be responsible (e.g., manufacturing, legal, public affairs, research)?
- How might the crisis escalate, and what would be the range of this escalation?
- Would you be in violation of any regulatory, local, state, or federal statutes, and what would be the implications?
- What are the legal ramifications?
- Would the crisis involve environmental concerns or affect the safety of the community?
- What would be the short- and long-term effects on the company, its production, and its ability to continue operating effectively, and how would the finances be affected?
- What impact would the crisis have on customers and their perception of your organization and its products or services?
- How might the investors be affected by the crisis?
- What knowledge do your employees have about the potential issue/crisis, and how would they be affected?
- How much and with what intensity would media be interested in such a crisis?
- Would such an issue or crisis just be the tip of the iceberg of a much larger and potentially more damaging crisis? It is important for you to examine the issue and see if it can lead or point to even greater problems such as known safety concerns, lax quality control standards, simmering employee relations problems, and other potential cans of worms. When you have such situations, you are opening yourself up for a protracted crisis, as every one of these becomes a potential story for the media and will be pursued.

So what are some examples of crises that might need a communications response? Here is just a partial list, yet it shows how wide a range there is, indicating that no company is really exempt from a crisis and hence the need to communicate effectively:

- Involvement in a government investigation
- Potential restrictive legislation
- New thrusts by the competition that endanger profitability
- Request for an interview by television's "60 Minutes," "20/20," or any investigative journalism team
- Product failure leading to injury or death of consumers
- Naming of the client in a multimillion-dollar lawsuit

- Plans for picketing or other demonstrations
- Extortion threats ranging from product tampering to bombs
- Disability or death of a key executive
- Hostile media queries
- Upheaval in the social environment
- Accidental contamination of places where people live and work
- Investigation by an agency of the government
- Mobilization of an adversary consumer group
- Conflict in the boardroom
- Fire, earthquake, storm
- Security concerns
- Product ban
- Employee problems (this could range from union strife to sexual harassment suits)
- Community concerns (is the planned plant expansion met with resistance?)
- Pollution and environmental concerns
- Pending lawsuits
- Regulatory changes
- Plant closings
- Layoffs
- Supplier problems
- Production problem
- Financial concerns (debt rating drops, stock price swings, poor earnings)
- Merger/Takeover
- Activist protests

Public relations professionals advocate going through your list and rating the crises on a scale of one to ten (ten being most likely) to prioritize the ones needing immediate attention.

It is important to mention another potential problem here, and that is the concerns associated with inflated egos. This happens as some individuals may actually secretly harbor a desire for publicity, and a crisis is just the way to accomplish that. Meaning, letting a crisis occur may actually be in someone's personal best interest. Take that concern into account early on as you look for ways to avoid a crisis.

Here are some other strategic questions that should be addressed as you initially determine potential problems and how best to handle them:

- What strengths do you and your company possess vis-à-vis the potential crisis?
- How might you minimize the issue?

- Can you form a coalition with others to attack the issue or crisis?
- Who will be there to help you, and how? (potential allies)
- Who might stand to gain from your misfortune, and how should this be handled?
- Who, outside the company, can be a resource or offer assistance?
- What speech or public-awareness opportunities do you have related to the issue?
- What additional information or research do you need on the issue?
- What backgrounders have been developed on the subject?

This is an excellent point in your preparation stage to review backgrounders the company has already developed and update those that are out of date. Also in all of the research you have compiled to this point and the issues that you have analyzed, do you see needs for new backgrounders to be developed? If so, now is the time in concert with public relations staff and even interns to develop a series of background papers so that you will have the information available should you be asked. And the process of developing the backgrounders forces the research process to be set down on paper.

Here is an example of what one company did for determining its vulnerability in a variety of situations:

CRISIS TYPE	VULNERABILITY	PRIORITY	ACTION
Cash	High and immediate	Top	Full attention
Industrial relations	High and immediate	Top	Full attention
Top management succession	Serious and current	High	Maintain awareness
Public perception	Serious and current	High	Maintain top awareness
Hostile takeover	Unlikely but possible	Moderate	Monitor
Sudden market shift	Remote	Low	None
Adverse international event	Remote	Low	None
Regulation and deregulation	None	None	None
Product	None	None	None[2]

As we began this section on finding your company's skeletons, or assessing your areas of vulnerability, we mentioned that one of the best ways to control a crisis is to avoid one in the first place. By examining your company with these various checklists and self-examination questions, you are possibly on the path to remedying potential critical problems and not having to deal with a crisis at all. If you do have a crisis, though, you are taking the first important steps to being prepared for it so that you can handle it effectively.

2

Form the Crisis Team

As any business person knows, the key to success comes from surrounding yourself with the best personnel. Almost any problem, be it low sales or budget concerns, can be solved by talented individuals. The same holds true for crisis communications—don't try to do it alone. Surround yourself with key decision-makers and knowledgeable experts so that critical viewpoints will be brought to bear on the situation. Step two in preparing for a crisis, then, is selecting the crisis communications team.

Of course, the key to having an effective team is not to wait until the crisis is upon you to begin thinking of those who should play a part. It is a good idea to have the team selected and meeting as you begin the early stages of crisis communication preparation. In this way you will benefit from experts from the outset and this support will have a strong positive impact on your final product.

One company, Crystal Cruises, chose as its crisis management team members the president, the senior vice president for marketing, the senior vice president for sales, the senior vice president for marine operations, the senior vice president for finance, and the senior vice president for Japanese media relations (as the parent company of Crystal Cruises is based in Japan). Now, add to this team the director of public relations and two key account managers from the company's public relations firm and you have a top-notch crisis communications team. (We will look at how this team effectively handled a crisis involving a fire in one of their ships in the case portion of this book.)

After you have gone through the steps of learning about your company in chapter one, you will be in a better position to begin labeling those individuals who should be a part of your team. Following the lead of other successful organizations, you will want to have the president of the organization and the director of public relations. A representative from the sales and marketing side of the organization will give you an important perspective of the consumer side of your organization as you begin planning. If your organization involves specific product lines you may want to have a series of individuals who could be involved depending on whether or not their product is involved in the crisis. For the purposes of planning you can choose one person from the product side of the company.

If your company has a large research and development department, you would want to include this perspective on your team. And finally, it is a good idea to have individuals representing the financial, personnel, and legal departments or areas of your company. Not every individual will be a standing member and called in during an actual crisis, but a broad grouping will prove invaluable as you enter the stage of finding areas in which you may be vulnerable and thereby head off a crisis before it occurs.

As you involve individuals in the planning process, you will not only be gaining valuable information to develop your crisis plan, but you will also learn how individuals work with one another and who would best handle the implementation of a plan during a crisis. Although some people behave differently in a crisis, you will have a general idea of their operating style.

The other positive effect of involving a wide group of individuals from a range of disciplines is that you will be starting the process of developing company support for your plan early on. As individuals participate, they will most likely "buy in" to the process and the plan, thus helping to facilitate the implementation of that plan should the need arise.

Once the general information is gathered, it is time to choose a small standing team of individuals and designated backups who will be your actual team. In determining the size, practitioners give us some guidelines and also suggest adding a newcomer to the group to give the person experience and training for the future:

As a general rule it is important to keep the task force as small as possible. The more people that are involved, the harder it becomes to reach decisions in an efficient way. The ideal number is about six to eight. Too small a group might lead to excessive caution, especially if those who are involved don't know one another very well. The key question in determining the size of the group is: "Is all the necessary knowledge present?"[3]

Each member will need to have knowledge about his or her respective field, be a decision maker, be a team player, and appear to work well under pressure or in a crisis mode. Practitioners note the importance of this team's not only working well in these respects, but also being able to analyze the incoming information and being able to develop a well-thought-out course of action. They must also be able to apply appropriately the crisis plan to the actual crisis. It is nearly impossible to anticipate every potential crisis and all will have their own subtle differences. For this reason, a plan needs to be flexible enough and based upon sound business practices and the philosophy of the company to be useful. The team members need to recognize this and have the authority to make decisions and take action.

It is also a good idea that members of the team be compensated for the extra duties they will be handling during the crisis, as these individuals will have to give up their outside interests and allow their normal duties to pile up during the crisis.

These individuals will then need to have specific crisis team roles besides providing information from their area of expertise. One individual needs to be selected as spokesperson with one or two others designated as backups. One individual should coordinate the team itself while another coordinates the physical arrangements (phones, communications, and the like). A member should also be given the responsibility of preparing the necessary statements and be backed up by others who can gather technical information should this be needed. And finally, a member should be designated to handle financial and legal considerations.

It is also important to look at the appropriate attributes of team members besides their technical abilities. Attributes that a team member should possess would include creative thought and being able to think independently as questions are many and answers are few during a crisis. Therefore a self-starter who will seek out information is very important. The individual should also be very flexible and be able to work well with all individuals whether it be employees, top management, government officials, reporters, emergency personnel, or other members of the team. The person should be tenacious in seeking out information and know where to go to get that information. In addition, the individual should be willing to accept responsibility. Good health and stamina are also important qualities, as a crisis can be extremely protracted. Rest may be at a premium during the event. This individual also should not have a large ego as this can get in the way of the team's effective handling of the crisis.

Your leader of the crisis team should possess all of the previous attributes in addition to the ability to listen well, keep focused on priority issues, plan and organize the follow-through for these issues, and work well with others. Creativity is of key importance along with the ability to accept the responsibilities and be able to achieve certain tasks by a deadline. All members of the team should possess ethical operating practices above reproach.

Public relations practitioners also note the need to have an individual from the outside be a member of your team and thus give an important fresh perspective to your group.

If your organization has offices or plants spread across the country or world where crises could also occur, you would want to designate a site coordinator to handle the gathering of information at the scene of the crisis. This information can be relayed to the command post for processing and dissemination. You will want to examine carefully the knee-jerk reaction of sending your CEO to the crisis site as spokesperson. As we cite cases throughout this book you will see that this is not necessarily an automatic response to a crisis.

Once the team is in place, they can assist in finalizing the plan you and your department have developed if there isn't a plan in place already. The team can then periodically meet to discuss possible crisis scenarios and even perform some practice drills.

This stage of the preparation process will be invaluable as you will discover different themes and angles in which a crisis could be played out. At a local nuclear power plant, the crisis plan is put through such a drill on a periodic basis and members of the press are even invited to participate. This fosters the opening of communications channels and allows team members some role-playing experience which will serve them well later should a crisis occur.

Your team, besides being well trained, should also be easy to reach since you can't plan when a crisis will occur. Team members should all have home numbers of each member in the group and should all know where and when each is traveling, whether it be for business or pleasure, and ways in which they can be reached. In certain crises, which your plan can state, you can have designated backups handle everything providing they are well trained and the crisis is one that your team has predetermined doesn't warrant calling individuals back from vacation. But there are going to be high-profile cases of a magnitude you have predetermined that will require the participation of all primary members.

3

Select the Key Publics

Once the crisis management team has taken inventory of potential problems the organization may face, and has outlined some initial responses to such situations, the task is then to identify the key publics with which communication must occur during a crisis. It will also be important to decide simultaneously which underlying message will be targeted toward each public.

One technique that may be helpful at this point is once again to bring the crisis management team together to discuss and make a list of the key publics. It is important to think beyond the most common groups and identify those that may even be indirectly affected in the event of a crisis. Depending on the size of the company, domestic or international, for-profit or not-for-profit, the list may differ from organization to organization. Below is just a partial list to assist in beginning the process:

- Board members
- Community and civic leaders
- Customers
- Shareholders
- Clients
- Neighbors (within the immediate business area)
- Financial partners
- Government agencies

- Regulatory agencies
- Vendors
- Certain competitors
- Family members
- Analysts
- Legal groups
- Media
- Subsidiary heads
- Employees
- Plant managers
- Union officials
- Retirees
- Pension holders
- Sales/Marketing personnel

Your list may differ, but it is important to develop as comprehensive a list as possible for your organization and industry. Not every public may need to be communicated with in every crisis, but having the broadest possible list will allow your organization to pick those specific publics in a given incident.

You may find it helpful then to analyze the list a second time to list the publics in order of priority with the most important public listed first. If this becomes too difficult a task, then listing broad constituent categories and dividing these categories into most important to least important may speed your crisis team on its way as it focuses on the most important groups.

To further define the various publics, you can divide them into four divisions:

1. Enabling publics
2. Functional publics
3. Normative publics
4. Diffused publics

Enabling publics possess authority and power while controlling an organization's resources. These publics include regulatory agencies, local community leaders, the board of directors, and shareholders. Functional publics may be employees, unions, and consumers. They provide labor and utilize an organization's product or service. Groups tied to an organization by shared values or similar problems are normative publics. These publics include professional organizations, political groups, and trade associations. Diffused publics are indirectly linked to an organization and include individuals or groups who are not members of a formal organization. The press and local citizens may be categorized as diffused publics. By categorizing publics in advance, an organization will be more able to deal with a crisis promptly and efficiently.[4]

In defining the key publics, whether by specific group or broad categories, it is helpful at this point to discuss the potential channels of communication to be used to get the message to these publics. While using a press release may appear to be the most obvious means of communication, it is by no means always going to be the most effective. Here again, the crisis communications discussion group needs to think of every possible channel of communication so that the most effective means will be matched with the appropriate target group.

Following is a list of channels of communication that can be used separately or in tandem to reach various publics:

- News conferences
- Press releases
- Interviews
- Teleconferencing
- Telephone calls
- Personal visits
- Interoffice memos
- Company newsletters
- First-class letters
- Telegrams and telexes
- Faxes
- Electronic mail
- Overnight mail
- Advertisements
- VNRs (video news releases)

And, while it may seem simple to note that one public or another is going to get a personal visit or phone call, it begs the question as to which person will be responsible for taking this action. Your team will want to examine the individuals and positions in your organization to determine the best person to make such contact. The public relations department, as with the press release, may seem to be the logical choice. But take, for instance, the board of directors as a potential public. Obviously a news release or advertisement is not going to be the most expeditious, effective, or appropriate manner in which to communicate with these key members of the organization. They will warrant either a personal visit or, at the very least, a phone call. They will also expect this communication to come from the president or chairman of the board.

The public relations department, on the other hand, may be determined to be the best group responsible for writing a letter (channel of communication) to the company's retirees (target public).

Of key importance at this stage is to make sure everyone is clearly aware of their responsibilities and that personality is taken into account when defining responsibilities. While legal counsel or the controller may be deemed the appropriate position responsible for communicating to a specific group, if the person possesses no communication skills whatsoever, then this should be noted and another position or individual given the responsibility or at least assigned a support role in the communication process.

An excellent way to see the importance of identifying publics is to examine the now famous Tylenol product-tampering case where, in the fall of 1982, Johnson & Johnson, the producer of Tylenol, was faced with an overwhelming crisis: Seven people died after consuming the cyanide-laced product.

Johnson & Johnson, a leading health-care organization with 165 companies in 53 countries around the world, employed 77,000 people during the 1980s. In the fall of 1982, Tylenol reported over one hundred million users, held a 37 percent market share in the over-the-counter painkiller market, and accounted for 33 percent of Johnson & Johnson's year-to-year profit growth.

Robert V. Andrews, assistant director of public relations at Johnson & Johnson, received a telephone call from a Chicago news reporter. The reporter informed Mr. Andrews that people in Chicago were dying from poisoned Tylenol and he wanted the company's comment. This was the manner in which Johnson & Johnson received the news that would eventually result in a $100 million loss for their organization.

First and foremost was the public's safety. In order to communicate factual and truthful information quickly, key publics had to be identified and notified. The media was at the top of the list, followed by the medical community, the Food and Drug Administration, the Federal Bureau of Investigation, and consumers. Throughout the crisis Johnson & Johnson maintained ongoing communication with each of these key publics.

Chairman James E. Burke set up a seven-member crisis management team which handled decisions on the ever-changing developments and coordinated all organizational efforts and communications. This team decided to withdraw all Tylenol capsules from the store shelves in Chicago and the surrounding area. An inspection by Johnson & Johnson and the Food and Drug Administration revealed two additional bottles containing contaminated capsules. This inspection highlighted the vulnerability of all capsules and resulted in a national withdrawal of all Tylenol capsules.

To show the public that Johnson & Johnson was doing everything possible, a full-page advertisement ran in major newspapers across the United States, offering consumers an exchange of capsules for tablets. In addition, Tylenol's manufacturer, McNeil, created toll-free consumer hot lines to respond to inquiries concerning the safety of Tylenol. Thirty-three telephones were installed, and during the month following the Chicago deaths, 30,000 calls were received from concerned consumers. Johnson & Johnson also offered free discount coupons worth $2.50 redeemable towards the purchase of any Tylenol product.

During the first week of the crisis there were 80,000 separate news stories in national newspapers, hundreds of hours of television and radio coverage, and over 2,000 telephone calls from media representatives requesting information. To aid in this massive press coverage, toll-free lines were established to enable news organizations to call and listen to pretaped statements. Approximately 730 calls were received from newspaper, television, and radio reporters.

Six weeks after the Chicago deaths, plans for the recovery of Tylenol were introduced during a sales conference at Johnson & Johnson's headquarters. Tylenol's manufacturer McNeil unveiled the triple-seal, tamper-resistant packaging. In addition, health-care professionals received 50 million triple-safety-sealed packages to distribute and help bring patients back to Tylenol. Johnson & Johnson also initiated a massive advertising campaign featuring Dr. Thomas Gates, medical director for McNeil.

By mid-December, Tylenol was on the road to recovery. Sales of the new capsules exceeded projection forecasts by 50 percent and tablet sales attained 80 percent of their levels prior to the crisis.

The key to the remarkable comeback of Tylenol can be attributed to swift action by the company combined with a clearly defined action plan. Following a strategy and developing the correct messages for the appropriate publics is clearly illuminated in this example.

4

Outline Key Messages

After your crisis team has been formed and has spent the time determining the publics with whom communication must occur during a crisis, it is then time to begin looking at what messages will need to be communicated. When you view news reports or press conferences, you will note that skilled spokespeople are very well prepared and seem to be communicating some very important points when they are asked questions. This is not by accident but rather by design. A well-planned crisis communication team and spokesperson will have a set of messages that they know very well and will endeavor to communicate them during a crisis.

For example, in 1991 during the war in the Middle East, English prime minister John Major held numerous press conferences. In my class on crisis communications I would show videotapes of John Major to the students as an example of skillful handling of a press conference. But one of the most important aspects of these sequences is that in every instance when John Major was asked a question, he would nod and acknowledge the question, provide a response, and include a clear message of concern.

Some of the messages that came through loud and clear were: opportunities for Saddam Hussein to have avoided the conflict; regular communications having gone on with the United States; the precipitation of war being clearly the fault of Iraq; and that no one wanted the war, but Iraq forced it upon everyone. These were not thoughts off the top of his head, but clearly thought-out messages.

The purpose at this point in developing your crisis communications plan is to sit down with your team and examine your business, determining those messages that you would want brought out during a crisis. For example, if you were involved in a youth organization that experienced a bus crash, you would have as some of your messages the prior success records of the programs and how many young people are served. The bus company involved would want to have emphasized the message of its prior safety record and that it quickly responds to correcting problems. In every instance during a crisis there will be opportunities to get out the positive messages of your company. This is not to say that you should not answer questions (this subject will be discussed in chapter 7), but what is important is that you acknowledge and answer the question, and in answering, provide your own message too. In this way you are active as opposed to reactive.

Here is a list of ways in which you can begin preparing your messages:

- How has your service benefited your clients? What is the safety record of your service?
- How has your product benefited consumers? What is the safety record of your product?
- What is the quantity of your product that has been purchased over the years? (If you have a track record of hundreds of thousands of good products then a problem with one or two may be put into perspective.)
- How has your organization supported the community in which it operates?
- How has your organization helped the employees it has hired?
- How many employees do you have? Has growth occurred over the years?
- What contributions has your organization made to the community, to research in the field, to civic, cultural, and social activities?
- What advances in the areas of research and innovation has your organization made?
- What are some of the successes of your top personnel?
- What is your organization's status in its industry?
- How has your organization handled previous crises?
- What have you done to prevent a crisis from occurring? (Note any safety changes, any additional monies spent on quality control, training of employees, and other ways of preventing a crisis from occurring.)
- If you have ever been involved in a crisis or helped another organization through a crisis, note how your employees handled the situation, helped victims, secured the area, and in other ways participated in the swift and positive resolution of the crisis.

- Prepare a list of words that are specific to your industry and have translations into everyday language made so that in the event of a crisis common language will be used, thus better transmitting unknown or confusing words.
- How has your organization investigated and handled any customer or client complaints?
- How has your organization handled any violation of safety codes and corrected such problems?
- Again, review any ways your company can be viewed as a good citizen, a leader in the industry, or as a provider of local jobs, and develop messages along these themes so that they may be brought out during a crisis.

The reason for doing this exercise is so that your organization, its history, and what it has accomplished can be put in perspective should a crisis occur.

Sometimes, though, no message is the best message. Even when you or your organization is in the right and has some positive news to report as a vehicle for delivering one of your key messages, it may be better not to, if in so doing, old negative messages may be dredged up in a public's mind and be rehashed.

The protracted public relations effort during the DC-10 crisis McDonnell Douglas faced in 1979 and 1980 illustrates this concern for rehashing old negative messages. After the crash of a DC-10 in May of 1979 much adverse publicity came the way of the company. And even when the company was vindicated by an FAA report in January 1980 proving that the planes met the toughest standards of safety, confidence by publics was still lower than normal. The concern, of course, that the company faced was the double-edged sword of wanting to set the record straight, but in so doing, would have to chance bringing up the negative perceptions of the crash at the same time.

The company spent a great deal of time with employee communications and concerted efforts with key publics such as travel agents. Even a hard-hitting brochure was developed to get the message across.

In the end, though, this final thought must be kept in mind: Although public relations programs may result in positive actions in the aftermath of crises, and although the temptation to set things straight with the media or impress important publics may be strong, some situations demand that the good deeds be done without giving due credit to the client. Reflections on the aftermath of an airline crash like the DC-10 crisis show that follow-up stories may lead to rehashing of previous accidents. Sometimes then, the best message is no message at all, as exemplified by the San Ysidro massacre at a local McDonald's when McDonald's suspended advertising "so as not to appear insensitive."[5]

Once you've decided whether or not you will be communicating a message, here are some sample messages that can be based upon the information you have gleaned:

- Before the accident today our manufacturing facility had a sterling record of safety with no hours of lost work due to accident in the last three years.
- Our organization has been cited by the _____ (fill in the blank) safety organization for being a leader in the field of safety.
- Our facility is reviewed by inspectors on a yearly basis and over the last six years has received the highest rating possible.
- Our equipment is serviced and checked on a monthly basis and prior to this accident there were no defects noted.
- Our organization publishes and distributes safety literature to our employees so that they can be involved in the safety process.
- Our organization has spent millions of dollars on reducing emissions and thus we are very concerned about the environment and we are doing our part to protect it.

For employee relations problems you might come up with a statement such as:

- Our organization believes in open communications among employees and management. Over the last two years we have been developing quality circles for groups of employees to work together, address problems, and come up with solutions.

It would also be important to add industry comparisons as part of the overall message package. For instance, you may have received three citations over a six-year period, yet the industry average may be ten per company over that same six-year period. Make sure this is highlighted, as it reinforces your safety record. By having all this information handy in message form (based on research and understanding of the organization noted in chapter one) you will be able proactively to handle the communications process during a crisis.

Of course you want to know of any succession plans so that investors' nerves can be calmed in the event of a crisis and they will understand that capable people are ready to step in and continue running the firm. This can be handled by having biographies of all top personnel readily accessible and a complete listing of those individuals who will succeed another should death or illness occur. You can then present messages in a timely and informed manner about the capable individuals who will be replacing a sick or deceased top manager.

This forces the company as a whole to ensure that it has done such planning, and again you are the catalyst for this very important process. In addition to having biographies on these potential successors, you will also need to note *why* they are qualified to fill in for the deceased CEO or other top corporate individual.

When you have your messages you will be in a position to turn a negative situation, such as having to lay off two hundred workers, to a positive one of thereby saving eight hundred jobs. Here is a way that this can be handled:

> Instead of reacting to the media's telephone calls—"Is it true that you are laying off two hundred workers?"—your communicator should be expected to look for ways to turn negatives into positives or, at a minimum, at least to neutralize negatives. In a proactive stance in this situation, your company could report everything that was done to try to save the two hundred positions and then regrettably conclude that laying off two hundred workers was an action designed to save the jobs of eight hundred other workers.[6]

The headlines may still read "Two Hundred Workers Laid Off" but at least you have endeavored to get the positive across as opposed to letting the media's viewpoint carry by default.

Here are some additional thoughts on the types of messages you may want to develop for a given public. These can help you begin to plan your messages:

- Employees: There is a good possibility that they will hear about the crisis first from a news source. You should still plan to communicate directly with them within the first twenty-four hours as to current status, company policy, and to assure them that you will be keeping them up to date. Assume that this information will get back to the press (even if it doesn't), so be open and honest without providing confidential or sensitive information.
  Remember that this will be the most likely group that the media will target to get information—expect it. So keep them informed and remember that the press will get a story with or without you—and if you are involved you have a chance to control the message and the crisis.
- Customers: Assure them that the situation is under control, and make sure it is, and estimate any delays in shipping products so that your customers will have confidence that they will be taken care of in a timely manner even if slightly delayed.
- Investors: In no way should this public be misled. They need to be informed about the occurrence and you need to engender their confidence and support. You can do this by letting them know what management is doing to control the crisis and always explain in understandable language what is happening and what your organization is doing to control the crisis (again, make sure it is). Keep them regularly apprised of the situation as it continues.

- Government and community leaders: Involve them as necessary and keep them well informed and current. They will want to know if any aspect of your crisis can spill over and affect their duties and responsibilities. Therefore provide information as to these concerns.
- Insurance companies: Inform them immediately and involve them in the process so that they become a part of the solution, not a part of the problem.
- Lawyers: Involve them early so that they can help and guide you.
- Families and victims: If there are families and victims, they should be communicated with quickly and in the most compassionate way possible.

The whole purpose of this chapter is to stress the importance of planning messages ahead of time, as in doing this you will be freed to manage the communications process during a crisis rather than wasting time tracking down information. Most of this information is readily available and can be gathered before the crisis, so now is the time to start outlining your messages. Steven Fink summarizes this advice in the following way:

> What you are striving for is what you should always be striving for: to control and manage the message, control and manage the communications, control and manage the crisis. You want to issue the story or the statement your way, in the way that will tell the truth and make your company look best. You want to issue the most positive statements you can in a proactive way, rather than allowing yourself to be placed in a position to defend against negative, reactive questions from the media.[7]

5

Gain Company Support for the Plan

As your plan is coming together, and especially upon its completion, you will want to begin gathering internal support for your plan. One of the ways this can be accomplished is through the backing of the CEO and top management. But there are other ways you can gain support for your plan because without your company's support the plan will not work.

There are instances where companies have had plans and have sent out, in the midst of a crisis to speak with the press, a junior spokesperson who has been told to say the following: "We are on the job, we've implemented our crisis plan, and the following actions will be occurring." In reality, however, nothing had happened with the plan and nothing had been done. The spokesperson obviously loses credibility and the company itself is in a greater crisis than before. But this problem can be traced back to a plan that has not been bought into by the organization and therefore has not been implemented. You need to avoid this problem by ensuring that all individuals responsible for the implementation of this crisis communication plan are involved in the process, buy into it, and understand their responsibility for its implementation.

You may be fortunate enough to have an enlightened CEO and management team that already appreciate the importance of crisis communications and therefore support for your plan will not be difficult. You may even have a plan already developed that has everyone's support. If so, you are indeed fortunate. However, many companies do not have crisis plans, or may speak of having crisis communications and think it's important but have done nothing about it and have nothing in writing. You as the public relations practitioner will now have the challenge of educating top management and ensuring internal support for the plan as it is developed.

One of the ways you can do this is simply to show them this book and the cases in the back along with the plans as a way of pointing out that other successful companies are doing this. In all the cases, the companies that have come out in a good position after a crisis have been those that understand the importance of crisis communications, have a plan, and implement it. If that isn't enough, take your CEO to public relations practitioner meetings where guest speakers specifically address public relations from the viewpoint of the CEO. This may seem very basic but if your top management does not understand or appreciate the importance of public relations, and hence crisis communications, you need to begin the education process immediately. Otherwise all of your best efforts will be for naught.

There is also a need to build personnel and backup personnel into any good crisis communications plan. This not only serves the purpose of ensuring that there will be enough people to handle the various communications in the event of a crisis, but that you will already know who these individuals will be. Additionally, you will have already considered the individuals who can best fill in and support the efforts if any of the primary players are unavailable.

There is also the added benefit in such a personnel backup system of beginning the process of buy-in to any plan that is developed. For example, in order for the CEO to accept the role of spokesperson, the individual must first agree to the plan, which calls for a spokesperson. So by labeling people's roles and having them agree to these roles ahead of time, you are, in fact, selling them on the plan and gaining their support.

If you are working with an agency it is important to keep them on retainer so that you have their expertise available to you with the additional people power which can be brought to bear quickly in a crisis. By having them involved early on, you will additionally have their support, which will further help your ability to deal quickly should a crisis occur.

Once the plan is in place, people have been identified, backups listed, and assignments made, it is time to gain acceptance of the plan. Without the buy-in of key people and the organization as a whole, the plan is worthless.

Obviously, the first place to begin the buy-in program is with the CEO and the management team. Start at the top and gain their support and the rest should fall into place. In gaining their support, you will want to be sure to train them and other top management personnel so that they understand not only the crisis communications plan, but also their role in it. As their training and understanding increases so, too, does their support of the plan. Your prior relationship combined with the CEO's understanding and appreciation for public relations and crisis management will have a great impact on ultimate acceptance. Once you have the top managers trained and they support the plan, spend some time developing the backup personnel within the organization and train them in the plan also. Make sure all involved are aware of the plan and have been trained. Finally, brief the entire organization on the crisis communications plan so that they are aware of its overall workings, who the key people will be and the roles they will play. Having the whole organization understand how the company will respond in a crisis will greatly help the overall communications process and the smooth, proactive handling of the crisis should it occur in your organization.

6

Develop External Support

Contrary to popular opinion and your perception thus far, the media are not your worst enemies, but actually important allies that should be nurtured. The media may publicize some embarrassing information about your company—that is their job—not necessarily to embarrass you, but to report news. If you do something that is newsworthy, embarrassing or not, it will most likely be reported. But if you have done your homework, you should be able to anticipate potential problems before they occur, and thus can deal more effectively and confidently when the media come calling. Better yet, why not work with your company's management team and correct the potential problems and thereby avoid any crisis or embarrassing situation altogether.

The media, too, may be major positive components in your plan, because they can become an effective channel of communication to get your messages and information transmitted in a hurry, and for basically no cost. How? Quite simply, by being open and candid and having your messages clearly determined, the media can play an important role in making your communications plan work. So let's look at ways the media can offer external support for your plan.

You can greatly help or hurt your cause depending on your relationships in the past with the media. If you have had negative dealings or you are viewed as uncooperative and antagonistic, the press will probably not deal very sympathetically with you during a crisis.

On the other hand, if you have spent time nurturing the press as part of your overall plan to develop external support before a crisis, you will be in a much better position to deal positively with the people who report the news.

This means getting to know the individuals at the various TV and radio stations, newspapers, magazines, and trade journals most likely to cover your company during a crisis. Spend time reading and listening to their reports to understand how they handle situations, their style, and any biases.

Practitioners advise meeting reporters informally during a noncrisis period and getting to know them and their needs. Visiting them at their place of operation is recommended, as is asking some of these questions:

- How can we (your company) be of assistance to the reporter or news organization?
- Do you have a current fact sheet or folder on our organization for your reference?
- Do you know what we do? Let me explain. . . .
- Is there information on our industry I can provide to you?
- I am not here pitching a story—but would certainly like to invite you to visit our facility and meet some of our key personnel.
- What stories would you be interested in or how may we help you write a better story?

And by providing your home number to the reporter, you will reinforce your sincerity to be there when *they* need to reach you. Remember, it is a two-way street. Credibility is the key.

Staging a drill is another good way to develop external support. Invite key outside groups to participate in the drill and offer suggestions on how it can be improved. They then become allies of yours involved with the solution—not the problem. A power company conducts these drills on a regular basis at their power plant.

We have noted that the press is not the only way to prepare externally ahead of time. Other key publics need to be part of the solution and not the problem. A key group we have noted before is that of local community leaders, politicians, and influencers of public opinion. If your company is viewed by these key publics as a supportive member of the community that has acted as a good citizen and a provider of jobs, then these individuals will be more apt to support and work with you should crisis occur. On the other hand, if you are viewed as a polluter, or a company that is not actively involved in the community, not a supporter of civic concerns, you will not have engendered any support from this key public. To turn things around and help yourself, you will want to spend time developing your relationship as a good citizen and involve key decision makers and politicians in how your organization would handle a crisis and how it would communicate. Involving these individuals in your plan, letting them know how communications would occur, and what role they would have, if any, in that communications process would greatly aid their support of you and your organization and speed a smooth communications process during a crisis.

Truly the importance of developing external support can be summed up by the thought that planning and preparation for a crisis should occur when there is no crisis at all. Spending time building goodwill with the press, key influentials, and your other publics while you have the time will greatly help you and your organization to be better prepared for a crisis when it occurs. Spend some time communicating with the media and with your key publics to make sure they know that top management in your organization are available to them for interviews, tours, policy statements, and other forms of communication.

A company truly helps itself when it is proactive in its planning and open and candid about how it operates, its role in the community, and its interaction with key publics. By making the company accessible to the media, the organization is on the road to creating good communication. Some companies still seem to act in a defensive manner. There are daily reports of organizations that almost act as an ostrich does with its head in the sand, thinking that by ignoring the media and not communicating with the key publics the crisis will blow over. This is truly not the case and the contrary is clear—that those companies that are straightforward, candid, and have spent some time nurturing relationships with the media and other external publics, and then communicating with these publics quickly and honestly during a crisis are the ones that come out ahead and keep their image intact if not enhanced.

7

Train the Spokesperson

This chapter will help you define the individual(s) that will be needed for your company/situation(s) and the training required to prepare him, her, or them for the spotlight. As we are admonished to remember, the public rarely judges the performance of an organization based upon facts, but rather on perceptions and emotions.

It is extremely important to choose the right spokesperson who is capable of portraying a positive image. Companies involved in a crisis often assume that the CEO is the best person for this role. However, there are times when the CEO is not the best person to give informed answers. For example, when the crisis involves much technical information, you may need to have an individual with the appropriate technical background to answer questions. There were two spokespeople, for example, during the Three Mile Island nuclear disaster: Harold Denton from the Nuclear Regulatory Commission and Governor Thornburgh. Denton handled the technical questions during press conferences, while Thornburgh dealt with subjects pertaining to the health and welfare of citizens.[8]

What is of critical importance is that the spokesperson speak with authority from management, be a communicator, and possess an understanding or appreciation of media relations.

Whether you choose the CEO, a senior level technical manager, yourself, or a combination, you will want to assess the ability of the individuals to communicate, their knowledge of the situation, and their understanding of the organization. Being a spokesperson is no easy task and there is no room here for egos. The individual will also need to be able to remain as detached as possible even though virtually no one is completely free from getting personally involved.

As the cases in this book will point out, CEOs can be very effective as spokespeople. They, in a sense, personify their organization and in times of crisis it helps to mitigate the situation when the company, business, or organization can be viewed as "people." It is much easier to attack an inanimate object and more difficult to attack people during a crisis. People *can* make mistakes and be forgiven—who forgives an organization? Additionally, besides presenting the human side of the organization, the CEO is the person in charge and this can have quite an impact in communicating during a crisis. While a lower level spokesperson may simply appear as a conduit of information, the CEO appears as the policy maker, which makes his/her statements that much more meaningful and powerful.

When anyone other than the CEO speaks, there is the chance of leaving in the observer's mind the question, "Is that all of it or is there more information that this person is not aware of?" The CEO, on the other hand, is usually viewed as the source—knowing all the information. However, as was mentioned earlier, there may be times when the nature of the situation is so technical or specialized that the CEO cannot explain all the minute details. This is when bringing in a technical expert can be helpful. I would not advocate delegating all the spokesperson duties to this individual for all of the reasons cited earlier about needing the CEO, but a technical support person can augment what the CEO is saying.

Also, in certain crises, it may actually be wise to keep the person in charge of the organization at a distance, as they may need protection (as with the head of Union Carbide being jailed in India when traveling to the Bhopal crisis site), or may become so immersed in the situation that he or she forgets why the message is being communicated.

Once you have decided on the spokesperson or spokespeople, you will want to conduct some training and simulation exercises. A brief session can be done in a few hours, while an outside training group may develop a program lasting up to two days. The idea is to take as much time as necessary to make the spokesperson feel comfortable, not only handling questions, but also clearly presenting your organization's key points and sounding sincere and credible.

One aspect of the training session, or the first phase, would simply be to put the individual in a "hot seat" and take direct questions from other staff members. Note how succinctly your spokesperson answers the question and makes the transition to get your organization's points across. Ask yourselves if the individual has command of the facts and knows when to stop talking. Sometimes the hardest thing for a respondent to do is simply to answer the question and wait for the reporter to move on to the next one. Most difficulties occur when an individual continues on or starts conjecturing about what might happen. Teach the spokesperson to simply answer the question, state the known facts, bring out any appropriate key messages from your list, and then stop talking. This is where the simulation becomes so very important and helpful.

At this stage of the preparation, it is important to ask yourself what are the worst possible questions that media can ask you or your organization. And what would then be your response? As you develop your responses, be mindful of how they will play in the press. We will talk later of developing succinct statements or "sound bites" that will most likely be picked up by the media. But make sure all statements pass the following public-perception test:

- Do they appear intelligent and well thought out?
- Do they show concern for the welfare of your various publics?
- Do they show compassion?
- Do they seem to offer a solution?
- Do they present your company in a good light?
- Do they make you seem responsible?
- Do they show you as being flexible?
- Do they give your publics confidence that you are in control?

After spending some time handling questions and analyzing the answers, begin phase two of the training, which involves videotaping the responses. Here, the spokesperson can see how he or she looks and sounds when being interviewed. Note the person's eye contact, inflection, and appearance. Is the person believable? Are there any nervous gestures or mannerisms that are either distracting or that present the individual in a negative light?

You may want to spend some time practicing for interviews similar to the style of "60 Minutes." While an interview of this nature may never occur, it is important to understand this form of journalism that uses close-ups and aggressive questioning as a way to see an individual become nervous and flinch or sweat, so that you can best prepare for it. A person unprepared for this type of interview would not likely present himself or herself in the most positive manner. On the other hand, those individuals who understand the "60 Minutes" system can handle themselves confidently and effectively. One way to do this is always to be courteous and be perceived as cooperative. Sometimes even a dull interview can additionally help you. By being dull and not getting excited (just the response that is usually hoped for by the media), you make it difficult for reporters to get sound bites (short statements that end up being aired on television or radio because they capture the essence of what the reporter is trying to convey). By not providing what the reporter wants, the entire motivation for conducting the interview may be lost, and you will have deftly avoided a very unfortunate presentation of your organization. All of this, of course, takes much practice.

If you truly understand the medium, the reporter, and the audience, and have practiced, you will be much better prepared to handle any press inquiries. Here are some checklists to assist in the process:

● BEFORE-INTERVIEW CHECKSHEET

Before an interview takes place, it is important to focus on the objectives of the interview from the standpoint of your organization, the reporter(s), and the viewing audience. This guide sheet will help you collect your thoughts and stay on track.

- What is the subject of the interview?
- What is the purpose of the interview?
- Why was your organization chosen?
- Who else is being interviewed?
- How long will the interview last?
- What is the interviewer's style and past examples of his or her work?
- What are the political and social leanings or biases of the interviewer?
- What is the motivation behind the interview?
- Who was responsible for assigning the interview, and why was it assigned?
- List the primary messages you want to communicate.
- If print media, what is the type of publication to be utilized (daily, weekly, monthly)?
- What is the coverage area?
- What is the estimated number of readers, viewers, and/or listeners?
- What would be the public's knowledge and interest about your industry and company?
- Are there other related events to which the public or the interviewer might tie your organization?
- Are there any reasons why your organization should not participate in the interview?

It is also important to examine the format of the interview ahead of time. Knowing whether it will be live or taped, edited or not, are important considerations. Will you be part of a panel or will there be phoned-in questions? Consider, too, the type of program if it is a talk show. Some may use you and your organization to attract viewers at any cost without concern for facts. Avoid being set up—not all exposure is necessary. Again, here is a checksheet to follow to help evaluate the format.

Television and Radio

- Format (News, talk show, panel discussion, press conference, one-on-one, telephone inquiries)?
- Investigate the style.
- Location (studio or remote site)
- How long is the program?
- Is it live or taped?
- Will it be edited?

Print Media

- Where will the interview be conducted?
- Will photographs be taken?
- When and where will the story appear?
- In what section of the paper will the story appear (this will indicate the importance of the story)?

Pay particular attention to the section of the paper in which your story will appear. Is it in a hard news area or soft? Do you know anything about the reporter's other articles? Practitioners caution that the "most adroit, successful interviewer—but also the most dangerous to the neophyte—is the openly friendly and empathetic reporter."[9] One cannot afford to let down one's guard in an interview and be guided into making damaging and unfortunate statements.

A final note in preparing for any interview is to give the spokesperson time to prepare physically. If time allows, take a breather, maybe catch a nap. At least take the time to have something to eat, put on some fresh clothes, and freshen up (if the speaker is male, make sure he shaves—a "five o'clock shadow" can make your speaker seem dark and less open). You can usually have the luxury of setting the time of the press conference or will at least be called by a reporter saying what time he or she will be visiting your company. Use the time to prepare mentally and physically—you will not only feel better but you will look better and will present yourself in a more positive light, and thus help communicate your message better.

Aviva Diamond runs a Los Angeles-based communications company that helps train corporate spokespeople. She provides suggestions on everything from the type of suit and tie to leaning slightly forward in the chair. She, too, emphasizes stopping and waiting for the next question rather than "droning on in unedited narrative."[10] She additionally uses the famous Richard Nixon "I am not a crook" speech to point out the importance of eye contact. There are also many other important points in this speech that can be used to help train spokespeople such as avoiding the use of negative terms and denials. As opposed to "I am not a crook" or "Our company is not a polluter," the spokesperson should use the positive statement that "We are concerned with the environment and will do everything within our power to correct the situation."

Below is an excerpt from a training session with the vice president of a plumbing parts supply company showing the before-and-after of some comments used for an interview. Not only was the corrected version easier to understand and full of facts, but it was also more concise—eighteen seconds shorter. You can also see clearly how predetermined messages are brought out during questions and answers.

● **BEFORE**

Interviewer: What kind of ideas do you have to help people cope with the drought?

Response: I think one of the first areas to look at when they, they . . . we've been through this once or twice before, and the first problem that arises is everyone wants a quick fix to the problem. And the easiest way to resolve the problem is to probably go back and look at what you have in your house today and what can be repaired without going to any new products. For example, a faucet that's leaking, the best solution to the problem is to buy a 10 cent washer and repair it, as opposed to buying a $30 shower head that might restrict flow slightly. In the case of our product, a toilet is one of the areas where the most water is wasted. Probably the largest area for wasted water in the household would be the toilet. And as close as we can estimate, about 25 percent of the toilets out there leak. Now what's the best way to solve it? Fix the leak first, and you're going to save a tremendous amount of water, probably more than you could through any gimmicks of lower-flow shower heads or bricks in the tank or anything like that. (speaker clears throat) The next step would certainly be to look at those products. But the first thing is to repair what you currently have and get it working right. And that will save the most water.

● AFTER

Interviewer: How can [your products] help the drought?

Response: The toilet is one area where you can really save a lot of water. Over 78,000 gallons of water can be wasted through a leaky toilet a year. That's more than the water you see in a typical swimming pool. So a toilet is a major culprit for water waste.

Interviewer: But it's very expensive to get it repaired isn't it?

Response: Oh, it's very inexpensive. A product like ours, Fluidmaster's products, five or six dollars, can repair the problem and fix the leak.

Interviewer: I understand from people in another state that nothing can repair the problem, that all your valves break down after six months.

Response: Well, that was a unique situation. What we've done is give a grant to the university to research the problem of chloramine in the water there. This is a problem that all the plumbing industry faces there. What we've found is a new solution we feel will resolve that problem. We'll be announcing that very shortly and turning the information over to other manufacturers.[11]

Though this is clearly not a crisis interview, it gives one the idea of how statements can be broken up and facts intermingled to get a point across. It also shows how a negative ("Your valves break down") can be turned into a positive ("It is a problem with the water, we are researching a solution and will provide results to others").

Diamond also highlights some important points in dealing with a hostile press:

- Keep your composure. Don't take the interview personally or get emotional.
- Avoid personal attacks. Challenge statements, not people.
- Use the NAB approach ("nod and bite") of acknowledging a hostile question and then guiding the answer into one of your key messages.
- Speak with conviction in your words, voice, and manner.
- Admit mistakes and move on.
- Choose the question you want to answer if a reporter gives you a series.
- Humor can be used to defuse a situation if handled properly.
- Don't lie. While you do not have to tell everything you know, you must tell the truth.

However, if it is only a matter of time before you will need to divulge any additional information, it is better to get it all out in the open initially. There is a rather morbid anecdote used to illustrate this among practitioners of whether one would prefer to have a limb amputated in one two-hour procedure by a professional, or inch by inch over a few weeks by someone of questionable abilities.

By being properly prepared in our knowledge of our company and the messages we wish to communicate, along with having a trained spokesperson, we will be better able to handle the sometimes difficult task of communicating in a crisis. We become the expert surgeons who can make a bad situation less painful in the long run through our knowledge of communications. If we lose control of the situation, as is later illustrated in the Exxon *Valdez* case, the process not only becomes more intolerable, but others begin determining our own destiny. A good spokesperson and a well-thought-out plan can help keep you in control.

When you are ready to begin the selection and training process, remember these key points:

- Is the individual technically qualified to communicate the risks involved?
- Can your spokesperson obtain and provide factual information quickly?
- Does the spokesperson have the communication ability and the authority to speak?
- Does the spokesperson project an air of confidence and competency?
- Will this spokesperson present information in a clear, concise, and competent manner?
- Will people understand what has occurred, what is presently happening, and what decisions are being made and how your organization is prepared to deal with the situation?
- Does the spokesperson communicate concern for people in a compassionate manner?

8

Structure the Command Post

Not all crises will warrant a command post, but usually the very nature of a crisis situation and the need to control the flow of information will necessitate having some type of central information operation. It cannot be overemphasized, as was stated earlier, that containing the crisis, maintaining the control of information, and speaking with one voice are of paramount concern during this critical time. A command post will allow the organization to achieve these objectives because it will function as a central point through which all information will flow; a place where key members of the crisis team will be able to meet, discuss, and effectively handle the situation; and a site where press conferences can be held to disseminate information to the public.

Examine your office or headquarters to determine its suitability for handling individuals and information in a crisis. You are looking for an area that can be used to gather your team for the purposes of discussing the crisis, implementing the plan, and monitoring progress and results as the crisis proceeds. You will want to avoid using someone's office, as you will need some space away from the regular operations and one that can be secured. You will also want to have it large enough for extra phones, computer terminals (if appropriate), televisions, diagram boards, and other tracking devices. You will want this room separate from another room or area, which will be used for media relations and possibly press conferences.

For press conferences, a large room, approximately 1000 square feet is recommended. A room this size will handle up to thirty reporters and therefore most situations except those of the largest magnitude. The room should be arranged so that the speaker is at one end of the room with his or her back to a plain wall or set of curtains. It is important to keep distractions to a minimum to increase the credibility of the spokesperson. Thus a square room or speaking from the longer side of a rectangular room is not recommended as camera angles will most likely pick up other reporters and camera crews.

Having a simple logo behind the speaker is a judgment call on the part of the organization. While it allows the name to be seen by millions through images sent by broadcast and print media channels, it may be best to let it go unseen as any negative aspects of the crisis may become inextricably tied to the logo and thus have a negative impact on public perception of the organization.

It is also important, unless another room of similar size is available, to have tables and chairs around the perimeter with phone and electrical outlets. By providing these simple logistical support items for the news media, your organization sends the important message that you are in control, organized, and prepared to meet the challenge. An underlying message will also not be lost on the visiting reporters—that your organization wants to work with them in getting the word out by making their job a little easier. This positive and collaborative approach can pay dividends of goodwill for you and your organization as the situation proceeds.

Your facilities should also include files of the contingency plans, scenarios, and instructions, along with crisis team members' phone numbers. By providing a proper environment, the organization is taking the first major step to proactively managing the crisis.

● HANDLING INCOMING CALLS

Your organization needs to be prepared to handle the upsurge in phone calls that will surely come during a crisis. Examine your current phone system to determine how many incoming lines you currently have and what call load would be required to generate busy signals for those attempting to reach your organization. The key is to avoid having callers receive a busy signal as this can exacerbate the problem.

It is wise to have support personnel be involved on your crisis management team who can be assigned the task of handling the phone system. They can interface with the phone company prior to the crisis to develop a contingency plan for added phone capabilities if your current system will not handle the increased load.

Your phone experts can also provide information on the most efficient way to have phone lines installed in the press conference room for the media personnel.

● PICK THE RECEPTIONIST

Receptionists are hired to answer incoming calls initially and direct them to the appropriate individuals—a task that is increasingly being handled through automated phone mail systems. The receptionist is usually not trained to handle the stress and understand the critical importance of his or her position in the event of a crisis. This is why it is important either to ensure that the receptionist is properly trained to handle the crisis calls, or have another individual in the organization designated as the receptionist in the event of a crisis.

You may even want to have some backup receptionists for either your current individual or the designee to facilitate the prompt handling of all incoming calls. Moreover, it is suggested that one individual handle crisis calls and another handle normal business calls. If your organization uses an automated system, it would be best to augment it with a "live" person initially answering the calls because individuals calling during a crisis will want to hear a person, not a machine.

The key concepts to be noted are that prompt handling of all calls is extremely important and that no comments are to be made over the phone except by the designated spokesperson. A receptionist may be tempted to comment on the crisis or, acting in a friendly and efficient manner, answer an inquiry, but this must be avoided. Efficient routing of calls to the spokesperson is the singular requirement.

You will, however, want to track incoming calls for the purposes of damage control and determination of public sentiment. There is, at the end of the book, an appendix showing an example of a log sheet that can be used to track calls by those handling phone inquiries during the crisis.

● REMOTE SITE COMMAND POSTS

We have confined comments thus far to dealing with a command post at the central office or headquarters of an organization. What if the situation warrants an off-site command post?

Dow Chemical, for example, has two specially equipped forty-foot truck trailers that can either be piggybacked on flatbed railcars or hauled by semitrailers. This allows the company to get a command post to the site of a chemical spill within hours. These vans are more than just portable conference rooms, however. They are designed to meet the need of the crisis and, as such, have a small laboratory, a technical library, self-contained breathing units, tools, generators, sleeping and washing facilities. The emphasis here is on handling the crisis and getting data on the situation. While some decision making and information dissemination may occur on site, it is recommended that information be sent back to the primary command post so that these functions can occur at the headquarters.

By having a mobile unit, the temptation would be for the CEO to leave headquarters for the remote site. In many instances this would be a mistake. An example is Union Carbide's CEO Warren Anderson who, in 1984, went to India to be at the site of the Bhopal disaster. According to analyst Steven Fink, this dash across the globe was by no means sound crisis management. It was, he contends, a "foolish, knee-jerk reaction which removed him from his essential management and communications responsibilities for nearly a week and landed him in jail" due to entering a hostile environment.[12]

While we will examine a case later on in the book that shows, in the case of Ashland Oil, that being on site can positively help resolve the crisis, it is important to remember that keeping the integrity of a central command post, albeit with a hotline to the disaster site, is of critical importance.

● WHEN BEST INTENTIONS PROVE INADEQUATE

It is appropriate to note how situations can change in spite of all the correct preplanning. In November 1984, Humana Hospital in Louisville, Kentucky, was the site of the world's second artificial heart transplant. Correctly sizing up the situation that this would be a media event, the public affairs staff at Humana took steps to prepare for the press. A command post and press area were set aside in the hospital's small auditorium. The anticipated handful of local reporters turned out to be "well over one hundred people crammed" into the small space.[13] The hospital quickly secured conference center facilities seven miles from the hospital to handle the press. By installing a direct communications link to the hospital and providing video and photographs for the news media, the event was a success and brought much goodwill to the hospital.

This example also points to the fact that not all crises are negative. The very nature of this event, because of its unpredictability and crucial importance, made it a crisis, but it was a positive one. The hospital public affairs staff rightly gauged this and took advantage of the situation to build good perceptions for Humana. Here, too, would be an appropriate time to have a logo behind the spokesperson to link the affirmative aspects of the situation with the company symbol and thereby constructively develop public perception.

9

An Agency Perspective:
Pros and Cons of External
Consultants

While many companies may consider it normal cost-effective business to shy away from hiring an outside consultant to aid in the management of a crisis, undertaking such a collaboration, whether it's with an individual or an agency, may prove more profitable in the effectiveness of a company's ability to communicate to the public during a crisis.

An internal communications staff, whose daily workload is focused on one client—the employer—can lack objectivity over time. And this can be especially true at the time of a crisis.

During a crisis an internal staff may find it difficult to see the whole picture objectively, as an outsider would. Because the staff is personally wrapped up in the situation, they may exaggerate the crisis unnecessarily, or may just as easily not give enough credit to the role of the company in its industry and the impact the crisis has on the public.

Regardless of the situation, bringing in an outside consultant to help manage and/or advise during the crisis may help broaden the communications staff perspective to deal with the crisis, adding a dose of objective realism.

Any external consultant entering a company is, to a certain degree, perceived to have more credibility than the in-house staff. The reason for this assumption is the notion that consultants work outside the corporate world in a number of different industries. Moreover, outside consultants, overall, do not have to be mindful of the same organizational politics that insiders do. Thus, consultants can help implement a crisis plan that will not fall victim to quite the same political red tape as would an internal staff's plan.

After taking the leap of faith by hiring an external consultant to help manage a crisis, the company must take precious time to consider the qualifications of the consultant. Although time may be of the essence and political factors may influence the need for choosing a consultant quickly, haste may prove detrimental. If the consultant has never actually experienced a crisis, the consultant's reaction to the crisis may be more damaging than not having hired an external consultant. It is necessary that foresight lead the consultant search, and not hindsight, especially during a crisis. Leave crisis management to those who have implemented such programs before.

While at times an external consultant may be a detriment to the efforts of an internal staff, the consultant may enhance the crisis management proceedings. The consultant may complement the staff, thus doubling the strength of successful crisis management. Whether it's perception or reality, consultants may lend a more secure sense of control to all management levels of the crisis program staff.

During peaks in the workload, such as during a crisis, an external public relations consultant may be the most cost-effective way to manage the increased activity. Far less expensive than hiring additional public relations professionals and their support staff, a consultant hired on a project basis will provide the previously mentioned bonuses to the crisis situation, plus prevent the financial constraints of having to maintain the employment of an extra public relations staff once the crisis and the management plan are complete.

External consultants may also specialize in skills needed to carry out the crisis communications plan. Whether it's financial relations, government relations, or another specialty, the professional expertise of a consultant may provide specialized skills that are strategic to successful crisis management.

The addition of a consultant also increases the number of media contacts the total public relations staff can communicate with directly. If an agency is hired, for example, their contacts with the media are more diverse and widespread, since account executives are communicating with a multitude of media for more than one client. Because of this interaction with a diverse number of media in, perhaps, a number of different industries, the agencies may have a clearer, more up-to-date and wide-scale understanding of what the media expects.

But there are concerns one must be aware of when bringing in an agency or outside consultant. One of the most difficult factors to implement during a crisis is the need to inform employees about the history of the crisis and plans for a public remedy.

When using consultants, the company has now added another audience that must be privy to the same information, if not more than what was provided to all company employees. Not only does the consultant add to the possibility of misunderstanding, misinterpretation, and exaggeration, but the mere presence of the consultant may promote hard feelings with the communications staff.

Involving a consultant during the moment of crisis can further bring about a feeling of discrediting the staff by creating a perception of incompetence. The internal and external perception of such an arrangement suggests that the staff is not capable of managing an effective crisis communications plan professionally.

The biggest risk for the consultant is the threat of losing the account, while the threat for the staff is losing their employment.

Of key importance for both the organization and the agency is to ensure open and honest lines of communication. An agency hired to assist with a crisis could not be expected to do it without a complete understanding of the organization and full access to all relevant information (even sensitive data) and key decision makers. Otherwise, it would be tantamount to trying to type without a typewriter.

An agency would also want to be careful not to be put in a position of being hired to correct a wrong situation—meaning that the client has done something wrong and an outside agency or consultant is being brought in to clean up the mess (this can be read as "cover-up" and clearly goes against all the ethical practices of public relations practitioners).

An organization bringing in a consultant would preferably want to do so before a crisis occurs so that the company benefits from the preplanning expertise of the agency, ideally to the extent of avoiding a crisis in the first place. However, no matter when the agency or consultant gets involved, it is critical that specific objectives are discussed and decided upon for which there will be some form of accountability. Ask these questions:

- Just how will the agency be able to assist?
- What track record do they have in crisis situations?
- What resources can they make available to you that your organization doesn't already have?
- How will the agency go about handling the crisis?
- Can they develop an acceptable plan for you (assuming you are holding discussions before a crisis)?
- Who from the agency will be working with you—junior level with no experience or senior level and seasoned?
- What will it cost (charged by the hour or by the crisis)?
- Will they be on site during the crisis?

Jim Lindheim, senior vice president and director of public affairs for Burson-Marsteller in 1985, additionally supplies some thoughts on the client/agency relationship from the agency perspective:

- The agency should be on site during the crisis, whether it takes a day or two or runs into the weeks.
- The agency should become an integral part of the crisis team, yet control should always be firmly in the hands of the client.
- Because the agency plays an advisory role and the client makes the final decision, the agency will be reluctant to make any guarantees on results.
- The agency will help the client to communicate quickly and honestly, prepare for the worst-case scenario, and help the organization to avoid appearing impersonal.
- The agency isn't going to be a magician who can make the problems disappear, rather the agency will be in the background helping the organization to work through the crisis, solve it, and communicate.

Lindheim gives us a final perspective on the role of the agency and fact that crisis communications is quickly becoming a specialized field in which organizations are looking for expert support: "Actually [crisis communication] is turning out to be a field or specialty of its own. It's almost like a total reversal of the usual public relations situation. Most of the time, our clients hire us to get noticed. In crisis communication, they hire us to get un-noticed."[14]

Part II

During the Crisis

10

Handle Immediate Needs

When a crisis strikes, the first response by you and your organization should be to ensure that the situation is brought under control and that all the facts are gathered. This comes under the heading of handling immediate needs. In the situation of a bus crash involving young people, immediately attend to the needs of those injured and contact authorities. Your priority is the safety of all those concerned.

We will look at a case later on in this book that involves a fire on board a cruise ship. Again, in this situation the immediate need was to ensure the safety of the passengers and the crew, to stabilize the ship, and bring the fire under control. Only then was the communication plan put into effect. The first priority was the immediate safety and security of the passengers.

For your purposes, the crisis team will want to have a listing of local authorities to contact in case of emergency, and be trained for the safety and security of all individuals if a crisis occurs.

Here is an example of a checklist and procedure sheet that can guide you in examining what you would need to do to handle the immediate needs of a crisis, as your main concern is knowing that your organization is capably handling and correcting the situation. If the situation is physically handled well quickly, then the task of communicating becomes that much more of a positive and easy task. Although this list is specifically aimed at youth service organizations, the way in which situations are handled is useful.

● PROCEDURES TO BE FOLLOWED IN THE EVENT OF SERIOUS OR FATAL ACCIDENT OR ILLNESS

No two emergencies are the same. While the various steps and suggested actions outlined represent sound procedure, your own good judgment should be the final authority until you are able to contact a superior. Know what is contained in this booklet and keep it with you for reference in the event of an emergency.

Handling Emergencies

Generally, your responsibilities include:

- Prevention of incidents before they happen. Become familiar with and put into effect the preventive measures suggested. Think ahead of time what unfortunate incidents might occur. Emergencies will be very rare if proper care is taken.
- Handling the situation at the time, notifying the necessary people after the incident, and working with the media.
- Be sure that one other adult is familiar with emergency procedures in case something happens to you.

Serious Illness or Accident

- Secure medical aid from the nearest professional source (doctor's office, medical center, or hospital). Never try to treat injuries that require professional care.
- If it is necessary to place the person in the hospital, do so, then:
  - Notify your office. Have details ready (name, age, address, etc.).
  - Parents or next of kin should be notified by the executive about the accident or illness and what steps have been taken to aid the injured or ailing individual.
  - If the incident occurred outside the local area, advise the immediate family how they may contact authorities or the physician looking after their loved one.
  - Have the attending physician or hospital administrator talk to the parents. Be sure they are satisfied with the medical arrangements.
  - Once a person has been admitted to a hospital, regardless of the reason,

do not remove him or her until the patient is medically released, unless the parents make different arrangements and take full responsibility.

—Secure transportation, if necessary, for parents or next of kin to the location of the injured or ailing one.

—Arrange to secure personal effects for safe delivery home.

• In some instances, it may be desirable to have a staff person or parent stay with him or her.

• If an illness is contagious, ask the doctor about the symptoms and for means, if any, of protecting other people. Then set up a system to check continuously on the other members of the group. Confer with medical authorities to determine whether it would be better to remain where competent medical aid is nearby.

• If there is a good possibility of others becoming ill after they return home, prepare a letter or call parents of all youth, pointing out that possibility.

In Case of a Missing Person

The person in charge should have a roster including names, addresses, and phone numbers of the total group. Leaders of subgroups should have lists of those in charge.

• Determine by a quick search that the person is really missing. Arrange for the search to continue while you are taking the steps listed below.

—Notify the nearest authority. If that authority is other than the police or sheriff's department (i.e., park ranger, fire department, rescue team, etc.), notify the appropriate police authority yourself.

—Notify your organization's top executive. He or she will notify parents, advisors, and school officials.

—Have all the details and be prepared to give as much of the following information as possible:

1. The location (including address) and contact phone number.
2. Name, address, and age of the person involved.
3. Occupation if he or she is an adult.
4. Name, address, and number of parents, guardians, or next of kin.
5. Names and addresses of leaders.
6. Background information on the event—date, time of day, etc.
7. Complete details of how the person disappeared, including his or her known movements and actions while still with the group.

When proper notifications have been accomplished, return and cooperate with the authorities. Then, when the immediate emergency has passed or you are relieved, write or dictate a statement with all the facts as you know them.

It is helpful to secure complete factual information at the scene, including names and statements of witnesses, leaders, members of the group, and public officials. Completing documented reports, supported by diagrams, helps establish future corrective guidelines and training experience.

Safe Driving Practices

- Do not drive unless you meet all of the qualifications, which include having a valid driver's license for the vehicle you are operating. If you are driving an occupied passenger bus or van, you must be twenty-one years of age.
- Check the vehicle's mechanical condition and operate only if it meets your standards and those of the organization.

In general, these standards require that you must:

- —Operate under the applicable state laws covering school buses.
- —Inspect the vehicle daily and at fuel stops.
- —Control passengers' activities for their safety.
- —Be sure you or another adult have knowledge of first aid and that a first aid kit is accessible in vehicle with all recommended contents.
- —Carefully supervise loading and unloading, especially when children must cross the street.
- —Stay within permissible passenger load.
- —Pull off the highway to stop.
- —Follow guidelines that establish maximum amount of hours to drive in a 24-hour period, but in no case drive when fatigued. The use of more frequent driver changes is suggested.
- —Obey all traffic laws.
- —Remember that your maximum speed is 55 mph.
- —Include the bus company's vehicle number (e.g., 1504) and label each bus by school and/or group.
- —In the event that more than one bus is in a convoy, a staff member should be in the last bus of that convoy.
- —During bus trips one chaperon should sleep while the other watches the driver, and then reverse every few hours.
- —Weather conditions and progress reports should be made to your organization's office during a major activity.

- Buses should be loaded by a staff member. The passenger list should be updated at the site to accommodate seating rearrangements so that each bus has an accurate list of passengers. The tour leader and office should be notified of all changes at the time of departure.
- Medical facilities should be identified enroute to all functions.
- Multiple sets of emergency phone numbers, procedures, contacts, and consent-to-treat forms should be aboard each bus and kept in a safe place.
- There should be a complete roll call and checkup at mealtimes, after fuel stops and rest stops, and at bedtime to make sure all youth are present.

When we look at communicating with key publics in the next chapter, we will see the importance of notifying the employees immediately. Yet, depending on your plan and given crisis scenario, dealing with your employees may be one of the initial actions you will need to take in handling immediate needs and concerns—in a sense, dealing with employee concerns may have to be moved up to the first step of bringing the crisis under control.

This can happen when the crisis at hand can so demoralize your employees that the very effectiveness of the business is at stake. An example of this is the twenty-one-week union strike in 1990 at the New York *Daily News*. The tension of the situation put everyone on edge to the point that minor concerns ballooned into major problems and the picket line literally split employees up. Those who didn't strike were embroiled in the conflict and were gossiped about.

If your crisis scenario could involve the figurative paralysis of your employees, then handling their needs will be one of your first concerns.

11

Notify Key Publics

Once the crisis has occurred and you have taken the immediate steps to bring the physical situation under control and ensure the safety of affected individuals, it is time to activate your crisis communications plan and to notify your selected publics.

Depending on the detail of your plan, you will have noted different publics to be notified for different crises and at the same time you will know which message you will want to communicate to each of these publics and the channel of communication to be used. What is most important at this time is swiftly to begin the process of candidly and openly contacting your key publics and providing as many details as you have available.

Even if you do not have all the facts, it is important to open up the communications process and indicate just that with the following statement: "The situation has occurred, and while we do not have all facts available, we want you to be aware of what we do know. We will provide further details as they become available." Begin letting your publics know how they can reach you should they have questions and concerns. By communicating quickly and candidly and opening up two-way lines of communication you will be speeding yourself through the communications program and building a sense of confidence among your publics.

Following are some examples of ways in which publics were notified during a crisis and the various channels of communication employed:

56

- Car companies facing a recall of a product may want to notify customers by using certified mail. This would allow for timely notification and additionally provide some assurance that the communication has been received.
- Johnson & Johnson, on the other hand, when faced with the Tylenol recall needed to alert its distribution centers very quickly to remove the product from retailers' shelves, and so it used electronic mail.
- Another fast form of communication (which additionally allowed for immediate feedback) was employed by Unocal during its proxy fight with T. Boone Pickens. It started with full-page advertisements in selected newspapers to encourage shareholders to vote via a toll-free (800) number through a service of Western Union called Datagram, and concluded with vote transmission to Unocal via telex. The time needed from call placement to vote reception was thirty minutes.
- In the area of investor relations, it is important to notify not only shareholders but also the institutional investors in times of crisis. The 1987 Wall Street crash had a significant impact on how institutions deal with their investment publics. We find that investor attitudes and the market environment changed greatly, thus making it more important than ever for publicly traded companies to release quickly to investors any information of a material nature regarding corporate activities.

To illustrate, both Lone Star Industries and Consolidated Natural Gas Company stepped up their investor relations communications in the wake of the October 19, 1987, crash. For example, Consolidated Gas held analyst briefings and began sending bimonthly white papers on a variety of topics including the recession and the marketing of new technologies. Besides sending these papers to analysts and investors, stockbrokers were also included on the distribution list so that their customers could be involved in the communication process.

The CEO of Lone Star, for its part, was involved in the communications process by having a question-and-answer section in the company's annual report. The vice president of investor relations complemented this approach with phone calls and one-on-one meetings with the company's large institutional shareholders such as pension funds, investment firms, banks, and insurance companies. The results of these targeted efforts resulted in major institutional investors holding their positions during the months following the crash.

Keeping a current list of all key institutional investors (see chapter three), along with following up with analysts are important aspects of shareholder relations. You should also keep these points in mind during the crisis:

- Follow up by phone with major institutional investors and analysts after releasing significant news. Anticipate their questions and have responses ready.

- While it may be painful to admit mistakes (à la product recall and the like) or present poor earnings reports, it is important to get all the facts out immediately. Let the investors and analysts get the information quickly and address what the company is going to do to correct the situation.
- Use employee publications and reprints of trade media coverage as support material sent to the investors and analysts before and during a crisis. Help them to understand the "big picture." An organization overview or fact sheets that discuss products, markets, management, and facility locations also may prove helpful
- Be candid with analysts and provide a clear perspective of the growth strategy of the company.

By remembering that open communication builds your credibility and heightens investor confidence you will be on your way to communicating well with this key public in a crisis.

During a crisis, owing to your concentrating on the media, your organization may be tempted to overlook such audiences as your employees and their families, who need to hear your message. These most important publics, which include organizational plant and division supervisors, union representatives, and sales people, cannot be forgotten during a crisis. The employees can be a very potent support force in your communications efforts if they are involved in the process.

This is not to imply that the employees become spokespeople (remember, we have shown that you should only have one spokesperson), however, your employees can be conduits of information and are going to be able to reassure their public contacts if they are properly informed.

It is critical that employees are communicated with in the most expeditious and effective manner. Smaller firms can have an employee briefing. A memo will work for other firms, while a video release, teleconference, satellite broadcast, or closed-circuit TV will be most useful for larger, more broadly spread organizations.

ESL, a subsidiary of TRW, came up with some employee communication strategies after a crisis involving a gunman who terrorized one of its offices:

- Management has to be involved and committed to providing open, honest, and current information.
- An internal crisis communications plan should be in place and be rehearsed.
- Have key company personnel identified ahead of time.
- Use established internal media that have proven to be successful.

- Work toward decentralized communication by using employee groups cooperating with management.
- Review the messages to ensure they are clear, consistent, and relevant to what the employees need to know rather than what management feels they should know.
- Support the communication process with other functions such as counseling and the like to ensure the overall well-being of the employees.

The case study of the disgruntled former employee at ESL who went on a six-hour siege of terror at the plant facility exhibits how good communications with one of your most important publics, your employees, can foster a better and faster resolution of a crisis.

On February 16, 1988, around 3:00 P.M., a former employee allegedly armed himself with nearly one hundred pounds of ammunition and weapons and gained access to one of the company's buildings. During the reign of terror, seven employees were killed and five others were injured.

The president of the subsidiary handled the explanation of what few facts were known at an initial group meeting for employees. All other inquiries were routed to one phone location for handling by the selected spokesperson.

The next day, a memo from the president was hand delivered to the desks of all employees. The memo explained what had occurred the day before and noted that counseling services would be available. Additionally, the memo announced that the president would meet with all employees at 10:30 that morning. At that meeting the names of the deceased were confirmed and other information was provided.

In the subsequent days numerous other channels of communication were opened up to ensure information was being quickly and effectively relayed to the employees. Funeral announcements were posted on the various company bulletin boards. The company's weekly newsletter contained special articles on the incident including updates on the injured and plans for a memorial fund. A hotline was also established to handle calls from employees and family members.

It was noted that all of the communications response and support that the employees received during the crisis greatly helped them deal with the situation.

The clinical coordinator for the counseling group further emphasized this belief when she noted that it was extremely reassuring simply to have someone in authority stand up and show some control of the situation.

You can also help employees through a crisis by:

- Communicating candidly and regularly. If legal concerns in any way supersede that, make sure you inform employees of this fact.
- Encouraging employees to share their concerns and begin channeling the emotions brought on by the crisis.
- Being careful about revealing personal views, however, as predictions and speculation only fuel the problem.[15]

12
Work with the Press

Good relations with all your publics, and this includes the media, means open, honest communications, which sometimes leads to playing devil's advocate. In other words, you not only represent your company to external audiences, you also must provide your insights from these publics to your internal audience. It isn't always easy, and it can be quite frustrating, but it is the essence of good media relations. And it is especially crucial during a crisis.

Here are just a few reasons why it is good to work well with the media:

- There is more of a chance to be active rather than reactive.
- There is a better chance of your being able to control the message.
- There is a much greater chance of correcting misinformation than if you don't talk with the media.
- Not meeting with the media sometimes makes you look as if you were not in control of the situation and may even appear rude, which will not help your cause.
- The media may be the best way to communicate quickly with many of your other key publics, thus making them an important resource.

Before we look at how to deal with the press correctly, let's examine what can happen if not handled correctly. The following situation occurred March 30, 1979, during the Three Mile Island crisis:

Relations between reporters and Met Ed (utility company) officials had deteriorated over several days. Many reporters suspected the company of providing them with erroneous information at best, or of outright lying. When John Herbein arrived at 11:00 A.M. Friday to brief reporters gathered at the American Legion Hall in Middletown, the situation worsened. The press corps knew that the radioactivity released earlier had been reported at 1,200 millirems per hour; Herbein did not. He opened his remarks by stating that the release had been measured at around 300 to 350 millirems per hour by aircraft flying over the island. The question-and-answer period that followed focused on the radiation reading—"I hadn't heard the number 1,200," Herbein protested during the news conference—whether the release was controlled or uncontrolled, and the previous dumping of radioactive wastewater. At one point Herbein said, "I don't know why we need to . . . tell you each and every thing that we do specifically." It was that remark that essentially eliminated any credibility Herbein and Met Ed had left with the press.[16]

The White House then stepped in and controlled the briefing process by having the NRC issue technical statements, the governor of Pennsylvania's office would comment on protective action, and the White House would handle comments on federal relief efforts. The worst-case scenario of communications and press relations during a crisis gone totally awry occurred as "the utility had no role whatsoever in the dissemination of public information, that privilege having been lost along with its credibility."[17]

One of the key things to remember in dealing with the press is to be honest and open. While you don't have to reveal confidential or sensitive information that may impair the rapid resolution of the crisis, you need to tell the truth in every instance.

As mentioned in chapter 6, working with the press begins long before a crisis occurs if it is to be done properly, and preparation is key to good relations. Let us go back to that subject and look at developing press relations in greater detail.

After assessing what your potential media audience is, you can begin compiling a list of local, regional, national, and international contacts in the following ways:

- Ask to review crisis plans and contact lists of fellow public relations practitioners within your organization, companies similar to yours, or members of professional communication societies in your area (e.g., PRSA, Public Relations Society of America; IABC, International Association of Business Communicators; WIC, Women in Communications; to name but a few organizations).
- Go to the library and review local, regional, and national media guides.

- Contact your local chambers of commerce to see what media are members.
- Use your area telephone books. Many newspapers, cable television outlets, and news media outlets may only be listed here.

This list must be sufficient not only to reach the local community, but also include a global audience. Since news is transmitted around the clock and bureaus are strategically placed so that personnel can be on the scene as soon as possible, local news organizations are thus well equipped to provide instantaneous coverage to networks. Also, do not underestimate the power of the amateur photographer or individuals who possess video camcorders.

Once you narrow your focus, devise a brief questionnaire that encompasses the information needed in an emergency:

1. Secure names and telephone numbers. Get the editor's/director's numbers, as well as the reporter you normally deal with on a daily basis. Make sure your numbers include day, evening, home, fax, beeper, and cellular phone numbers.
2. Ascertain publications/on-air deadlines. Know exactly when the media require their information.
3. Learn what the appropriate format needs to be. Is it a news release they want, or a fact sheet that can be read in thirty seconds?

After compiling this information, prepare a template (e.g., a standard generic release that has blanks left in it allowing it to be used at a moment's notice by dropping in the relevant facts). You should have at least two releases. The first, written in broadcast format, is to provide details to your external audience about what has happened, who has been affected, and what your company is doing to address the problem. The second is a brief paragraph for internal audiences (e.g., employees, shareholders, customers). Type up your sample commercial or public service announcements, news releases, editorials, et cetera. Also develop a form which you will use to record the name of the reporter, the name of the news media, the information shared, and when and where to contact them. If possible, store all material on a diskette as well as make hard copies for reference.

You are then ready to verify the accuracy of your action plan and get feedback on this information.

- Depending upon your company's policies and procedures, distribute the list to your spokespersons, your boss, fellow public relations professionals, and public relations professors in your area. Giving each a reasonable deadline,

have them thoroughly read your contact list, and ask them to return it with their suggestions.
- Personally visit each local news media on your list and have them verify the information. Provide them with the information they will need to contact you.
- Make appropriate changes.
- Test it at an unannounced time.
  —Have someone in your company develop a scenario on paper so that you can write your response.
  —Develop a scenario yourself to test your crisis response team. Observe their responses.

Compile your list and make copies to keep at your office, in your car, at home, and in your briefcase or portfolio. Make sure a copy is included in the company's crisis plan.

When a crisis does occur, it is time to communicate or, in other words, it is time to put the plan into action.

If a news conference meets your needs, you should hold it at a place and time convenient for the news media (consult your media guide). Send a media alert by news wire giving the date, time, place, and a brief message detailing the reason for the news conference. Prepare kits that include material appropriate to the media (news releases for print media are different from broadcast), and include a short biographical sketch of each speaker. Brief your speakers, and conduct a mock news conference where possible questions are posed. Provide for refreshments, extra paper and pencils for the news media, as well as a check-in list at the door so you can follow up with those who could not attend.

Begin on time, as everyone has deadlines. State the reason for the news conference, and ask that questions be held until each individual has spoken. Introduce each speaker in turn. Moderate the question-and-answer session so that questions can be directed to the appropriate individual, and get the conference completed on time.

If you determine that a news conference is not the best alternative, send out the following as soon as possible:

1. Using your generic broadcast release to external publics, contact and notify a news wire service that you are faxing or delivering a release. Depending upon your area and your business, the most useful will be Associated Press, United Press International, a regional news wire, and/or business wire service. List your name and contact telephone number, giving an approximate time for the next update.
2. A news release updating the format established in your plan for the print media should follow, giving more detail.

3. A broadcast news release updating your first release should be sent within four hours of the first to news wire and broadcast news media (and every four hours after that if new information is obtained).

4. Distribute your thirty- and sixty-second commercial/PSA copy to area television, radio, and cable TV outlets. Provide contact telephone numbers for those affected by the crisis.

This initial release of information should occur within twenty-four hours of the event. After that, your situation may need to include the following:

• A tour of the affected site for news media.
• Photographing and/or videotaping for review or media use.
• Conducting a speaker's bureau for presentations to area businesses/organizations.
• Assisting the CEO with a shareholders' meeting.
• Preparing a publication to report on the crisis for one audience, or preparing targeted material for each audience.

After your first seventy-two hours, you will still handle massive amounts of information, but unless it is an unsolved problem you should be on the downhill side. If you have not reached your audiences with your message within that time frame, chances are that other news, not to mention your publics' other concerns, will take precedence. That is why being prepared and carefully handling your most important public, the media, is so important.

Despite what your opinion may be of the news media, they are there to do a job, a job granted to them in the Bill of Rights. Freedom of the press. And they are there not only to do their job, but also to do the best job they can. Let's face it, their byline, or their face, or their voice is read, seen, or heard daily.

So what do you do when faced with an individual who will not take the facts presented and looks for an "angle"?

1. Calmly, politely state that this is the information you possess. You will be happy to provide them with additional information when it becomes available.

2. You appreciate their need to have a different approach for their news media as everyone else is reporting the same situation. Can you arrange an interview for them with someone from the company?

How do you deal with an aggressive reporter?

1. Give the information in a calm tone of voice, presenting a relaxed countenance (this takes a great deal of practice, not to mention patience). Tensing up will only provide a nonverbal message that this individual is getting to you and that you may have something to hide.
2. Restate the information in another way, or ask the reporter to restate his or her question.
3. Tell them that you appreciate their attention to detail, but firmly inform the reporter that this is the information you have and that you will provide them with an update at a specific time. Thank them for their interest and let them know that you have to attend to other reporters' needs.
4. Deal with persistent reporters seeking the identity, for example, of a minor or an adult volunteer by simply informing them that you cannot release names owing to their right to privacy (unless of course the individual has notified you of waiving that right).

What if a reporter asks a question that you have no information about and cannot answer?

- Never say "no comment."
- Tell the reporter that you do not have the information available right now and will get it to them by an agreed-upon deadline. And do it.

What if a reporter asks a question regarding a legal matter?

- Refer to the statement approved by your legal department, or state that, because of company policy, a trained spokesperson from that department may have to answer.

The bottom line in all these scenarios is not to let your ego or emotions get the best of you. You can only come out the loser in any such situation or confrontation.

Don't concentrate an inordinate amount of attention on the daily media coverage. Remember, too, that the media are still just some of many publics. And while their presence will be felt daily, you should be careful not to forget the other groups that need information.

Also, try to avoid the mindset that the media are intruders who've created the problem by devoting so much time and space to it. It is the media's job to report news, and since they are less familiar with the problem, they may seek to fix blame in a crisis. While you may not want this, you should never avoid responsibility. Your organization is expected to act responsibly and respond with swift action and correct information.

It's worth restating that you need to learn to stop talking—a good reporter will ask a question and then let you talk, rarely stopping you—in the hope that you will feel uncomfortable by the silence and thus keep talking. Eventually, you may start answering questions that haven't even been asked and possibly expand the communications crisis at hand by opening up an entirely new avenue for the reporter to travel down. While you need to answer the questions, you don't have to answer questions that have not been asked. By all means, learn to answer the question and stop.

It is also important to remember that people tend to recall the answer more than the question and thus some of these phrases may help redirect a question to the message you wish to communicate:

- That is a good question, but in answering I feel you need to know . . .
- That is possibly one way of looking at it, but first it may be helpful to look at it this way. . . .
- I'm glad you brought that up because here are some important facts to understand. . . .

A word of caution in using this technique is that if you never come back to addressing their question, you may begin to damage your relationship with the press. It is a two-way street—they need information and you want to provide it; however, you are in control of what is said and there is nothing wrong with making sure your message is delivered as you answer the question.

You also don't need to repeat questions, as this sometimes reinforces a negative question posed by the reporter. And be careful about being drawn into a negatively worded question that may put you on the defensive and make you react instead of following your own agenda.

Here are a few examples of such questions for which you should be prepared:

- Is it true that? . . .
- When you said _____, didn't you really mean? . . .
- What did you mean when? . . .
- What is your response to? . . .
- Didn't you? . . .
- Did you know that? . . .
- We understand that? . . .

These questions need to be answered, but in *your* way, not the reporter's. We discussed this earlier when examining training the spokesperson, but it bears repeating that even with a negative question you can turn it around, make it positive, answer it, and deliver one of your key messages. It just takes practice and knowing your messages quite well.

As you are preparing to answer questions, and during the actual interview, make sure your message is worded in such a way that it will get picked up as a sound bite (statements that broadcast media replay as part of a newscast). Every day on the news you can see examples of how an interview is summarized by a reporter and then highlighted by a sound bite from the person being interviewed. You will want to have your messages constructed in a similar manner to facilitate getting them picked up and aired.

Remember these tips when working with the press:

- Use imagery when making a statistical point. While numbers will quickly be forgotten, graphic comparisons won't, such as "enough water to fill Lake Michigan" rather than referring to number of gallons.
- "No comment" should be avoided at all costs. When you have nothing to say—say so—or if you can't respond, say why. And if you don't know, say that and tell the reporter you will get back to him or her (and do so).
- Do not make any comments "off the record," as you must assume that everything you say—especially during a crisis—will be used by the media. Avoid being lulled by a reporter into "painting a picture off the record" to give them a better understanding of the crisis. This may seem innocuous enough, but again, everything you say can end up in print, so you need to proceed along that basis and make all statements, comments, background information, and the like with the full expectation of seeing them in print.
- Don't "stonewall," which means you are constantly stalling the press—not providing them with any information or comments. Again, we spoke before about the fact that a reporter will get a story with or without your help so stonewalling presents the worst of all situations for you: A story will still appear, and since you didn't influence it by providing any information, it will most likely be a negative story, or at least one that does not communicate your key message(s). And because you stonewalled, you have hurt your relations with the press.
- Try to learn about the reporter(s) ahead of time. You can usually see a person on TV, hear them on the radio, or read them in the paper on a regular basis so that you can get a feel for the style with which they report and determine whether they have any possible biases.
- Don't let the interviewer put words in your mouth.
- Don't let the reporter confuse or fluster you with multiple or run-on questions. Be patient and let the interviewer finish. Then begin your response by saying, "You've asked several questions, which I'm happy to answer. Let me start with your main point first." Then *you* determine what that main point

will be. Remember, you are in control since it is you who has the information that people want.

- Try to avoid too many silent gaps during an interview between the time you are asked a question and when you respond. You can have some pat phrases on hand to use to fill the space and still give you time to formulate your response. ("Thanks for asking that . . . that's a good question . . . let me see if I understand your question.") Remember, too, you don't have to repeat the question—which may give emphasis to a negative message—yet you can acknowledge it in a positive vein.
- Logic, of course, dictates not losing your temper or becoming angry under any circumstances. You may find yourself creating another crisis to contend with.
- And finally, you may find it quite helpful to analyze newscasts to review how others deal with reporters. You can tape good interviews and record some of your own practice sessions and compare. Practice does make perfect in dealing with the press.

Again, note the importance at this stage of the crisis of working to contain the current situation and avoid opening up another "can of worms." We have spoken before about learning how to make a statement and then be quiet—even if there is a pause before the next question. At this critical stage of the crisis you may be asked to speculate. You must resist the temptation. No one can fault you for not speculating and simply saying that it is too early to guess what might have caused the situation and that this information would be forthcoming once an investigation has been concluded (if you say this, make sure you hold an investigation and that you do provide the results). But you can be faulted if you speculate and then open up an entirely new line of questioning by the press. Remember, if you have been open and honest and there is nothing left to say, then the press will go elsewhere for a story—you don't have to provide it for them.

The bottom line is to get off the front page in a day or two at the most. By controlling the situation and working effectively with the press, you can do that.

When the crisis is over it is time to evaluate your dealings with the media:

- What worked? What did not?
- What unforeseen event happened that should be included to update the plan?
- What coverage did the crisis receive?
- Was the coverage primarily favorable toward the company? If not, what was the underlying reason?

- Did any rumors/incorrect information get printed? What was the source?
- Was the news media receptive toward public relations' role in the crisis?

As you say your last thank-you to the news media, you will be tempted to return to the annual report, overdue new-product release, volunteer campaign, and other postponed tasks. Getting caught up is paramount in your mind right now, so evaluation is a fading concept. But now is the time to review, when things are still fresh in your memory.

13
Track Public Opinion

As the crisis proceeds you will continually want to track the reporting and public presentation of all information. This is a critical part of the crisis communications process as it allows you to see how and if your messages are getting out. While you will do a thorough evaluation after the crisis is over, you need to be taking straw votes regularly during the crisis to allow for modifications of your plan if necessary.

One way to track opinion is right through your telephone. Your switchboard should be set up to handle comments and inquiries from individuals stating support or disapproval for the situation or your handling of it. It seems that in most crises there will be a large number of people wanting to comment and you should be prepared to handle these comments by noting the date and time the call was made, the individual's name if they will give it, and the phone number. Inform them that their comments have been noted and ask if they would additionally like a call-back from one of the crisis team members who can comment more fully on the situation. It is important to note that switchboard and receptionist individuals should not make comments but merely make note of calls being received.

A mail log will be another way you can track people's perceptions of your company's handling of the crisis. Mail should be logged in on a similar sheet to the phone log. Again, if an individual requests information back, make sure you supply it to them. In any case, a standard acknowledgment letter should be sent out noting that you have received and processed their comments. This form of good follow-through can only help the perception of your company even if the comment was a negative one.

Yet another way to keep track of public opinion will be through the media itself. Your command post, with radio and television capability, will give you an opportunity to keep track of what is being reported. And in many instances talk shows will pick up on the crisis and have call-in opinions from listeners. These too will give you some insight as to what perceptions are developing in the minds of various publics.

You can also make use of the press log as McNeil Consumer Products Company, the makers of Tylenol, did. Using the press log they tracked public opinion where queries had jumped from the normal range of seven hundred to eight hundred per year to two thousand in the month of October alone:

> The press log, which was researched and updated for accuracy, included the name, title, news organization, phone number, address, etc. of every one of the 2,500 plus calls on the Tylenol story in the first several months, as well as everyone who wrote a by-line story, which we researched from the clips as they came in. It was used in numerous ways to communicate with the people closest to the story including inviting them to the video press conference (via satellite) which was our initial event in the Tylenol comeback. Some 600 reporters turned out, making it the largest press conference . . . ever held.[18]

And finally, getting press clippings will allow you almost daily input for this tracking process. But we are warned as practitioners that clippings in and of themselves might not reflect a public's opinion. Clippings can eventually "become the accepted view of what the crisis is about. This is an area where even experienced communicators err. Do not confuse the press with the public. Reach out beyond yesterday's headline and communicate with your key publics—whenever possible, directly."[19]

Sometimes the only way to avoid dancing to the tune of the media is to insist on objective measures of the impact of events on key audiences. Your own ongoing evaluation of public opinion can help you tell your story to the press. By using your telephone and mail logs showing responses and attitudes, you can show how some views may be incorrect. More formal methods of research such as surveys can also be used in profound and protracted crises. It is important to analyze what is being reported about the crisis and your organization. Statement analysis involves looking at what is being said and what perceptions seem to be developing from these reports. Don't assume everyone understands your organization just because you have supplied them with a media kit and some fact sheets, and held a press conference.

Organizations have gone to the extent of evaluating actual comments by the news media in their reports during a crisis. This is important because your organization needs to be concerned about misquotes, misperceptions, and incorrect information being disseminated. You may not want to force a correction on every incident, but you will want to be aware of any facts being misrepresented and contact the reporters so that future articles reflect the information correctly.

This analysis can be facilitated by listing the important facts, noting any possible misperceptions reported, and analyzing any resulting conflicts. How you communicate will then be based upon the importance and magnitude of the misrepresented facts.

If incorrect information is being reported and misperceptions start to develop, work to correct them swiftly. On the other hand, if you have succeeded in getting on and out of the front pages in a day or two, be careful to weigh the costs of potentially reopening the crisis by pushing too hard for corrections.

Part III
After the Crisis

14

Critique and Evaluate

When the crisis is over, it is time to turn your attention to evaluating what occurred and laying plans for any future communications needs. Before you begin the process, however, make sure that the crisis is truly over. When we start examining individual cases, you will see that your determination of the crisis being over is not necessarily how others perceive it. And in this area, perception is reality.

For example, when we look at the Union Pacific train derailment, we will learn that the crisis communications were not over when the fires from the burning tank cars were out—but rather nearly a week later when the tracks were repaired and the line reopened.

And Exxon's woes with the *Valdez* spill did not end with the problems in Alaska. Rather, another communications crisis flared up when the ship attempted to make port in Southern California for repairs.

In essence, then, you need to be continually evaluating the crisis and your plan and the subsequent responses to stay on top of the situation.

When, to the best of your team's ability, you determine the crisis is over—meaning the media have gone home, the command post is shut down, and there are no lingering secondary issues that have sprouted up (if so, deal with them in the same intensity as the initial crisis)—then it is time to evaluate.

This may be the hardest part of your crisis as you will most likely be quite physically and emotionally drained. Your team members, too, will feel drained and want nothing more than to have a break and get back to their "real jobs." But all of your "real jobs" depend on correctly and completely wrapping up this crisis. So while everything is still fresh in everyone's minds, reconvene the team and examine how the crisis went.

Ask these questions:

1. Was the crisis itself handled quickly and effectively? If not, why not?
2. Were the immediate needs handled and the safety and well-being of others dealt with swiftly and capably?
3. Which publics did you communicate with and with which message?
4. Did you miss any publics? Did any need to be added to your plan as the crisis unfolded? (If so, why did your plan initially miss this/these public/s?)
5. How did the command post work?
   - telephones
   - fax
   - security
   - ability to handle media needs
6. Did the communications efforts work according to plan?
7. How did the team members interact?
8. Were any more members needed? Fewer members?
9. Were any departments underrepresented? Overrepresented?
10. Do you feel your messages were communicated?
11. What do you feel the perception/image of your organization is now? And how is this different, if at all, from before the crisis?
12. Were there any miscommunicated messages?

As you approach these last few questions, you and the team may feel unprepared to answer—and that is to be expected. But attempt at this point to get all of your perceptions related to message transmission and public image down on paper. Then you will want to survey as well as possible your various publics to determine if your perceptions are correct or incorrect. You may want, should you have the resources, to commission a formal survey or opinion poll. At the very least, you will need to review the news clips and phone log sheets, and send out questionnaires to a sampling of your publics (employees, stockholders, community leaders, and the like).

Ask these key groups the following questions:

- Did you have enough access to the facts?
- Did you feel the facts were delivered in a timely manner?
- Did you feel that all information was accurate?

• Do you have any ideas as to how we can better supply you with information in the future?

You will also want to approach those reporters involved in communicating during the crisis and ask similar questions—most importantly, did they get the information they needed for their stories in a timely and complete manner?

If all of this sounds vaguely similar to the research stage, or first step of the four-step process of public relations, your perception is correct. As public relations practitioners know, effective communications are based upon first researching, then developing an action plan, communicating that plan, and finally evaluating the results. And although we are in the evaluation stage of the crisis communications, you are in essence beginning the research step of a new cycle of communications.

As you learn of miscommunicated messages, burgeoning misperceptions, or even a tarnished image as a result of the crisis, you can begin developing an action plan to communicate the correct message and clear up any of these problems.

Conversely, you may find yourselves pleasantly surprised at some new positive images befalling your organization as a result of the crisis. No need to pat yourselves on the back and chalk it up to luck; your careful planning and execution allowed that to happen, so determine ways you might communicate this message or image and enhance it further.

It is clear, then, that by evaluating quickly and effectively after the crisis you will be able to check the accuracy of your plan and make any revisions if necessary. You will also be starting the first step, if necessary, to beginning a communications plan designed to correct any misleading impressions or enhance positive new images of your company.

15

Epilogue: Get on with Business

We have spoken throughout this book about the fact that you never know when a crisis may occur and you can never really be sure which company or organization will be affected. This was never more clear than when Dow Corning became embroiled in its own crisis through controversy surrounding its silicone breast implants. The information regarding this incident is just becoming known as this book is being completed, and so a complete case cannot be presented, but we can at least discuss and illuminate one more time that no company is exempt and no problem can be completely written off as having no potential for a crisis.

In this instance complaints had arisen over a period of time about side effects that occur in some women who have breast implants. Crisis management experts caution that whether or not there are facts to prove that silicone breast implants are safe is beside the point if people *perceive* a problem to exist. According to news reports and analyses, the need for Dow to show a human and concerned face is extremely important to those who are involved. To this point, Dow has been rather aloof and the spokesperson's responsibilities have been delegated to an individual within the subdivision. Whether or not this is according to plan has yet to be determined.

One aspect that was initially good was the installation of a hotline for individuals to call should they have concerns. However the FDA put pressure on Dow after it was learned that counselors were spending more time convincing people of the safety rather than simply taking information, and at this writing the hotline has been shut down.

Ironically, one thing that has come out through news articles is that Dow has a history of showing concern even in the face of it being a poor business proposition. For example, their silicone lenses, which were not profitable, were still produced when it was learned that they were the only good source for preventing infant blindness. The company therefore has a good track record in showing concern for public needs and this story not only needs to be told, but this type of involvement and expression of concern for consumers needs to be brought out.

The fact that Dow is not receiving high marks from communications critics may be having an impact as we are already starting to see some changes in the way they are handling the situation. Communications are becoming more proactive and there is a significantly higher amount of information being released to the public.

The case with Dow further shows that crises can occur at any time, to any organization, and that matters can get quickly out of control if not handled swiftly and effectively.

At the same time, it is also important to note that crises do end—one way or another.

Once the crisis is over, you have followed the plan, critiqued and evaluated the entire situation (through meetings of the crisis team), it is simply time to close the books on the incident and move on with life.

In many crises, such as a bus crash, a devastating earthquake, or fire where there is loss of life, there may be scars that will last forever for those who have been associated with the crisis. However, the communications that have been handled well will greatly propel the healing process for your organization.

One thing that always keeps people going during a crisis is knowing that tomorrow will come and all things will pass. So if you have done your best in handling the crisis, communicating in a timely and effective manner with your publics, and been open and honest, you need to move ahead with the current needs of your company. While the emotional scars may last a lifetime, the effect on your company will in time subside, and if there is any comfort in this thought, then it should be passed on to the other members of your crisis team.

Again, borrowing some sayings from the Boy Scouts, "be prepared" before the crisis occurs, "do your best" to handle immediate concerns to rectify the situation and communicate with the appropriate publics, and finally, get on with the business of doing a "good turn" daily for your customers.

Part IV

Case Studies

USAir/SkyWest Crash at Los Angeles International Airport

February 1, 1991

Diane Reesman, public relations specialist for the City of Los Angeles Department of Airports, related the events surrounding the first major incident at Los Angeles International Airport since 1978. What happened and how the public relations bureau handled the crisis provides a good case study.

● BACKGROUND

Los Angeles International Airport (LAX) serves approximately one hundred airlines and handled 45.8 million passengers in 1990. There are approximately eighteen hundred flights each day and the Department of Airports regularly conducts mock disasters including practice rescue drills in preparation for a real incident.

● THE INCIDENT

On Friday evening, February 1, 1991, a USAir 737 carrying eighty-three passengers and six crew members slammed into a SkyWest Metroliner carrying ten passengers and two crew members on Runway 24 Left at LAX. The 737 was just landing when the crash occurred. As an investigation later showed, an air traffic controller forgot that the Metroliner was holding for takeoff on the runway. The smaller plane was engulfed by fire and the two planes skidded a distance of 1,540 feet before coming to rest against a building adjacent to Runway 24L.

The fire department arrived on the scene within one minute of the crash and it took approximately thirty minutes to extinguish the fire. Only then was it learned that the Metroliner (second plane) was involved, as it was almost completely disintegrated. A triage center was established and ultimately there were sixty-seven survivors.

● EMERGENCY LOGISTICS

Agencies responding to the incident included the Los Angeles City Fire Department, Los Angeles City Police Department, the Department of Airports (operations, police, construction and maintenance, public relations bureaus), National Transportation Safety Board, Los Angeles County Coroner's Office, American Red Cross, USAir, and SkyWest.

The Los Angeles City Fire Department and the airport police set up command posts on site from which regular briefings were held. Radios, portable bathrooms, and cellular phones were all brought to the command center. (Since the media monitors the radio frequencies, sensitive information was transmitted via cellular phones.) The airport's construction and maintenance bureau erected a wall to screen the morgue area from the view of airplanes taxiing to and from terminals and runways.

Planning meetings were held at the command post every hour from Friday evening through Saturday. Meetings were held every three hours on Sunday. All agencies and bureaus were represented at these meetings.

American Airlines allowed the use of its hangar facilities to store the pieces of the airplanes and the National Transportation Safety Board began its investigation.

The fire department brought in a chaplain and psychologist as part of the response team. It is important to note that psychological debriefings continued for one month after the incident. Psychological support was available not only to the victims and their families, but also to assist response-team members who were feeling the trauma of the situation. At the time, response-team members would simply be doing their job and "not thinking about what was actually happening," but sometimes the stress would force them to obtain assistance.

● COMMUNICATIONS

As part of the communications plan for air disasters, the lead agency for disseminating information will change as the incident progresses. Initially, the airport's public relations bureau handled inquiries the night of the crash. They concentrated on providing only confirmed facts—which were sometimes hard to come by. They also coordinated the first press briefing where the chief of the fire department and the mayor of Los Angeles addressed the media. A press pool was formed and escorted to the crash site by fire department and airport public relations staff immediately after approval was granted by the National Transportation Safety Board. This took place approximately five hours after the incident. A second press pool was formed and escorted to the crash site on Saturday, February 2, at approximately 1:00 P.M. The public relations bureau, with a staff of fourteen people, made five representatives available to speak with the media. Besides these staff interviews, the bureau coordinated the availability of outside experts, as needed, for certain details and sidebar articles.

As the incident progressed, the media focused more on the airlines involved, the fire department, Federal Aviation Administration, and the National Transportation Safety Board.

During the fifty-two hours of the incident, the public relations bureau logged some five thousand calls from the U.S. and around the world.

Beginning the second day (Saturday) of the incident, the fire department assumed the lead communications role with the National Transportation Safety Board (NTSB) having veto power. By the end of the second day, the NTSB assumed the lead communications role and held press conferences for another five days at a nearby hotel.

● MEDIA RELATIONS

According to Diane Reesman, who heard about the crash at home at 6:10 P.M. and arrived on site at 7:40 P.M., there was a news "feeding frenzy" during those first hours where reporters "wanted it all and wanted it now." Media helicopters circled the crash site for approximately ninety minutes before the FAA cleared the airspace for safety reasons. The press was also able to get information through the press pools (one on Friday night, the second on Saturday afternoon). Reporters additionally rented apartments nearby so they could take photographs from the balconies looking toward the crash site.

● **AFTERMATH**

The NTSB stayed on site for one week before returning to Washington, D.C. to conclude its investigation through interviews and hearings. It was ultimately determined that human error was the cause of the accident due to an over-worked controller who forgot that the SkyWest plane was still on the runway when the USAir 737 was cleared to land. Since the accident and subsequent investigation, there has been relatively little coverage by the media regarding the event.

The Exxon *Valdez* Oil Spill

● **THE INCIDENT**

On the evening of March 24, 1989, the seas in the Prince William Sound were calm and the weather was good. The Exxon *Valdez,* a 987-foot oil tanker, left the harbor of south Alaska's Valdez and headed for California. At approximately 11:30 P.M., the local pilot who had guided the tanker out of the port went off duty and the third mate manning the bridge was given permission by the U.S. Coast Guard to change course in order to avoid icebergs.

Twenty minutes later the oil tanker plunged into rocks and was grounded on Bligh Reef in Prince William Sound. Approximately 11 million gallons, or 240,000 barrels, of Prudhoe Bay crude oil poured out of the gashes in the tanker's hull and spilled into the sound. According to one estimate, the oil slick was roughly one thousand feet wide and four miles long, spreading southwest from Bligh Reef and up the coastline to the Aleutian Islands, some eight hundred fifty miles away.

The spill occurred during the semiannual migration that provides Prince William Sound with the largest concentration of migratory fowl in the world. Millions of birds, seals, otters, fish, and whales fell victim to the pollution and perished. This environmental disaster—America's worst oil spill—became international news and the world waited for Exxon's response.

● EXXON'S RESPONSE

In 1989 Exxon was one of the five largest companies in the United States, with sales of nearly $80 billion. At the helm of this megacorporation was CEO Lawrence G. Rawl, the son of a truck driver and an ex-marine. Rawl had been employed by Exxon for thirty-seven years before assuming the responsibility of CEO and was generally viewed as a vibrant and visionary leader. He was also noted for having a strong disdain for publicity and the media. This was probably the guiding factor behind the handling of the crisis.

No organization can eliminate public scrutiny, but Exxon—a company with vast public relations resources and experience—was given poor marks by public relations observers for being late and lax in informing the public. Several hours after the disaster, the media asked for a statement from Exxon's headquarters in Houston. They received a vague and uninformative response. According to Exxon's headquarters, the Exxon Shipping Company, the manufacturer responsible for oil tanker transportation, would have to answer the media's questions. A week after the spill, Exxon had still not addressed the issue. Dennis Stanczuk, media relations coordinator, responded to questions posed by journalists by stating that his boss had forbidden him to answer any questions. More than a week after disaster, Brian Dunphy, another Exxon Shipping spokesperson, could not verify the extent of the damage or what was being done to rectify the situation. Top Exxon executives declined to comment, thereby increasing the impression that the company was not responding vigorously.

To deal with the disaster, Exxon set up its media center in Valdez, Alaska, a remote town with limited communications operations. Exxon explained that they had located the information center in Valdez because the media would best be served from this location, and filtering news through operating companies in major metropolitan centers would not be the most effective means of communication. Rick Hagar of *Oil and Gas Journal* wrote in an editorial that the Valdez center's infrastructure was unable to handle the vast number of inquires from reporters and the public. Hagar also made the point that handling media out of a major city such as New York or Houston would have been logical and convenient for the media and probably would have been more manageable for Exxon. Robert P. Irvine, APR, executive vice president of Jack Guthrie & Associates, voiced a different opinion. He believed that Valdez was the most logical location because that is where the media were. Public statements by Exxon were often erratic and contradictory. At one news briefing, an Exxon spokesperson said there would be minimal environmental damage, while others in the industry said the damage would likely be substantial.

A series of lower-ranking Exxon executives were sent to Valdez to act as spokespersons. Rawl did not immediately fly to Alaska because according to him, he was technologically "obsolete." Going to the site would have diverted his people's attention away from the immediate need of cleaning up the spill. The first news conference conducted by the president of Exxon Shipping concluded in a battle with fishermen and journalists. The president of Exxon U.S.A. was then dispatched to Valdez. Six days after the incident, Rawl appeared on television with a factual story describing the kinds of chemicals that Exxon would utilize to clean up the oil spill. He made no apologies to the fishermen whose livelihood had been adversely affected and showed no emotion over the tremendous environmental impact of the disaster. Ten days after the spill Exxon released a full-page advertisement in newspapers around the world that expressed their concern and guaranteed to do everything possible to clean up the oil. Although Exxon apologized for the disaster, it did not accept responsibility for the incident. On April 14, three weeks after the incident, Rawl finally went to Alaska.

During the last week of July 1989, the damaged oil tanker was moored in San Diego harbor. Of all the damage caused by the March 24 disaster, the repair of the tanker was the easiest and the least expensive, about $25 million to repair. Exxon will pay $1 billion in civil penalties over ten years and $125 million in criminal fines. These fines amount to only two days' profits for Exxon, which earned $5.01 billion in 1990 and the $1 billion payout spread over ten years will cost Exxon approximately $600 million in 1991 dollars. The human toll of the cleanup involved 10,000 workers, 1,000 watercraft, 70 airplanes and helicopters, 134 aquatic biologists and toxicologists, 2 archaeologists, and a historian.

● THE CRISIS COMMUNICATIONS PLAN

Exxon may not have been prepared for such an expansive disaster. Their crisis management plan allotted only five hours for the containment of an oil spill. The main flaw was that the plan for a five-hour crisis was underestimated. Thus, when the spill occurred, nearly two days elapsed before the plan was put into action.

In order to prevent this crisis management failure, an organization must simulate predicted crisis situations, familiarize staff and executives with the stresses of potential and inevitable crisis situations. During such an exercise the errors in the plan can be discovered long before a real crisis hits. Crisis communications plans are virtually worthless without the proper measures of simulation and rehearsal. Practicing the execution of the crisis communications plan is part of the plan itself, and is strategic for gaining control when a crisis does occur.

While planning is a necessity for a crisis communications plan, the effectiveness comes from having all crisis management team members, especially spokespersons, know their individual roles and responsibilities. The *Valdez* incident reaffirmed the need for companies to set up a preexisting crisis communications plan, test the plan, and respond quickly and compassionately.

The Ashland Oil Refinery Disaster

In 1988, Ashland Oil, Inc., was the nation's thirteenth largest oil company and its second largest independent oil refiner. This was also the year Ashland Oil experienced the company's most publicized crisis of the decade, a 750,000-gallon diesel oil spill into the Monongahela and Ohio rivers.

In January of 1988, a defective storage tank made from forty-year-old untested steel was moved by the company to a different location and ruptured in the process. Within seven days, an oil slick had spread over one hundred miles into the Ohio River basin, threatening to contaminate the water supplies of 750,000 people in four states.

Ashland Oil, Inc., chairman John R. Hall faced the crisis head-on. According to Hall, it was just a human reaction on his part and his colleagues'. "Our attitude was: 'Hey, guys, we've made a mess here. We've got to clean this thing up and we've got to try to do anything we can to help all the people who have been inconvenienced, to try to minimize the impact.'" As soon as Hall learned of the cause of the spill, he rushed to Pittsburgh to oversee the control of the crisis. He made himself and other top executives available for questions and he accepted complete responsibility for the spill. Hall brushed aside the cautious advice of his lawyer and made a public apology, admitting that the company had made an error in its usage of the tank. Ashland requested and paid for the Battelle Institute to complete an independent investigation. Without knowing the results of this investigation, Hall called a press conference to reveal the findings. Battelle announced that a flaw in the steel caused the rupture.

Following the crisis, Ashland Oil made a grant to the University of Pittsburgh to provide funding for a study assessing the long-term environmental impact on the waterways. Researchers concluded that no significant long-term effects on the river system were expected, but recommended additional monitoring of a few areas. Ashland provided the funds for further observation of the waterways.

Hall's handling of the situation received positive recognition and approval. The Louisville *Courier-Journal* commented that "the company has come away remarkably unscathed, and it may well emerge with a better public image than before the disaster." The 21 April 1989 edition of *The New York Times* quoted a crisis management consultant's review of Hall's handling of the crisis: "[Hall] was a little slow out of the blocks, but after a day and a half he began to move heaven and earth. . . . He pledged to clean everything up, he visited news bureaus to explain what the company would do, he answered whatever questions were asked. Within twenty-four hours he had turned the perception from 'rotten oil company' to 'they are pretty good guys.' " Hall even received praise at the source of the spill in Pittsburgh. Carnegie-Mellon University's graduate school of industrial administration presented Hall with the honor of "Outstanding Crisis Manager of 1988."

This crisis cost Ashland Oil approximately $40 million in fines and legal claims, $10 million coming directly from the company, and $30 million paid for by insurance. Hall had only one regret concerning how he handled the crisis. He remarked that he should not have waited until the second day after the spill to make any public statements. He did this only because he believed he would have better and more accurate information to share. When handling a crisis, he said, "you really need to respond pretty quickly."[20]

Crystal Cruise Line—Fire at Sea

Norman Sklarewitz, a Los Angeles–based travel and business writer, presented a textbook crisis communications case when he described an incident involving the *Crystal Harmony*, a $200-million cruise liner. The incident occurred on Monday, October 1, 1990, at 5:32 P.M. Pacific Standard Time when a fire started in the auxiliary engine room of the 49,500-ton vessel.[21]

There were no deaths or injuries from the fire, but the ship, part of Crystal Cruises—a wholly owned subsidiary of NYK Line, Inc., Tokyo—was stopped dead in the water. This information, along with the fact that there were 920 guests and 540 crew members aboard, and only nominal emergency power, was reported to the director of public relations of Crystal Cruises at 7:15 P.M. The director of public relations received the information at home from the senior vice president of sales who had been called on the radio phone by the captain of the cruise ship.

The disaster was labeled a shipboard crisis, per the plan outlined in the company's crisis communications manual,[22] and the director of public relations wasted no time in setting this plan in motion. She began calling the other members of the predetermined crisis management team (CMT): the president of Crystal Cruises and designated company spokesman; the senior vice president for marketing who was also the CMT coordinator and alternate spokesperson; the senior vice president for sales and alternate spokesman; the senior vice president for marine operations and the on-site coordinator; the senior vice president for finance who acted as financial and legal liaison backup; and the senior vice president for Japanese media.

The plan called for at least one of the key CMT members to be present at all times, although the director of public relations felt that this situation would require all team members. However, since several members were traveling and unavailable, the senior vice president for sales became the person in charge, with the director of public relations acting as backup. (These backup designations were also defined in the plan under the heading of crisis management team responsibilities.)

Messages were left for the other members of the team and they arrived as soon as possible. Those who could not make it in time were replaced by other key individuals and were joined by two members of the cruise line's public relations firm—the group supervisor and the senior account executive.

The conference room at the office was the designated center of operations and the director of public relations began preparing this room and making additional copies of the crisis manual while waiting for the other team members to arrive. It was discovered, though, that the phones serving the conference room would not be available as the switchboard, which handled calls to the room, was shut down for the night. The team needed an outside direct line for communications, so an office of one of the vice presidents was used instead, although it was more cramped.

The first update for the team came at 9:30 P.M. over the speaker phone as the captain informed the team members of his announcement to the passengers and crew. He had ordered the crew to their emergency stations and informed the passengers of the fire but that it posed no danger to them. Once the fire had been controlled, the captain then dismissed the crew from their stations at 8:50 P.M.

The captain then informed them that the ship was without power and electricity other than emergency generators. Therefore, toilets, water, air-conditioning, and galley refrigerators were not working. The passengers were then told to make themselves as comfortable as possible on deck and the ship would supply complimentary beverages and snacks.

With the team aware of the facts involved, the ship-to-shore communications were shut down to allow emergency communications only, and action to correct the situation was commenced. One of the team members began the process of securing tug boats from South America to tow the disabled ship back to port. By 2:00 A.M. the next morning, the necessary tugs had been located in Cristobal, Colombia; Panama; and Venezuela. However, it turned out that three of the four engines had been started by Tuesday afternoon so that the tugs were not needed. With the ship under some power, it was estimated that she would reach Cristobal on Thursday, October 4.

By late Monday evening, the entire team was assembled at the command center, but in order to maintain consistency, the acting coordinator remained the same. The team now turned its attention to preparing for media coverage. There was concern about the incident getting a lot of play as there had been some other unfortunate incidents with other cruise ships in the prior months. However, since the ship was still well off the coast of Panama and the phones were shut down for emergency purposes, the ship was not accessible to reporters or camera crews. This gave the CMT time to prepare press releases and communicate with the key publics. During Tuesday, then, the press release was written and faxed to Japan for approval. Other advisories were prepared for port agents, employees, suppliers, and travel agents, as the next scheduled sailing of the *Crystal Harmony* would have to be canceled.

By 4:30 A.M. Tuesday, the communiqués were completed and the public relations staff began preparing a set of sample questions most likely to be addressed by the press together with appropriate answers. And at 5:45 A.M. the first press release was faxed to the Associated Press, Reuters, Business Wire, and major East Coast papers. Selected consumer magazines and free-lance travel writers were also provided the information. The team's goal was to communicate directly with the press as opposed to having the media get the information from other sources as had been the case in the past with incidents involving ships at sea.

The media in the Midwest received the release between 5:45 A.M. and 6:45 A.M. with the West Coast being informed beginning at 8:45 A.M.

Some secretarial support became available around 5:00 A.M. and reservation agents who had been called at home also began showing up early so that the company would be prepared to begin handling the inquiries. As the employees arrived, they were given a copy of the news release and a memo explaining the situation. Everyone was informed not to take outside calls or phone out. It was made clear that only authorized personnel would speak for the company. Key members of the CMT were available to answer questions from the employees before they went to their work areas.

A follow-up press release was then prepared and disseminated at 4:30 P.M. Tuesday and presented information on the ship's status as it made its way to Colombia. A third release was issued two days later as the ship arrived in port and the passengers disembarked. This release also provided information on three chartered jets that would take the passengers to Los Angeles, Atlanta, and Seattle for connecting flights.

And the last release came on October 9 with the announcement that regular sailings would resume on October 27. With this last release, the team completed the communication of its four major messages.

The incident generated a rather light media response with no television or radio coverage and only minimal print coverage; those papers that did run stories kept them to three or four paragraphs. No press conference was called as the key media noted that the press releases and phone calls were sufficient. Phone inquiries totaled eighty.

The president of the cruise line was available at the October 2 employee briefing and at the arrival of the ship in Cristobal. The president was joined by other key executives at the ship and brought full refund checks for all the passengers. The passengers also received a letter apologizing for the inconveniences and were offered $500 in credit for future cruises or special services already purchased.

The response to the company's handling was quite positive. The media had never seen a cruise line handle a crisis this way before and 280 passengers signed a letter expressing their appreciation for the handling of the incident. The next sailing of the *Crystal Harmony* was sold out and bookings for the rest of the year were near capacity.

The management team of the company reviewed the plan and the crisis and was pleased with the way it had been handled. The only changes that were made for the future were to include secretarial support early on and install a private line in the conference room so that it could be used.

Red Cross Response—The San Francisco Earthquake

At 5:05 P.M. on Tuesday, October 17, 1989, as millions of people around the world tuned in to watch game three of the World Series, an earthquake occurred along the Loma Prieta fault line, providing a live example of what an earthquake can do. Scenes of fires, the collapse of a section of the Nimitz Freeway, and another on the San Francisco Bay Bridge replaced views of Candlestick Park and the game.

And, although just two weeks prior another natural disaster in the form of Hurricane Hugo had swept through the Caribbean and South Carolina leaving a larger path of death and destruction than the San Francisco earthquake, the media did not have the access to affected areas and thus, few images were available for evening newscasts. The opportunity for access was completely different in the San Francisco earthquake and the stage was set for much coverage and the need for effective crisis communications. This media coverage would generate problems not encountered with Hurricane Hugo. This case outlines a few of the problems precipitated by the vast amount of media coverage.

One minute after the Northern California earthquake occurred, American Red Cross staff and volunteers responded. The San Francisco Chapter volunteer staff crawled out from underneath the table where they had taken refuge and began the job of preparing emergency shelters and food for earthquake victims (shelters were opened one to two hours after the earthquake occurred). They were joined by other area Red Cross volunteers, some of whom were staffing first aid stations at Candlestick Park. Initial damage assessment provided an evaluation of disaster-caused human needs, while radio communications were used to obtain vital information.

Volunteers and staff trained in disaster relief were recruited from across the country through the computerized Disaster Service Human Resource System (DSHR) at Eastern Operations Headquarters in Alexandria, Virginia as Western Operations in Burlingame, California had no electricity or telephones. Supplies to keep the operation going were sought and would continue throughout the relief effort.

As the Red Cross disaster relief operations continued, caseworkers accessed updated damage assessment information in order to determine whether an individual or family would need long-term shelter, clothing, replacement of basic household furnishings, or assistance with medical needs. While the American Red Cross is mandated by Congress to provide relief to the victims of disaster, it receives no government funding. Disaster relief and all other programs are funded by contributions from United Way and direct private donations from the American public. Thus, the public affairs function of the American Red Cross has both a primary and secondary goal in meeting the needs of disaster victims. The primary goal is to provide disaster victims and their families with information about Red Cross services and how to access them. The secondary goal is to develop, implement, and evaluate communication strategies that enhance the Red Cross image in order to provide both the human and financial resources necessary to meet disaster-caused needs.

Very little education about the role of the Red Cross in a disaster was done in the San Francisco Bay Area for several years before the earthquake. This included not only the public, but also the news media and local government. Part of the problem was that the Red Cross public relations department staff changed frequently, resulting in lack of continuity. An untrained and inexperienced staff compounded the situation.

When public affairs personnel trained in disaster relief first arrived to coordinate efforts in the San Francisco Bay Area (Region One), they were not located at disaster headquarters. Although groups usually work as a team during a disaster, this did not occur during the San Francisco earthquake. Donations poured in faster than they could be counted. This meant that public relations personnel did not have an accurate accounting of what had been raised. Despite the unusual, overwhelming response from the public, the fund-raising group did not issue a statement to curtail public appeals. About two weeks into the relief operation, the media and area governments began to demand a specific accounting of what was being raised and spent.

In Santa Cruz County south of San Francisco, the situation was totally different, but the needs were just as great, since it lay closer to the fault line. A large Latino population, some of them undocumented aliens, had little or no political representation. Out of this emerged a suit against the county, creating a bitter situation between the Caucasian and Latino populations. In order to accomplish the task at hand, the Red Cross had to deal separately with each group, even though they were accused of compromising their neutrality.

The Latino population preferred living in tent cities rather than a building because many had lived through the Mexico City earthquake. In that area, buildings were old and not prepared to withstand an earthquake, so aftershocks destroyed what minutes before had appeared safe. In addition, few Red Cross personnel spoke Spanish and most were unfamiliar with the dietary preferences of this group.

Relief efforts for Hurricane Hugo and the Northern California earthquake were not just spread out geographically. Human and financial resources were stretched beyond the ability to cope, as these disasters were on a relief scale Red Cross had never previously faced and resources were drained.

To better illustrate the communication problems encountered by the Red Cross, Kim Schwartz, director of marketing/communications, provides three separate eyewitness accounts.

Peggy McGinley, director of media relations for the American Red Cross Los Angeles Chapter, who was the Red Cross public affairs officer for the San Francisco/Oakland area, known as Region One, during the first three weeks following the earthquake recounts the following:

I was on a plane the afternoon of October 18, less than a day after the quake. I checked in, was briefed at Western Operation Headquarters and assigned to the San Francisco area. I reported to Bob Howard, who was the public affairs officer for the entire Red Cross Northern California earthquake relief effort at that time.

When the telephones came back on, it was all backed up with many, many calls. When it was finally possible to get through, the cellular telephone I used was crucial as I could be reached no matter where I was.

The lack of existing public relations efforts in the area resulted in the public expecting Red Cross to do more than what our role is following a disaster. We are there to meet emergency needs. This was complicated by public relations not being consulted by the chapter early on about potential problems and not being housed in the disaster headquarters, but at the chapter.

The media response was outstanding during the first two weeks. It was a PR person's dream. Red Cross was chosen ABC's Person of the Week, the first time an organization received that distinction. The media thought very highly of Red Cross as they would focus on the positive stories of Red Cross aiding the disaster victims.

But certain local media became more difficult towards the end of my three week assignment, asking intense questions, "What is being raised? Where is it going?" San Francisco Mayor Art Agnos also wanted an accounting. And the social service agencies we normally refer the homeless and longterm assistance cases to felt Red Cross would take care of everything.

Hope Tuttle, Director of Public Affairs for the American Red Cross Seattle-King County Chapter, who was the Red Cross public affairs officer for the Santa Cruz County and surrounding area south of San Francisco known as Region Two during the first four weeks following the earthquake provides the following:

It was like working on two separate jobs. I dealt with the rural, migrant farmer problems, while Peggy worked with the metropolitan and suburban populations.

This disaster had me dealing with more different kinds of media than on any other operation and the national media interest continued longer than I had ever experienced. Days would begin with a 5 A.M. live broadcast to CBS Morning News and would end with a live radio interview from my hometown at 10 P.M. Geraldo Rivera's people called wanting to interview 40 disaster victims to be part of his talk show. They gave us two days warning. We obtained half that amount, some of whom were not only victims, but also Red Cross volunteers. It was hard to find people willing to do this, because grief had really started to set in (about two weeks after the earthquake). The media were extremely thick in the area and people were tired of talking about it. The program turned out well. I made sure that all the Red Cross people had identification, or dressed in Red Cross clothing to illustrate that Red Cross had been, and was, right in the community—it was really neighbors who were helping neighbors.

I also conducted two VIP tours. Mrs. Quayle, the Vice President's wife came to dinner at the shelter housed in National Guard tents. The Secret Service came a day and a half before she arrived to check out who she would talk to, what food she would eat, who would cook the meal, where she'd walk, where the lights would be, etc. Some of the undocumented aliens were very nervous because she represented government at the highest level. We made sure anyone who wanted to stay out of the "limelight" could do so.

Mick Jagger was the other VIP. His manager had a home in Boulder Creek, in the middle of the quake zone, so he became interested in what Red Cross was doing. Jagger was holding a concert in Oakland and he arrived by helicopter. He toured the tent shelter with the Red Cross and then downtown Watsonville with the mayor of that town. He was shocked at the destruction (half the downtown was totally destroyed). He seemed genuinely concerned about the town's survival and how it would affect jobs. He gave the American Red Cross $500,000—$250,000 to earthquake relief and $250,000 to Hurricane Hugo relief efforts.

Both the VIP tours took time and energy but were necessary to ensure that the story of the disaster, its victims, and the recovery was known. By having Public Information staff work on arrangements for the visits, it allowed those who were giving direct services to do so with a minimum of interruption. There were two major problems that impacted our work. One situation had occurred quite some time before the earthquake but did affect us. The situation was political and pervasive. The Latino population had little or no representation in county government and sued over the issue. They won, but it created two angry sides. We couldn't deal with both of them at the same time, so we had to deal with both separately. This made the job more difficult because we had to continually reassure people of our neutrality.

The other major issue is that undocumented aliens who had applied for the United States amnesty program to become citizens were confused about the Red Cross role. Their paperwork stated that they could receive no government aid. Their experience in their own countries led them to believe that the Red Cross is tied very closely to the government. Other undocumented aliens were afraid to register their true names for the same reason. Caesar Chavez agreed to make public service announcements to assure victims that all information given to the Red Cross is confidential and that the Red Cross is not part of the United States government.

Most of the Latinos would not enter any building as they remembered that the aftershocks of the Mexico City earthquake in 1986 had themselves destroyed buildings. The county government arranged for the National Guard to set up tents in a baseball field in Watsonville and this became another Red Cross shelter site. One media story out of Oakland pictured only Latinos living in tents and featured a Caucasian family in one of the shelters in a building. They didn't explain that people could reside at the shelter of their choice. We didn't get bad local reaction as the area news media asked about the situation and cleared it up.

What was essential was that the Santa Cruz chapter was well-prepared, started relief work immediately, and worked cooperatively with Red Cross paid and volunteer staff brought in to assist. Larry Gilliam, the Red Cross Public Affairs Chairman, was a disaster victim himself and had a newborn baby, but he continued to assist when needed. Local chapter volunteers lent a hand when they could get time off, including a husband-wife team who helped take photographs and write feature stories for the media and the volunteer newsletter.

It stuck in the local residents' craw that the earthquake was portrayed as the "San Francisco earthquake," when the fault was in *their* area and the damage was more widespread. We used the volunteers' photographs to produce a special photo montage showing local pictures and correctly identified it as the Loma Prieta earthquake. This small gift to paid and volunteer staff who had worked hard and long on relief efforts really seemed to make a difference.

The next account is from David Giroux. Giroux, then assistant manager for the American Red Cross Pine Tree Chapter in Bangor, Maine, was assigned for six weeks to Hurricane Hugo and later assisted Red Cross earthquake relief efforts for two weeks. Giroux now works in the media relations section of External Communications at Red Cross national headquarters in Washington, D.C.

I worked with Elizabeth Quirk, Disaster Services specialist with the American Red Cross Sacramento area chapter who was the Public Affairs officer for the entire Northern California relief effort at that time.

Organizationally the biggest concern was dealing with the financial development issues—dealing with an outpouring of public support and what was the American Red Cross doing with the money. A lot of our work was backtracking to see what was missed early on from a communication angle.

We had an unprecedented level of public attention to the earthquake. This was a perfect example of how media visibility can drive public emotion and a number of factors contributed to this. Hugo cut a swath through the Caribbean in which nothing survived. But the media couldn't get access to the islands and even into remote areas of South Carolina so there were very few visual images available.

Contrast that with the earthquake happening on worldwide television, with people seeing their worst nightmare happen to San Francisco. Pictures of the stadium where the World Series was taking place were contrasted with scenes of fire and a car plummeting off a bridge. And it wasn't just primetime viewing, the media was able to access any area they wanted. It was an uphill battle explaining to people that needs exist all across the country, but everything was overshadowed by the earthquake.

With the scope of these disaster relief operations, we were bringing in thousands of workers, and helping disaster victims. These numbers increase the chances that problems and communication errors will occur. Not to mention the people who misrepresent themselves as Red Cross personnel while selling food, ice, or other products. This threatens the public level of trust. The two disasters together presented us with a level of performance we didn't have experience in, but it forced us to raise our standards. We now have some valuable experience in catastrophic disaster planning and communication, so we'll be better prepared for the next one.

In dealing with the media and the public, before the disaster, it seems that we didn't communicate effectively about what services we provide and role we play in disaster relief and preparedness. We weren't communicating clearly how people could help, so the issue of contributions wasn't always handled well from the start. Our own spokespersons didn't always understand the policies and procedures on gifts designated for a specific disaster. Public perception is in fact *everything*, with the first 24 or 48 hours following a disaster determining whether you succeed or fail.

The other important factor we learned is that the technology being used by the news media—our most ravenous consumers of information—is something we need to adapt just to keep pace. We are making that investment now in order to help disaster victims and the public.

And finally, Henry N. Tuttle, the former public relations director for the American Red Cross Massachusetts Bay Chapter, provides the last view. Tuttle stepped in as director of public affairs for the American Red Cross San Francisco Bay Area executive unit in March 1990. He is now the communication director of the American Red Cross Northern California Earthquake Relief and Preparedness Project.

> I arrived to see headlines screaming "Did Red Cross Do the Right Thing?" The department had been previously handled by another Red Cross staff member who had no public relations experience, and unlike the other Red Cross executive unit personnel the communications department had never been fully consolidated. My office was a storage area filled with boxes and few files. I rearranged an office staff of one internal communicator and secretary and ended up with only a secretary. This meant I handled both the chapter public relations and the public affairs job for the earthquake which still needed someone in that position. By May, I had hired a staff of two additional personnel; one to handle internal communications and another to handle external communications.
>
> I had to convince the Public Relations Committee and its Chairman Rod Hartung, Vice President of Public Affairs for Chevron, that attention was now being paid to the function as they were frustrated with the current situation. And I must add, Chevron helped an awful lot.
>
> A five part image recovery plan was begun to curb criticism of Red Cross. This involved an internal audit of Public Affairs in Northern California, external marketing research and finally matching that public perception with internal capacity. Mary Ackerly, Director of Corporate Communications for the American Red Cross Metropolitan Atlanta Chapter, came out to handle this effort for three months. Another research company had done a study for a local nonprofit and had included the American Red Cross for comparison before the earthquake. The results showed that Red Cross suffered a ten percent drop in confidence among the public. As of the 1991 survey, Red Cross has a 95% familiarity rating and 89% favorability rating.

● RETROSPECT

The American Red Cross had a policy of permitting the public to help a particular disaster, but if all disaster-caused needs had been met in a community, any surplus funds would be held in reserve for future disasters. In response to public dissatisfaction with this policy caused, in part, by media misrepresentation of Red Cross policy, the Red Cross made a decision to keep all funds donated for the earthquake in northern California—including over-subscriptions—for use in relief and preparedness following the northern California earthquakes. A blue ribbon committee chaired by John B. M. Place, the retired CEO of Crocker Bank, recommended that the then available $32.9 million be split into four categories of relief projects, including some that went beyond the traditional types of Red Cross relief: 1) traditional Red Cross disaster relief; 2) external grants project; 3) case management project; and 4) chapter preparedness project. Four months later the Northern California Earthquake Relief and Preparedness Project was formed.

Two million dollars went to assist chapters with case management in the wake of the earthquake, with another $2 million going towards preparedness efforts. With funding from the relief and preparedness project, an effort was made to create training for communicators, as well as a crisis textbook to be used for reference.

Training began during the fall of 1991 with over one hundred Red Cross communicators trained during that time period.

A five-day intensive effort is involved by the participant. Public Affairs I, a course that covers how to handle a local disaster, is followed by Public Affairs II, a course that details the issues, concerns, and staffing necessary for a national disaster. An in-depth, probing media training, an overview of Red Cross forms, and fund-raising basics round out the training.

The text used during this course was "Communication During a Crisis—A Guide to Effective Public Affairs." Published in October 1991, this guide quickly ran through its first printing of over three thousand copies. The book contains an introduction which outlines the Red Cross mission, defines communicators' roles, details the audiences and sensitivities to be addressed, and discusses coordinating efforts. The action steps section takes the individual from preparedness through completing the job. Sample fact sheets, news releases, and public service announcements are included for reference. Sample scenarios, as well as an appendix of reference material, are attached as part of the guide. Guidelines are also given for donor designation. The language is specific and encourages donors to contribute to the Disaster Relief Fund, which can be utilized to respond to any disaster.

The American Red Cross continues to place a strong emphasis on recruiting staff and volunteers who are bilingual, and has updated disaster training to include sections on dealing with clients of other cultures.

Chrysler Minivan Crisis

In early 1991, *Consumer Reports* magazine reported problems with Chrysler minivans equipped with the A604 Ultradrive four-speed automatic transmission. This report propelled Chrysler into a crisis communication mode to handle what they felt was a direct attack on their most lucrative product line.

In 1990, Chrysler held 47 percent of the U.S. minivan market with 380,374 of the company's 1,698,068 U.S. vehicle sales being minivans. Chrysler, as well as most U.S. automotive manufacturers, makes little profit from North American passenger car sales. Their primary source of profit revenue is from Jeep and minivan sales. Therefore, Chrysler could ill afford to lose the bread and butter of their company's sales. During a satellite telecast to dealers, Chrysler Corporation chairman Lee Iacocca remarked, "We have a very serious problem right now that could drive us all out of business if we don't address it—and I mean fast. . . . Without minivans, we don't eat. It's that simple."[23]

Chrysler had problems in 1989 with an A604 design defect that caused internal fluid leakage through a seal resulting in clutch failure. Chrysler completed a production change in the logic of the transmission's electronic controller which corrected the problem. According to its top engineers the problem had been resolved and the transmission was reliable. Yet some early 1991 transmissions had bad surface finish on the reaction shafts which damaged the reaction shaft bushing. It so happened that in a blind test by *Consumer Reports* the 1991 minivan that was acquired for their test contained one of these few defective transmissions. Chrysler proposed that the problems with the A604 transmission were blown out of proportion and the problem had been re-solved.[24]

Chairman Lee Iacocca was directly involved in communicating to key publics during this crisis. During a telecast to company dealers, Iacocca commented, "In 45 years in this business, that's the one vehicle (the minivan) I am proudest of. Hell, it's almost a sacred trust. And because of that, we have to come out swinging."[25] And swing he did. Chris Theodore, executive engineer for power-train engineering, was appointed the A604 troubleshooter. Chrysler executives met with the *Consumer Reports* staff to confront their accusers head-on. A public relations hotline was set up at their Michigan office to handle consumer and media inquires. In addition a survey was conducted to determine the impact on the general buying public.

Chrysler also acutely recognized that one of their key publics was their dealers and Iacocca conducted a teleconference to explain the serious nature of the crisis and to let the dealers know how to handle the situation. First and foremost was attending to the immediate needs and in this case the need to correct the defective transmission. "When it comes to the minivan, we play offense. If it still has problems, find 'em and fix 'em," Iacocca instructed the dealers. He also informed them that they should use other reports from different auto magazines that showed a completely different and positive review of the minivans. He went so far as to say, "If anybody badmouths our minivans, take it like you would an insult to your sister."[26] Iaccoca's swift and direct response enabled Chrysler to be on the offensive rather than the defensive during a time of crisis.

Union Carbide

We spoke earlier about the Union Carbide crisis regarding the CEO flying to the site in Bhopal, India. Let us examine this case further in the context of identifying potential problems ahead of time and knowing how to communicate when the crisis hits.

The tragedy occurred on December 3, 1984, when methylisocyanate gas escaped from the Union Carbide plant in Bhopal, India. Over fifteen hundred people were killed by the poisonous gas and thousands more were injured.

The company faced immediate problems. They were not able to ascertain complete information about the event until days after it had occurred because telephone lines were jammed and airplanes were filled to capacity. These fact-gathering problems were further exacerbated by a perception that the company was generally responding to the communications aspect of the crisis by staying locked behind closed doors and occasionally releasing information to the media.

The appearance that the company was not being up-front and sensitive created a negative perception of the handling of the crisis and began to manifest itself in other ways as the stock price began to drop.

One aspect that becomes clear in this crisis is that the tragedy might never have even occurred. Note what one crisis communications expert stated about knowing of potential problems ahead of time:

The Bhopal crisis, though it burst unexpectedly, was not without warning. As usual, there was nonperformance by low-level managers, in this case the operators of the Bhopal plant. A company audit in 1982 warned about problems at the facility, but top management's attention was focused elsewhere. Mr. Anderson was trying to reorient the company from its historic dependence on commodity chemicals, like the pesticides produced at Bhopal, toward consumer products, like Glad plastic bags, Eveready batteries, and Prestone antifreeze it was already marketing. Those at the top were concentrating on strategic planning, not operations. [27]

Further, CEO Warren Anderson noted at a press conference some three months later that conditions at the plant were so poor that it should not even have been allowed to operate.

Subsequent studies revealed additional safety concerns including:

- Inoperative equipment
- Housing built in a toxic environment (next to the plant) due to political pressure to ease overcrowding
- And Union Carbide's problems weren't limited to India as a leak occurred at one of its chemical plants located in West Virginia eight months later. Upon inspection it was determined that the plant was in violation of safety standards. Only two gas masks for every six operators were available to the employees caught in the chemical leak.

With these numerous problems, the potential for a crisis was enhanced and it is no wonder negative perceptions developed, especially given the delays in communication and the back-to-back leaks at plants on opposite sides of the world.

A Shooting in San Diego

Here is one man's account of a crisis that occurred at Alvarado Hospital Medical Center in San Diego, California, and his handling of the communications during this very trying episode. On January 29, 1979, a shooting occurred in the San Diego, California area where a sixteen-year-old female sat in a house across the street from an elementary school on a cold and cloudy Monday morning. She proceeded to open fire upon children arriving at the school. During the shooting a custodian and a principal were killed and approximately fourteen children were injured. The local hospital where the individuals were taken became the site of the aftermath and became the crisis center in which the spokesperson had to communicate and bring some semblance of control to the confusion.

Spokesperson Nick Sylvester had been at the hospital for six months and was handling the marketing and community relations. He had begun right after another crisis had occurred and was responsible for bringing together a team and developing a plan to handle future crises which seemed to center around the emergency room activities.

Through the program he developed, he noted the location of a command post in the lobby and away from the emergency room. In this manner he was able to allow proximity to the crisis without interfering with the resolution of the crisis and the safety of the patients.

He then included in his plan individuals who would have the task of being "runners" relaying information between the emergency room and the command post, thereby allowing communication to flow from the emergency room, the source of information, to the command post, where the information would be disseminated to the press. Sylvester then spent his time establishing contacts with the media. Through personal visits and by being "diplomatically persistent" he was able to make contact with the appropriate individuals and the media with whom he would deal during a crisis. These individuals included assignment editors, news editors, and reporters.

When the crisis began, Sylvester had in place a plan for the command post, relaying information and opening up lines of communication with the media.

● THE CRISIS

Upon the arrival of the injured at the hospital, everyone's concern was for the condition of the children. Sylvester was in the position of making sure the next of kin were notified prior to releasing this information to the media. The plan called for three additional PBX operators to be on call should an emergency arise, and these individuals were thus brought in. Other telephones and extensions were activated during the crisis. The PBX operators were trained in handling the flood of calls and it was their responsibility to differentiate between the media inquiries and the calls from the concerned parents. Again Sylvester astutely determined the need for handling the concerns of the different publics. Parents naturally wanted to know the condition of their children and the media wanted the overall status of all the injured.

It was a tenuous situation for Sylvester dealing with the needs of the media and the rights of the parents and their children. The first day of the event information was handled via the phone and command post information. A news conference was then held with the doctors providing information to reporters about the condition of the injured. Sylvester acted as the backup coordinating spokesperson.

At the news conference the doctors and Sylvester updated the media on the condition of the injured individuals and Sylvester spoke for the administrator. This was again part of the crisis plan, as it had been prearranged that Sylvester would be the appropriate individual to speak on behalf of the hospital. The hospital administrator during the crisis moved to an office down the hall so that he was in close proximity and could be part of the crisis team, but delegated the spokesperson responsibilities to Sylvester.

A special room was set aside for the radio reporters. It was decided that the children would not be interviewed as it was hospital policy to avoid the disruption this would cause for the patients. It's important to note that state codes protect the right of privacy and prohibit hospitals from letting individuals know the identity of patients. After much discussion, however, a parent agreed to speak to the media and provide them information, thus satisfying the needs of the press.

A potentially critical situation occurred when a member of the press tried to break in through a back door and get into one of the patients' rooms. Fortunately, the reporter was stopped before any contact with the patient was made.

During the crisis period, over three hundred inquiries were received at the hospital and four to five news releases were developed. Sylvester truly learned that the media cannot be ignored during a crisis. Information needs to be provided to them frequently and in a factual manner. They become a part of the overall team that is concerned with communicating the information as rapidly as possible to the various publics. The media likewise frequently view public relations personnel or the spokesperson as a necessary evil because they have to go through indirect channels to get the information. By understanding this relationship Sylvester was better able to handle the crisis at the San Diego hospital.

He leaves us with some important comments to summarize his experience as a spokesperson:

- Being honest and up-front is one of the most important items, as has been noted throughout the book.
- Once the crisis is over it is important to get on with business.
- Do the best you can in the situation. Follow your plan and then proceed. The media will be much more supportive of you and your efforts if you truly work with them and try not to thwart their need for information.
- If you don't have an answer, get back to them with one in a timely manner.
- It is important that all public relations practitioners fully understand the dynamics of the relationship between the media and the organization.
- Evaluate how the crisis was handled.

Sylvester noted, too, the importance of having a spokesperson designated and trained prior to an event occurring. In some of our cases we note the chief executive officer is that spokesperson. In the case of the San Diego hospital another individual, in this case Sylvester, was the designated spokesperson, yet coordinated with the overall operations manager of the hospital.

When a crisis is not occurring, the practitioner should be preparing for one by establishing good relations with the media. This comes through cordial contacts, knowing the right people, and communicating the positive messages about your organization. When a negative situation such as a crisis occurs, the positives will sometimes downplay the negatives of the situation and the crisis may have minimal impact upon your organization's image.

Also Sylvester noted the need to be a good community player. Meaning, your organization should do things for the good of the community on a regular basis, as this again makes for a positive perception of your group.

And finally, Sylvester underlined the need to have a plan ready before a crisis occurs, with the correct contact names and phone numbers so that you can begin handling the crisis in an effective manner and do it right the first time. This will allow you to stabilize the situation, provide the information to the appropriate publics, and conclude the crisis in an expeditious manner so that your organization can get on with business.

A Midwestern Bank in Crisis

Here is an interesting case to examine, as the crisis began as a result of a proactive approach by a midwestern bank to reassure its publics of its solvency and become somewhat of an "expert institution" on what to look for in a bank.

With the close scrutiny banks had been coming under, the holding company produced a series of pamphlets designed to educate the public on the differences between healthy and sick institutions.

The pamphlets and information were well received by the public, but for some reason the customers of the bank interpreted the discussion of banking problems as specific to their bank. They began withdrawing their deposits and the bank quickly found itself in the middle of a crisis.

Fortunately the bank knew what to do and had spent time prior to the crisis meeting with local newspapers and developing external support. They responded quickly by contacting the press and a follow-up story appeared, explaining that the bank was doing quite well, which cleared up the confusion.

Because of the problems facing the banking and savings-and-loan industries, every comment, financial report, or new service charge is magnified. That is why it is so important to be prepared, to know the industry, and to have a plan.

Strategies that came into play in this situation included the following:

- Knowing what the issues facing the bank and the industry were
- Being ready to articulate these issues by having researched them and developed backgrounders, fact sheets, and position papers

115

- Regularly communicating financial information—to avoid surprises
- Communicating directly with the customers—a key public
- Good relations with the media
- Simulating how other bank failures and public perception will affect your bank
- Having messages designed to meet these concerns
- Knowing how, when, and to whom to communicate these messages
- Providing media access to the bank chairman[28]

Child Abduction at Santa Ana Unified School District

Diane Thomas, APR, public information officer for the Santa Ana Unified School District in Santa Ana, California, relates a case she participated in that clearly shows the need to communicate with the appropriate publics, know your position by being prepared, and take into account the mental stress associated with any crisis.

In 1987 a young girl was abducted from an elementary school in Santa Ana, California, and her body was found a few days later, a victim of a tragic slaying. Here is how the Santa Ana Unified School District handled the crisis and communicated with its various publics.

Upon the report of the missing child at the school a series of events, per plan, went into effect. The school took the initial step of calling home and then contacting members of the family followed by classmates and neighbors to determine the seriousness of the situation before involving the police. School staff and members of the district's police services walked the neighborhood. The police were notified about a missing child, the district's superintendent and public information officer were alerted. Initial police reports indicated a serious situation so it was determined by members of the crisis team (public information officer, assistant superintendent of elementary education, and the special education director) that the communications and crisis operations would need to be set up at the school site.

As the principal was on leave during the week the crisis occurred, the assistant superintendent assumed the role of crisis coordinator and school site coordinator. The team used the vacated principal's office as the command post and began operations to assess the facts and communicate with the appropriate publics.

Thomas had developed good relations with the public information officer from the police department and this allowed for a smooth flow of information between the two groups. Early on, the police department held a press conference off site in a neutral location to avoid interrupting the instructional program at the school. The team then noted that its major publics would be classroom teachers, parents, other students at the school, the general Santa Ana community, members of the school board, and the media. Once these groups had been identified the crisis team began communicating messages through the appropriate channels to each of these groups.

School security was enhanced. The site was already fenced as it was on a busy street, and it had only two entrances. Security officers were brought in to guard the entrances and admit only students, teachers, parents, and other authorized personnel. One of the immediate needs was to communicate to the parents through the use of flyers that the school was a safe place to be. They were also reminded of safety tips for children walking to and from school. The parents supported this effort by bringing their children to school to ensure their safety as the abductor had not been apprehended. Parents were also informed that there would be a meeting in the evening with the police and a psychologist to keep them informed of any new events and to provide counseling.

Students needed to feel secure and loved and to have an outlet for their feelings. This was provided by the special education department's team of psychologists who handled classroom and individual counseling as needed. Teachers were also coached in how to respond to children's questions and how to spot children who needed further counseling. The teachers also needed to be kept informed and to receive methods for reducing their own stress.

Lines of communication were established and kept open between the police department, the crisis team, and the superintendent's office/board of education. Information flowed freely between these groups and all members were kept apprised of progress and events in the case.

The need for the media to acquire information and to report it quickly and accurately was astutely noted early on. However, the needs of the press had to be secondary to the needs of students, parents, and teachers in order to maintain normal operations at the school. Therefore the crisis team and the public information officer invoked California Education Code, which allows administration officials to prohibit nuisances or disturbances in the form of strangers on the school campus. The public information officer ensured that press conferences were held and she was available for questions and would allow other staff members to answer appropriate questions.

Overall this was an effective measure, except when a reporter intruded upon a private parents' meeting where the parents were receiving information and counseling. Once again the needs of the parents took precedence over the reporter's desire to gain access to a public building. The parents' meeting was private and their right to privacy prevailed.

This example is cited because only through Thomas's experience and knowledge of the education codes was the incident handled swiftly and appropriately. She conscientiously worked to provide the media appropriate information and protected classroom instruction because she knew that student learning could not be compromised.

In allowing other administrators to speak with the press, Thomas was careful to choose those individuals who understood the situation and had some knowledge about the importance of appropriate communications. Thomas is a firm believer that everyone is responsible for their own words and that they have to assume that everything they say will be seen in print, so she coaches anyone who is involved in media relations to think first before speaking. Simple to say, but challenging to do; yet the success of the way this crisis was handled indicated that her message was well received.

An example was not using words such as "children sobbing," which would truly grab headlines, but rather using words such as "the children are saddened" by the event, which softens the headline and makes a sound bite more difficult to capture.

During the crisis Thomas made sure that the clerical staff had short scripts so that they could answer general and immediate questions over the telephone and refer any specifics to the crisis team. Thomas had also taken the time to prepare the staff and administrators at other schools so that they would be prepared for what to expect regarding police investigations occurring on campus and for a little loss of control due to the events. All the preparation paid off, as communications and the crisis went as well as could be expected. The hardest blow to everyone was the fact that the little girl had been murdered, and this was taken very hard by all members of the team. The event began on Monday and concluded on Friday after the discovery of the body. School psychologists noted the need for closure, so a memorial service was held on Friday as a way of concluding the crisis, with the weekend being a natural separation for a regeneration on Monday. With planning and some luck, the outdoor event, including a release of white balloons, took place in privacy, with no press coverage.

Once the crisis was over the team evaluated each of the schools to determine backup command posts since they had been lucky this time that the principal's office was available. At other schools, had the principal been present, this would have been more difficult, so backup command posts were noted. The team also noted that everyone received counseling from the special education team, and this was important. The one group that did not receive counseling and should have was the crisis team itself. There was a great deal of stress and it was important for them to have the opportunity to vent their emotions so that they could more capably continue handling the crisis. They also noted that feedback occurred on a regular basis because they were dealing with teachers, students, and parents not only through flyers, but two-way communications in the form of meetings and personal contact. This allowed them to evaluate as they went along and learn of any potential misconceptions or incorrect reporting. The team was able to stay on top of the situation and bring the crisis to a close, though it had a sad ending. Thomas brings up the importance of psychological counseling and this illuminates the fact that all crisis management plans should have a provision for counseling, since the stress can be quite high.[29]

Union Pacific Train Derailment

According to Mark Davis, with the public relations department of the Union Pacific Railroad in Omaha, the following case occurred in 1986 and provides a look at how communications can be handled when a crisis lingers for several days and involves the evacuation of individuals. It also shows what to be aware of when other organizations and agencies are involved in the process, too.

In 1984, an eighty-car Union Pacific train heading from San Antonio to Ft. Worth, Texas, derailed at a bridge. Thirty-two cars derailed, including five cars containing butadiene, one with formaldehyde, and one with ethylene glycol. Some tank cars fell into a creek. Following the derailment, an explosion occurred and the ensuing fire continued for a week. The incident occurred next to San Antonio airport, thus disrupting air traffic. The first person on the scene was a train master, followed by Mark Davis and John Bromley of the public relations staff for Union Pacific. The accident occurred at 12:50 P.M., and he arrived at 5:00 P.M. This meant that reporters were there ahead of the actual crisis team. Yet the train master on the scene began working to correct the situation and bring it under control, as well as to coordinate with the local authorities. Upon arriving at the scene, Davis and Bromley teamed up with members of the city that had been notified and were brought together to control the situation.

This is an example of when a crisis goes beyond your organization and impacts upon other groups, and therefore the need to coordinate efforts is very important. Per city plans, an evacuation had to be effected until there was understanding of the content of the smoke cloud and the determination as to danger of any possible toxic gases from the crash. Experts were brought in and the team began mapping out its strategy for handling the situation and communicating the information.

The first order of business was to set up a briefing schedule so that the news media would have the most current information and on a regular basis. It was jointly decided by all parties that briefings would be held every hour. These hourly briefings occurred for a period of two days, then went to every two hours. What is interesting to note, according to Davis, is that the crisis team and the reporters together came up with the media briefing schedule and although conferences were held by the hour, they were not held on the hour. The most convenient time for the meetings was twenty minutes after the hour, thus giving them time for questions, compiling stories, and getting them to their agencies or appropriate offices for inclusion at the top of the news.

Davis and Bromley also coordinated with the television stations to come up with a mutually acceptable plan for interviews, so that live coverage could be carried but no preferential treatment given. It was clearly stated in the beginning, that all the information the crisis team had would be passed on, that there would be no reason to go off the record because there would be no information given off the record, and that they would provide all the information once and for all in a press gathering. This created an air of fairness and teamwork that allowed the smooth dissemination of information. It also helped that members of the crisis team and evacuees stayed in the same hotel for the period of the crisis, which meant there was much informal contact. Setting down these rules allowed everybody to coexist peacefully.

One of the immediate communication concerns was explaining what chemicals were involved and what dangers, if any, were posed by these chemicals. Experts were able to provide the information and let people know that the chemicals were not dangerous, yet all the terminology used was such that it was not easily understood by the public, so the crisis team came up with explanations and common language to explain what was occurring. This allowed for easy communication and the assurance that the message would be properly communicated and received.

Coordination was a regular factor between Union Pacific and the other agencies, and decisions were made jointly and efforts coordinated. Upon the flames being extinguished, the crisis wound down and the crisis team began dismantling its operations. After seven days the members of the Union Pacific crisis team and the other crisis team members had left San Antonio. This is where Davis learned some very important information, which he passes on to those studying crisis communications. Just because the immediate crisis appears to be over does not mean that your job as a communicator is completed.

It became apparent to Davis that as long as reporters were still on the scene the organization had an obligation to continue the communications process. This was exemplified by the fact that after the crisis team had left and repairs were continuing on the train tracks reporters stayed until the line was actually reopened, which took another seven to ten days. During this time the reporters were free to talk to whomever they chose, and at times they disrupted the necessary operation of getting the tracks repaired. In retrospect Davis noted that it would have been a good idea to continue to stay, offer updates, and be the liaison to avoid any disruptions and ensure that the proper messages were being communicated.

Part V

Sample Plans

Developing a Plan

The importance of crisis communications has been clearly stated so far. But if all you do is to familiarize yourself with the concepts, determine "it can never happen to us," and then file this book on a shelf, you have missed the whole point of this handbook. You need to begin writing down a plan and coordinating with others to work through different scenarios.

We will look at a few plans—some simple and some complex—of what others have done. This should help you gain some ideas. We will also look at some examples of how a crisis can come out of the blue at the most unexpected time. Those examples should serve to shake those of you who don't think you are in a vulnerable position or a high-profile industry. You, too, will then want to start developing at least an outline of how you will handle adverse situations.

The key to developing a plan is to get something in writing and begin making lists of activities that will need to be done, and in what order, during a crisis.

Marion Pinsdorf, who has studied the communications programs of airlines during flight disasters, offers some parameters for plans in this arena:

• Make available to the duty officer the names, phone numbers, and locations of all key airline officers, those who need to know in case of a crash, and members of federal and state agencies, such as the Federal Aviation Administration and the National Transportation Safety Board. Since accidents seem to happen perversely at the most inconvenient times—weekends, nights, and vacation times—standby phone numbers and alternates should be included.

- Establish functional priorities: Who should be called and in what order. It feeds any ego to call the CEO first, but lower-ranking managers may have a much greater need to know.
- Have statistics available on the type of plane, cruising speeds, number of seats, safety record, revenue, passenger miles flown without fatalities, names of crew, and other details that help position the airline positively despite the accident. Such background furnishes balancing information to accompany pictures of burning wreckage and grieving survivors.
- Release crash information as soon as the facts and names can be verified and the next of kin notified. Here the interests of airlines and press coincide: to get as much information out as quickly as possible. Quick release expedites coverage, minimizes drawn-out follow-ups, and quells rumors, which are usually more horrible than the truth.[30]

Items that should be discussed in developing your plan include some of the following (some items may sound very minute, yet some companies even plan down to this detailed level):

Who will communicate with employees?

Who will operate the phones?

What will they say?

Who will back them up?

Do you know how to add an 800 line within a short period of time?

Do you know how you will add extra phone lines or rededicate existing ones?

Who will run the copy machine when sensitive material needs to be reproduced?

How will rumors be handled
inside the company?
in public?

How will customers' needs be addressed?

Which hospital will be used for employees if needed?

Who will you coordinate with at the hospital for gathering information on conditions?

How will the hospital protect these individuals from media intrusions?

How will the hospital coordinate with you and the media?

How will you get to the site of the crisis if it occurs in the field?

Who will be assigned to the site coordination?

Who is on your team?

Who is the spokesperson?

Who will back them up?

Who will develop the plan?

Who will distribute it?

How will it be updated?

When will drills occur?

List some scenarios.

Where is your command post going to be?

Where will the media center be?

Do these rooms contain the following, as appropriate?

_____ accessible tables and chairs

_____ trash receptacles

_____ ashtrays

_____ paper

_____ pencils and pens

_____ copies of the crisis plan and team members list

_____ sufficient electrical outlets

_____ the capacity to be secured

_____ radio and television capabilities

_____ name tags

_____ clocks

_____ restroom/shower facilities nearby to freshen up

_____ refreshments

_____ fax machines

_____ a direct phone line

How will the early stages of the crisis be handled regarding information gathering and dissemination, as this is the most critical and sets the tone?

How will you involve the media as a resource in getting vital information out?

Have employees, except for the designated spokesperson, been briefed on avoiding making comments of any kind to the press?

Do you have the appropriate technical advisor(s) on call for each scenario?

Have you looked at different scenarios and do you have appropriate contingency plans?

Does everyone know their role?

Does everyone know where the plan book is?

Have you planned for a simulation?

Have you tried to correct potential problems?

Are you updating the plan on at least an annual basis?

Marriott Hotels and Resorts Public Relations Crisis Communication Plan*

In the event of an emergency, the property's first and foremost responsibility is the protection and welfare of its guests, visitors, and employees. However, high on the list of priorities is the communication of information about the emergency to the news media. You should make every effort to work with the media in a professional and timely manner, and provide them with accurate/approved information.

● PROCEDURES TO FOLLOW

When your hotel or resort is faced with an emergency situation that requires response to the media, the following public relations plan should be implemented:

1. The manager on duty (MOD) immediately notifies the general manager and the director of marketing. The MOD should contact the resident manager if the general manager is unreachable.
2. The general manager, director of marketing, or resident manager must con-

---

*Reprinted with permission.

tact Marriott's Western/Pacific regional public relations office, who will contact Marriott Hotels and Resorts' public relations office at corporate headquarters immediately.

3. Marriott's Western/Pacific regional director of public relations will discuss the situation with you in detail and help you prepare an appropriate public relations action plan, including official response, proper handling of any on-site media, immediate media calls, and follow-up media calls.

4. Once an action plan has been agreed upon and approved by a corporate public relations representative, it should be discussed with all the members of the executive committee as soon as possible.

5. The following guidelines will be part of the instructions you receive in the third step (above), and must be followed no matter what degree of emergency your property is experiencing.

   • The general manager (or his or her designee) is the only hotel staff member who should make any statement to the news media.

   • The property's employees should be strictly prohibited from making any statement, providing information, commenting on the situation, or talking with the media.

   • Switchboard operators and all other employees should refer media calls directly to the designated spokesperson, who should then provide the approved response.

   • Speculations and opinions are prohibited by employees to anyone. In times of emergencies, rumors run rampant and can have devastating impact on all persons involved and public opinion after the emergency.

   • When an emergency involves the police or fire department, it is on public record, and additional information requests should be referred to the investigating officer or fire chief. Under no circumstances should the name of a victim or the victim's condition be given to the media by the hotel spokesperson. These types of questions should be referred to the investigating officer or hospital where the person was taken for treatment.

   • No estimate of loss in terms of dollars should be released to the media until a qualified insurance adjuster has been on the scene to determine the extent of damage. This could take many hours or days, so the media should be told that the loss is as yet undetermined. Do not be pressured into giving your "best guess."

   • Do not allow members of the press to tour your property unescorted. The general manager should escort the reporter, photographer, and/or camera crew through the property only after he or she has discussed the situation with the regional hotel public relations office and determined the full intent of the reporter's story. If the general manager is unable to escort the press person, he or she should assign a competent manager who is briefed on every aspect of the emergency and the property's public relations position.

- Keep a log of all media calls and visits to the property related to the emergency and record what was said to each reporter or editor.
- Refer questions not directly associated to your emergency situation to the Marriott Hotels and Resorts public relations staff. Example: If you are being questioned about a suicide at the property, and the reporter wants to know how many suicides per year take place at Marriott Hotels and Resorts nationwide, you should refer them to the headquarter's public relations office.
- Keep the regional public relations staff posted on any significant changes in your emergency situation and/or if you need to change your approved statement.

● MARRIOTT'S WESTERN/PACIFIC PUBLIC RELATIONS OFFICE

Regional director of public relations   *Office:*

    Home:

Public relations coordinator   *Office:*

    Home:

Public relations assistant   *Office:*

    Home:

● CONTACT AT CORPORATE HEADQUARTERS

Marriott Hotels and Resorts public relations
Nonworking hours and weekends

When you reach the after-hours number, you will reach the corporate security desk, which is manned twenty-four hours a day. They will immediately contact a member of the public relations staff and inform them of your emergency situation.

● CONDUCTING CRISIS INTERVIEWS

The key to conducting a successful crisis interview is to stay *calm*. Reporters (from print and electronic media) see a nervous and panicky spokesperson as someone who is not telling the whole story or is not in control of the situation. Your general manger or spokesperson should try to be as relaxed and professional as possible at all times. Here are a few pointers to remember when conducting a crisis interview:

- Do not grant interviews until after the emergency situation is under complete control. Your general manager should not be conducting interviews when his or her services are needed rescuing guests or working with the police or fire department.
- Stick to the approved statement.
- Answer honestly only the questions you are asked. Do not volunteer information.
- Conduct interviews in a safe area of the property or off property away from the crisis scene.
- Do not conduct interviews cold. Get a basic idea of the questions the reporter plans to ask and orchestrate your answers in advance. Know the facts.
- If the police and/or fire department are still at the scene, let them know the media wants to conduct an interview and what your spokesperson plans to say.
- Request newspaper reporters to repeat back any direct quotes for accuracy.
- Be accessible to the press. If you grant a newspaper or TV station an interview, you are obligated to give equal time to other members of the press who are there for legitimate reasons.

● SUMMARY

Emergency situations are best handled by people who are prepared for them in advance, people who have a plan, and can implement the plan quickly. This plan, and the support from the regional public relations staff, will enable you to prepare for, and manage, any emergency situation.

American Red Cross*

In any kind of disaster situation—simple house fire or a major national catastrophe such as an earthquake or flood—information is important to those affected. Quick, efficient dissemination of critical information to everyone involved in or affected by the disaster can mean the difference between life and death. Over the long term, this can help make the management of the relief effort a much easier task.

In any disaster, the local chapters of the American Red Cross will be at the forefront of efforts to provide relief and comfort to victims. Red Cross communicators—those individuals responsible for public affairs, communication, and media relations—must get timely and helpful information to Red Cross clients, supporters, and other key audiences.

The preparation begins with an understanding of the dynamics of a disaster relief operation and of the different audiences that communicators need to reach, a clear appreciation of the mission of the American Red Cross, and a knowledge of the important role of Red Cross communicators in providing relief to victims of disaster.

This crisis communication plan explains these concepts and outlines the steps to successful communication during disaster relief operation. The plan

---

*This is the introduction/overview of an extensive and detailed guide. It is reprinted here with permission of the American National Red Cross.

has been designed as a comprehensive guide for paid and volunteer staff and is an adjunct to Public Affairs I and II.

This plan also recognizes that situations vary with the nature of the catastrophe, the local "landscape," and the extent of available resources. The procedures recommended here are intended as a guide for local and nationally assigned communicators. While each step in the process is important and should be followed, the actual methods for implementing them must be directed by the local disaster-relief operations director (hereafter referred to as the job director).

● DEALING EFFECTIVELY WITH A CRISIS

The action steps outline specific communication steps for implementing a sound, flexible public affairs program to adapt to a wide range of emerging issues. But despite your best efforts, a crisis situation may emerge. Crisis situations are complex; a tailored, strategic approach is needed to defuse a potential conflict that can hamper the efforts of the Red Cross on behalf of its clients.

A crisis occurs when unforeseen events threaten to harm the ability of the Red Cross to accomplish its mission. A communication crisis results when information—erroneous or correct—circulates in the community and obstructs your ability to convey critical information to Red Cross clients and supporters.

The strategies in the crisis scenarios apply to communication challenges that most often result from or occur during a disaster relief operation. Many of the same techniques may be used effectively to manage a crisis or deal with communication challenges related to other areas of service.

Be Aware of What is Happening—And Could Happen

Practice preventive communication by watching for signs of impending problems, and do not ignore the hallmarks of a situation spinning out of control. Practice proactive communication by communicating clear, consistent Red Cross messages on a regular basis, before the disaster or crisis ever occurs. When we take the time to educate our clients, supporters, and the news media, they are better prepared to understand our role and our needs.

● THE MISSION

In all communication with the public, the role of the American Red Cross should always be emphasized:

The American Red Cross is a humanitarian organization, led by volunteers, that provides relief to victims of disasters and helps people prevent, prepare for, and respond to emergencies. It does this through services that are consistent with its congressional charter and the fundamental principles of the International Red Cross Movement.

The mission of a major American Red Cross disaster relief operation:

Within the scope of the American Red Cross disaster services program, provide prompt, effective services to disaster victims to meet their disaster-caused basic human needs and to assist disaster victims without resources to begin and complete their disaster recovery efforts.

The mission of the Red Cross communicator in a disaster is clear and should be the guiding principle of all actions:
To develop, implement, and evaluate communication strategies that promote American Red Cross services and enhance the Red Cross image. To disseminate information to people affected by the disaster as well as others assisting with relief efforts.

● DEFINING ROLES

Chapter Communicator

The role of chapter communicator during a disaster may be assumed by different chapter workers, depending on the chapter's personnel resources, but the responsibility of that person will remain constant. The role of this person is to act as a manager of information flow, not as the controller. The communicator's job is to ensure that the right information reaches the target audience in a timely fashion. The chapter communicator should report directly to the disaster relief operation director (job director), who is the chapter disaster services worker responsible for managing all relief operations.

Public Affairs Officer

The public affairs officer (PAO) is a disaster-trained Red Cross communicator assigned to a nationally administered relief operation. The PAO works as a partner with the local chapter communicator(s) and other Red Cross disaster relief workers to develop clear, consistent communication about relief efforts. The

PAO reports directly to the director of the disaster relief operation (job director), who is designated by disaster services.

STANDARDS OF PERFORMANCE AND PERFORMANCE GOALS

The following are standards of performance for the public affairs officer:

- All Red Cross shelters are identified internally and externally as Red Cross facilities.
- The location of Red Cross shelters and any fixed and mobile feeding sites are provided within eight hours of the disaster's impact to local news media organizations, in order to inform disaster victims of the availability of these services.
- Daily reports are made to local news media organizations on the location of service delivery sites and availability of Red Cross services to disaster victims.
- Information on the opening of all Red Cross service centers is provided to local news media organizations not less than twenty-four hours before each center opens.
- Information on the handling of disbursing orders and containing the phone number of the accounting function is distributed to local vendors within seven days of the disaster's onset.
- Disaster services at national and the operations headquarters are provided with copies of all press releases issued by the relief operation on the same day as their release.

The following are performance goals for the public affairs officer:

OPENING A DISASTER OPERATION

- Within eight hours of arrival at job site, prepare and have approved by job director a fact sheet that includes information on shelter locations, Red Cross disaster activities, and Red Cross hotline and donation guidelines to be used for reference, media inquiries, news releases, et cetera.
- Within twelve hours of arrival, identify spokespersons and develop written talking points based on the fact sheet.
- Within eighteen hours of arrival, establish relationship with local chapter communicators or managers in the disaster-affected area and define responsibilities for dealing with local media.
- Within twenty-four hours of arrival, assess communication equipment needs

(e.g., typewriter, computer, fax, beepers) and submit request to job director for approval.

- Within twenty-four hours of arrival, compile media lists.
- Within forty-eight hours of arrival, determine the need for additional public affairs staff members in consultation with job director. Submit recommendations to staffing officer.
- Within forty-eight hours of arrival, develop a preliminary action plan for approval of the job director.

ONGOING

- Through the use of media and public outlets (bulletin boards, schools, stores, et cetera), assure that disaster victims have adequate information regarding Red Cross services.
- Respond to media inquiries promptly to facilitate timely placement of Red Cross stories and make every effort to assure accuracy and timeliness of media messages.
- Clear all media releases with job director or designee. Give a final copy of the release to the job director. Send copies of all media releases on the same day as release to operations headquarters and to disaster services and External Communication at national headquarters. Provide timely response to concerns about negative issues and information that may put public confidence in the Red Cross at risk or impede the organization's ability to provide disaster relief.
- Attend daily staff meetings with job officers.
- Submit a daily report of public affairs activities to the job director.
- Establish with job director the need for formal internal communication and appropriate channels.
- Assure that print materials meet Red Cross graphic standards.
- Be fully versed on Red Cross policies and issues relevant to service delivery and fund-raising.
- Ensure adequate use of Red Cross identification and in appropriate languages.
- Provide support and coordination for VIP tours and develop agenda, for approval by job director, for events that may garner public attention.
- Monitor media coverage and maintain daily media log.
- Coordinate responses to national media inquiries with national headquarters External Communication.
- Perform the duties of the public affairs officer according to acceptable standards of conduct, appearance, and technical expertise, and in a manner consistent with the mission and goals of the American Red Cross.

CLOSING AN OPERATION

- Compile a final narrative report and file it with the job director before leaving the disaster site. Refer to ARC 3015, Section XI, for format of report.
- Narrative report includes media logs, news clippings and other materials related to public affairs activities during the disaster operation.
- Appropriately recognize individuals who have contributed to public affairs efforts.

EXTERNAL COMMUNICATION—NATIONAL HEADQUARTERS

manager, public inquiry	director, External Communication manager, media relations manager, advertising media relations associate chapter communicator/public affairs officer (PAO)

American Red Cross External Communication staff members are available twenty-four hours a day to support public affairs efforts in a major disaster.

During Business Hours (Monday through Friday, 8:00 A.M. to 5:30 P.M. Eastern time), Call (202) 639-3200; During Nonbusiness Hours, Call the Red Cross at (202) 737-8300 and Ask the Operator to Page the Media Relations Associate on Call.

When Do I Call External Communication?

- Call when preliminary damage assessment reports clearly indicate that a major disaster has occurred.
- Call when national media (any news media that holds a nationwide audience) begin covering a disaster. External Communication is charged with handling national media contacts.
- Call when you first think a communication problem exists or is emerging. External Communication can answer questions about ongoing operations and provide counsel on resolving a potential conflict early on when it is still small.
- Call when a communication problem may spread to other chapters. External Communication can keep chapters informed about an issue so that communicators can respond to any questions with one voice.
- Call when you need counsel or advice on any disaster communication concerns. External Communication can serve as a sounding board for your ideas and can offer other solutions and approaches that can enhance your efforts.

- Call when you need a disaster public service announcement (PSA) produced for local broadcast.

INTERNAL COMMUNICATION—NATIONAL HEADQUARTERS

Internal Communication coordinates the flow of information to Red Cross national sector and field units and helps shape the content and communication products for management.

During Business Hours (Monday through Friday, 8:00 A.M. to 5:30 P.M., Eastern time), Call (202) 639-3474.

What Products or Service Can I Expect from Internal Communication?

- Internal Communication coordinates the writing and distribution of items for rapid communication, such as chapter information bulletins (CIBs) sent to field units by AMCROSS.
- Internal Communication writes and transmits regular or special executive bulletins (EBs), which communicate top-line management information to managers in the field via AMCROSS.
- All chapters, especially smaller units without AMCROSS technology, can use the chapter inquiry center. Callers may address questions to an Internal Communication representative or listen to prerecorded updates on the latest organizational news. Call 1–800–234–4ARC and select the chapter inquiry option.
- In cooperation with other units of national headquarters, Internal Communication coordinates special information kits and key management messages sent by overnight express or first-class mail.
- Internal Communication produces CrossLink and BioLink business TV networks, providing field subscribers with an opportunity to interact with Red Cross decision makers during a crisis.
- Internal Communication is responsible for *Cue-In*, the bimonthly management newsletter for Red Cross leadership.

When Do I Call Internal Communication?

- Call when you have a question about a CIB or EB, or any other internal communication vehicle.
- Call when you are unclear about Red Cross management policy during a disaster relief operation or crisis.
- Call Internal Communication when you have a comment or complaint about

the effectiveness and clarity of national headquarters communication with field units. You can also call a chapter inquiry center representative at 1-800-234-5ARC.

● IDENTIFYING THE AUDIENCES

In a disaster, victims and several other audiences need information about relief efforts. Each audience has different information needs and receives information through different sources.

Understanding these specific needs and sources is essential to ensure that information reaches the most people in a timely way and does not waste precious energy or resources. Before beginning the communication process, define who is in these broad audience categories and how best to reach them in each situation. In general, audiences include:

- Disaster victims—People who have been displaced, injured, separated from family, suffered damage to their home and belongings, or are otherwise in need of immediate assistance.
- Potential volunteers and donors—People who are prepared and willing to assist with relief efforts, but do not know whom to contact or where to go.
- Disaster workers—Individuals and organizations, including Red Cross personnel, already on the job assisting with the relief efforts who need to understand the scope and details of the assistance available so they can accommodate victims' needs.
- Government officials—City, county, state, and federal public officials who need to understand what the Red Cross is doing in order to coordinate efforts across the scene, or to communicate relief efforts to their constituents.
- Community leaders—Members of the board of the local Red Cross chapter, local United Way, chamber of commerce, et cetera, who are partners in mobilizing support for victims.

Generally, the news media will provide the broadest outlet for information, but direct communication not conveyed through the news media can often reach some groups in an even more timely manner. Direct communication may include personal letters or visits to community leaders, government officials, religious groups, or civic organizations. Public service announcements and news releases may also target the internal communication channels, such as newsletters, of specific groups or organizations.

In a major disaster in which the local chapter requires national or regional public affairs assistance, audiences for Red Cross communication are likely to be larger, more diverse in their needs, and more demanding in the quality and type of information they require. Relief efforts and the disaster itself are likely to attract more extensive—and more likely national—media coverage. As a result of the expanded scope of communication needs, local Red Cross personnel will experience increased demands on their time, resources, and abilities.

● SENSITIVITIES

It is easy to predict the increased demands that will be placed on Red Cross communication staff during a disaster. The public will be hungry for information, and our own organization will be operating in high gear. What may be more difficult to predict, however, is how these demands will affect the communicators themselves.

The public affairs officer must pay close attention to the sensitivities of local Red Cross chapter personnel. Chapter public affairs paid and volunteer staff members may be overworked, stressed, or exhausted. In the rush to assist victims, it is sometimes easy for frontline workers to become reactive and lose a sense of priorities. The local chapter communicator may be a technical person assuming the role of communicator and may feel overwhelmed. The chapter communicator may also be concerned about local media contacts that have taken years to establish.

At the same time, chapter staff must understand the roles of disaster workers assigned to the nationally administered operation. The public affairs staff assigned by the operations headquarters are Disaster Services Human Resources (DSHR) system members, probably from other chapters around the country. They understand the challenges of responding to disasters while maintaining normal service delivery. They may, however, need time to assess the particular needs of the local audience, while at the same time getting information to national news media.

● TEAMWORK AND COORDINATION

Once the Red Cross communicators understand each other's roles, they can focus on one of the most important elements of their job: consistency. Red Cross communicators at all levels must work together to speak with one Red Cross voice. This will require regular contact by telephone, fax, and personal briefings. Learn about your public affairs counterparts at the chapter, on the disaster relief operations, and at national headquarters. Share information, ideas, and resources. Find out how you can help them, and what they can do to make your best efforts more successful.

Westside Community Schools*

Omaha, Nebraska

● **CRISIS COMMUNICATION PLAN**

Guidelines for News Media Relations in Emergency Situations

This plan is intended to supplement other administrative procedures and guidelines for dealing with emergency situations. It should be reviewed on an annual basis, and should be distributed to all members of the district who could be affected.

● **EMERGENCY SITUATIONS**

It is always to the district's advantage to cooperate with news media, but never more so than during a crisis situation. Our schools are always open to public scrutiny, and that includes the media. Not all news is good news. But no news often has a far more negative effect on the public, so we will try to provide information in a timely fashion at all times. This plan is intended to be used in

---

*Reprinted with permission.

144

situations that, because of their scope or seriousness, become the focus of much media attention. The 1975 tornado is a case in point. The actual implementation of the plan should be determined by the size and nature of the emergency.

Situations can include:

- Serious accidents involving students or staff
- Acts of violence involving staff or students and/or non-district persons
- Natural disasters striking any district property
- Fires, explosions
- Strikes

● BEFORE AN EMERGENCY

- Designate an emergency communications coordinator (ECC) and an alternate ECC. The coordinator should not be directly involved in efforts to resolve the emergency situation itself, e.g., the superintendent, but should be someone who is familiar with working with the news media on a regular basis. (In most situations, the director of communications may be designated.) A backup person should be selected to act when the ECC is unavailable. Technical or other experts may be designated as spokespersons as well. All employees should know that the ECC, alternate, and designates are the only employees authorized to speak with the media.
- Members of the EC team will hold organizational and review meetings.
- Select one primary and one or two secondary locations to be emergency newsrooms (point of assembly for reporters), apart from the area designed for dealing with the crisis itself. The room(s) designated should be able to accommodate news conferences, with multiple telephones, electrical outlets and typewriters, and even refreshments. (The boardrooms of the ABC building are obvious first choices. Other locations should be designated in the event that those rooms are made inaccessible by the emergency.)
- News media identification badges should be made available for distribution by the ECC.
- A brief version of the plan should be distributed to all area news media.

● DURING AN EMERGENCY

- The emergency should be reported at once to the superintendent who will inform the ECC, who will activate the plan. The ECC will inform the other members of the team of the nature of the emergency. The superintendent will notify the board of education members and keep them up to date on a timely basis (they may be sought out for interviews).

- Employees should refer all news media inquiries to the ECC. Reporters should be directed to the emergency newsroom. Reports will be issued at the newsroom. Interviews will be arranged and updates gathered by the ECC and EC team.

All members of the team should be helpful and courteous at all times to the news media, but should refer all questions to the ECC. Depending on the situation, persons other than the ECC (e.g., the principal of the school where the emergency occurred) may be designated as spokespersons, and should then respond to all questions to the best of their ability. Answer honestly, but do not speculate or guess. If you don't know, say so . . . then get the answer as soon as possible. Be prompt in your dealings with the media; they have pressing deadlines. Always call the media back when you say you will, usually immediately after you have gathered the facts. Don't use educational jargon. Do not speak "off the record." Do not ask to see the story before it is used. Always inform the ECC or communications department when you have talked with a reporter. This eliminates possible contradictory statements. Do not give "exclusives" to members of the media. All should have an equal chance for gathering information, which is a key reason for having a media center and news conferences.

The media should be provided with the following information:

Facts—no speculation, and no cover-ups. In layman's terms, tell the key facts: who, what, when, where, why, and how:

- What happened? When? And where?
- How and why did it happen? (Do not speculate; if you don't know, say so.)
- Who was involved?
  Provide names only after next of kin have been notified of death or injury, and only according to the district's other policy on releasing confidential information.
- Extent and nature of injuries, property damage (no dollar amounts), continuing damage, and insurance coverage.
- Photographers (and others) should not be allowed at the scene if there is still danger in the area, but should be allowed in when the immediate danger has passed. They should be provided with stills of the facilities from the crisis preparedness plan file.
- Employees should be informed of the details of the situation as soon as possible, by the fastest means possible.
- Key community and political leaders should also be informed as soon as pos-

sible on an individual basis by designated personnel if the situation is serious enough to warrant it.

● AFTER THE EMERGENCY

- If the situation warrants it, make arrangements for the media to be personally escorted to the site.
- Arrange for other photographs if confidentiality prevents photographing the scene or people.
- Release to the news media, as soon as possible, district decisions relating to the incident, whenever it is deemed necessary. Where appropriate, express gratitude to the community, police and fire departments, emergency crews, and employees for their help. This places a positive ending on what could have been a negative story.
- The ECC or delegate should follow up by compiling a file of clippings, and a summary of how the crisis plan operated during the emergency, and what might improve the plan. This should be accomplished within two weeks, while the information is fresh.

● ANALYSIS

Some ways in which the plan could be made even more clear and helpful can be found in clarifying certain terms and having all reference documents be a part of the plan. For example, district policy on releasing confidential information is alluded to in the plan; this information or policy should be an addendum to the plan so it can be immediately referenced.

Additionally, the "designated personnel" who will contact key leaders should be designated in the plan, if not by name, at least by title/position. There are also many references to the situation warranting some response. These levels of response should be noted clearly by defining the degrees of crises that could befall the organization. Again, the key to a successful plan is to have the contingencies spelled out in advance to keep debate and interpretation to a minimum during the crisis itself.

Duke Power Company*

● INTRODUCTION

Duke Power Company employees work hard to design, build, and operate the safest and most economical power plants in the nation. The performance of our three nuclear stations speaks for itself. We are proud of the good operating record we've established over the years.

While the possibility of an accident happening is very slim, we must plan for the unexpected and be prepared. Duke's crisis management plan describes how the company would respond to activities at a nuclear power plant.

This response effort would include company personnel at the affected station and the Charlotte general office. Representatives from local, state, and federal agencies are involved. All of these plans are regularly tested and refined in drills and full participation exercises.

● DUKE POWER COMPANY'S RESPONSIBILITIES

Duke Power is responsible for actions and decisions required to restore the plant to a safe and stable condition. These actions include assessing the event's

---

*Reprinted with permission.

severity; supporting the plant's operations; managing the response effort; providing information to county, state, and federal officials; recommending any public protective action and communicating appropriate information to the public and media. (Decisions about public protective actions are the exclusive responsibility of local and state officials.)

● DUKE'S RESPONSE ORGANIZATION

Duke carries out its response activities in three key locations. At the affected station, plant personnel in a technical support center (TSC) are responsible for all site activities. These actions include: plant operations, equipment repair and maintenance, and environmental monitoring. In addition to plant personnel, representatives from the nuclear regulatory commission are also located in the TSC. Activities at the TSC are directed by the emergency coordinator, who is generally the station manager.

The crisis management center (CMC) is the off-site response organization. Once established, it relieves the TSC of overall management responsibility so plant staff can concentrate on returning the station to a stable condition. The CMC is directed by the recovery manager, who has the following duties:

1. Overall control of response activities.
2. Provides input and assistance to the Emergency Coordinator in the TSC.

The recovery manager's staff largely parallels the staff in the TSC.

● THE NEWS GROUP

The news group, which ultimately reports to the news director, is part of the recovery manager's staff. The news group is staffed and organized to provide information promptly about plant conditions and Duke's response efforts to a variety of publics. These publics include the news media, for dissemination to the public at large; local, state, and federal public information officers; and other audiences with specialized interest, such as regulators, elected officials, and members of the financial community.

News group participants, operating from the joint information center (JIC), communicate with the following audiences:

A. Media

Duke relies on the media to provide prompt, accurate information to local residents and the public at large. To provide access to current information on plant status, a media center is promptly established in the O. J. Miller Auditorium of the electric center. The news plan specifies that the only Duke Power representative empowered to announce new information about plant status is the public spokesperson. This "single spokesperson" concept ensures that the media—and thus the public—receives consistent information about the plant's activities.

B. Plant Neighbors and the General Public

News group members staff telephones in the JIC and at the affected plant to respond to questions or concerns from residents around the plant or from the general public. In the JIC, news group representatives are co-located with counterparts from the state and county to better respond to the public's questions.

C. Employees

Employees of Duke Power are informed of activities at the plant through computer mail generated from the JIC and distributed system-wide. Many employees also receive training in rumor control procedures and are instructed to refer any questions to the JIC.

D. Elected Officials

News group members initiate contact with local, state, and federal officials to provide information on plant status. Elected officials—or any other constituents—have questions on plant conditions.

E. Industry Groups

The news plan relies on major industry groups to distribute information on plant status to other utilities.

F. Regulators

Pathways of communications with federal and state regulators are also included in the news plan. Public information officers from FEMA and the NRC work out of the JIC. The NRC has technical staff in the TSC and in the CMC. Members of the North Carolina Utilities Commission and the South Carolina Public Service Commission are also updated on plant status.

● STATES AND COUNTIES

Because the states and local counties have responsibility for public protective actions, an effective response depends on close interaction among Duke Power and the state and county officials. To provide timely information to the state and county, their information representatives are co-located in the JIC. The states and counties issue their own news releases on activities in their community and participate in press conferences.

Additionally, if requested, a news group member is sent to each of the state and county operation centers to serve as a technical resource on plant activities.

News Group Position Summaries

News Director (ND)—Overall responsibility for the news group and coordinates the release of all public information about the emergency. Manages Duke's activities in the joint information center (JIC) and is the primary contact for all lead PIOs.

Public Spokesperson (PS)—Duke's official representative at press conferences; he is the only person authorized to announce new information on plant conditions. Located in the crisis management center when news conferences are not in progress.

News Coordinator (NC)—Collects and verifies plant status in the crisis management center, drafts news releases and secures approvals. Serves as the primary CMC information contact to the news director.

Assistant News Director (AND)—Responsible for the production and dissemination of Duke's news releases. Ensures flow of plant related information within the joint information center. Assumes the news director role in the joint information center during news conferences or other absences of the news director.

Staff Assistant (SA)—Ensures smooth and effective set-up and operation of the JIC and related facilities such as the media center and the media monitoring area.

State/County PIO Liaison (S/C PIO Liaison)—Serves as the conduit for information between Duke's news group and the state and county public information officers in the JIC.

CMC Technical Assistant (TA)—Serves as primary technical resource for the news coordinator in the CMC.

Technical Support Center Liaison (TSCL)—News group representative at the technical support center.

Media Coordinator (MC)—Ensures smooth operation of the media center.

Catawba Owners Liaison (COL)—Keeps Catawba owners informed of plant conditions for emergencies at either Catawba or McGuire. Located in the JIC.

Internal Communications Coordinator (ICC)—The point of contact for all employee information about the emergency and the response effort. Located in the JIC.

Investor Communications Coordinator (IvCC)—Responsible for communications with the financial community. Located in the JIC.

Governments Coordinator (GC)—Responsible for communications with elected officials in state, county, and federal government. Located in the JIC.

Technical Briefer Section Head (TBSH)—Coordinates the activities of technical briefers, and assists the AND in expediting accurate and timely communications with special audiences. Located in the JIC and media center.

Technical Briefer (TB), media center—Works with the media and industry/agency officials in explaining information about the plant status.

Technical Briefer (TB), rumor control—Responds to telephone inquiries received in the JIC from plant neighbors and the public at large.

Technical Briefer (TB), news center resource—Serves as primary technical resource in the JIC to the news director and the assistant news director.

Technical Briefer (TB), media monitoring—Assists in the review of media reports for technical accuracy. Located in the JIC and the media monitoring area.

Technical Briefer (TB), state/county EOC—Serves as the news group representative in the state/county EOC.

Technical Briefer (TB), community relations—Serves as the on-site news group representative. Reports to the affected plants information center.

Technical Briefer (TB), media notification—Notifies the media of the plant's condition and activation of the JIC.

Technical Briefer (TB), hospital—Serves as the Duke Power representative at the hospital.

Media Center Assistant (MCA)—Greets and registers media representatives upon their arrival to the media center.

Audiovisual Coordinator (AVC)—Responsible for media monitoring and the videotaping of all news conferences. Located in the media monitoring area (electric center) and in the JIC and media center.

Media Monitor (MM)—Records radio and television news programs and EBS messages. Reviews for accuracy. Located in the media monitoring area.

JIC Assistant (JA)—Responsible for the set-up and logistics supporting all news group facilities. Located in the JIC.

Secretarial Team (ST)—Provides clerical and administrative support for the news group. Located in the JIC.

News Release

Bulletin #_____

Date _____

Status as of _____ A.M./P.M.

THIS IS A DRILL

Charlotte, N.C.—Duke Power Co. reported an (alert/site area emergency/general emergency) at its (station) near (city, state) at (time) on (date).

The (event classification) was declared due to a _____. Here is what happened:

- (Time)   (Activity)
- (Time)   (Activity)
- (Time)   (Activity)
- Etc.

THIS IS A DRILL

For further information, call the Joint Information Center in Charlotte at 704/382-0644, 704/382-0655, or 1/800-777-0005.

Plant neighbors should stay tuned to their radios or TVs for further information. State and county officials would use the Emergency Broadcast System for any protective action recommendations.

NOTE: A Media Center is being (has been) established at the O. J. Miller Auditorium in the Electric Center in Charlotte. Facilities will be made (are) available at the center for media representatives.

Duke Power Company's
Joint Information Center

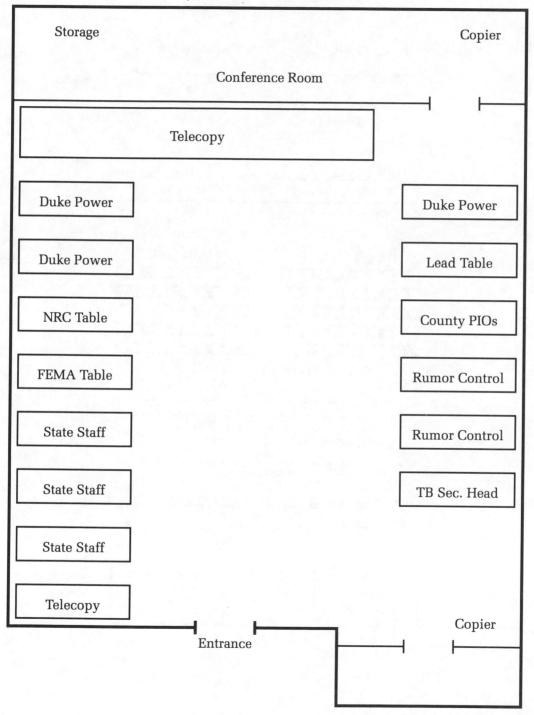

**Duke Power Company's
Media Center**

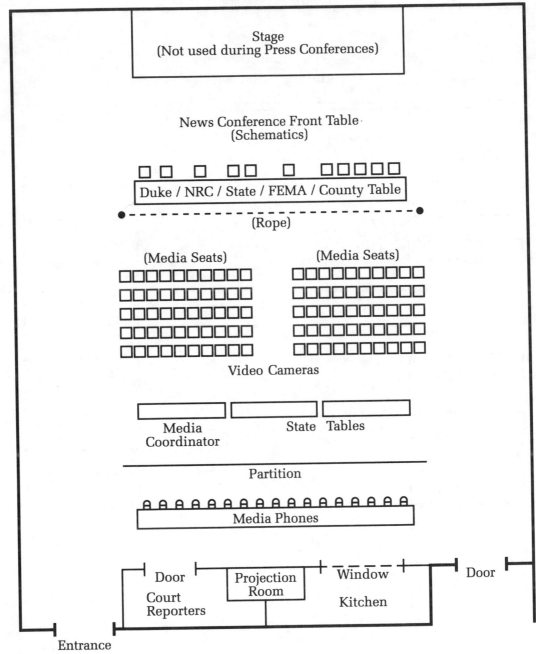

Union Pacific*

● PUBLIC RELATIONS DEPARTMENT PROCEDURES

Overall

The public relations department is responsible for the dissemination of information to the public pertaining to the Union Pacific Railroad. In the event of a hazardous material incident and/or release, the public relations department will work with the appropriate company personnel, all federal, state, and local agencies, contractors of Union Pacific Railroad, and customer representatives who have product involved in the incident and/or release, to ensure factual and timely information is made available to the appropriate media ensuring accurate and timely reporting to assist with the overall coordinated effort in safely resolving the incident.

Preincident

The public relations department will provide to the necessary company personnel names and phone numbers of the appropriate public relations personnel

*Reprinted with permission.

who should be notified in the event of a hazardous material incident and/or release. The public relations department will be responsible for the updating of this information and will notify the appropriate personnel when changes occur.

The public relations department will assist with providing the necessary training for appropriate company personnel in an effort to strengthen the emergency contingency plan.

Incident

After the public relations department is notified of a hazardous material incident and/or release, the department will consult with the appropriate company personnel and determine if the incident warrants a public relations representative be sent to the scene of the incident and/or release.

If a hazardous material incident and/or release is minor, with no immediate danger to the general public, the public relations department will notify the appropriate media of the incident in order to ensure factual reporting without going to the scene. If necessary, the appropriate company personnel would be briefed by the public relations department as to the appropriate method to handle local press inquiries at the scene. Any statements made to the media at the incident site should be indicated to the public relations department to ensure consistency with statements made to the media.

If an incident is major, a public relations department representative will be dispatched to the scene of the incident by the most timely mode of travel. In order to provide accurate information from the onset of an incident, while the public relations department representative is enroute to the incident and/or release, public relations representative from company headquarters will contact the appropriate media and provide the most current information and indicate that a public relations department representative is enroute to the scene.

After the public relations department representative arrives on the scene of an incident, the department representative will consult with the appropriate company personnel and incident commander. The public relations department representative will conduct a series of media briefings at one-hour intervals as pertinent information warrants. After initial incident information is provided to the appropriate media, updates will be provided at intervals of every two hours, as information warrants, until the incident and/or release is stabilized.

The public relations department representative will consult with all appropriate company personnel, all appropriate federal, state, and local agencies, all contractors provided by the company, and any customer product representatives in order to provide an accurate account of the situation.

The public relations department representative will work with all appropriate incident personnel and offer any assistance and guidance in establishing a media center, if such a center is warranted.

The public relations department representative will work with all appropriate incident personnel to ensure a coordinated media effort is maintained and the representative will attend incident briefings in order to ensure the coordination is maintained throughout the incident and/or release.

Post Incident

After the incident and/or release is stabilized, the public relations representative will work with the necessary company personnel during the incident evaluation and provide any suggestions that will assist in strengthening the emergency contingency plan.

Union Pacific also provides information on their training sessions for crisis communicators:

MANAGEMENT DEVELOPMENT PROGRAM

8:00–9:00 A.M.	Department overview
9:00–9:15 A.M.	Introduce staff
9:15–9:45 A.M.	Media relations
9:45–10:00 A.M.	Break
10:00–noon	Crisis communication
noon–1:30 P.M.	Lunch—Press Club
1:30–3:00 P.M.	Crisis communication
3:00–3:15 P.M.	Break
3:15–4:00 P.M.	Exercise
4:00–4:30 P.M.	Exercise review
4:30–5:00 P.M.	Wrap and Q&A

CRISIS COMMUNICATION

10:00 A.M.–noon & 1:30–3:00 P.M.

I. Definition and basic theory of crisis communication
II. Before the crisis
    A. Being prepared
        1. Know the railroad
        2. Know the issues surrounding the railroad
    B. Identify audiences
        1. Internal
        2. External
    C. Crisis communication planning
        1. Internal
        2. External
    D. Testing the plan
    E. Evaluation and plan modifications
III. Crisis
    A. Working the plan
    B. Evaluation
        1. As you go
        2. "Inside and Out"
IV. Post crisis evaluation
    A. Internal
    B. External
    C. Modifications
V. Setting up a communications area
VI. Assessing the effects the media have during a crisis
    A. Short term
    B. Long term

Los Angeles Department of Airports*

It is the policy of the Los Angeles Department of Airports to cooperate with representatives of the news media in their coverage of activities, events, and other stories of public interest at Los Angeles International, Ontario International, Palmdale Regional, and Van Nuys Airports.

The normal source for news media seeking information about airport operations or administration is the department's public relations office at each airport. Requests for interviews with members of the Department of Airports management, its managers of specialized airport functions, or its personnel should be made through the public relations office.

News media covering stories related to air traffic control, air safety, aircraft, or airline matters are advised to contact the Federal Aviation Administration, manufacturer, or airline involved. The Department of Airports is not a source of news information on these subjects, although the department's public relations office will, when requested, attempt to refer media to the appropriate contacts.

Although procedures vary somewhat at each airport, as a general policy, the news media enjoys the same access to public areas of the airport (ticketing lobbies, sidewalks, et cetera) as does the general public.

The airfield operations areas are subject to a comprehensive federally

---

*Reprinted with permission.

mandated and approved security program that denies access to all except those having a legitimate operational need to use the area. However, it is the practice of the department, during regular business hours, to permit news media access to limited areas of the airfield operations area (AOA), either under escort of the department public relations staff or accompanied by authorized representatives of airlines or other tenants.

During times of airfield or other airport emergencies, procedures exist at each airport for a central check-in of news media, identification of authorized press personnel, and transportation to the scene of the emergency. Access cannot be granted until the fire department or other on-site crisis management agency declares the area cleared for such access.

Certain areas both on and off the AOA are leaseholds of airlines and other tenants of the Department of Airports. Included in this category are airline maintenance hangars, ticket counters, etc. Media should make arrangements with the airline or appropriate tenant for access to such an area. In many such cases, the department's public relations office can provide a contact phone number.

Because of the scope of operations at Los Angeles International, certain public relations procedures specially apply to this airport.

Inquiries should be directed to the public relations bureau, 213-646-5260, Monday through Friday, 8:00 A.M. to 5:30 P.M. After hours and weekends contact: airfield operations at 646-4265 or airport police at 646-6254. A public relations representative will be contacted to return the call.

● PRESS CREDENTIALS

The public relations bureau recognizes media representatives with current press credentials issued by the Los Angeles Police Department or the Los Angeles County Sheriff's Department. In the event of an incident that is wider than Southern California, it is at the discretion of the manager of public relations or commander of the on-site crisis management agency which other forms of news media credentials to recognize. Access to restricted areas will be based on the possession of the approved credentials and other applicable pertinent safety and airport regulations.

In the event of the following situations, these guidelines apply:

● BOMB THREAT

The Department of Airports asks for the cooperation of the news media in its effort to reduce the number of bomb threats. Experience has shown that publicizing threats often encourages others to be made soon after the incident.

The department characterized two types of bomb threats:

1. Specific—threat against a particular aircraft, flight, or building
2. Nonspecific—all others

The airline subject to the threat will determine whether the threat is specific or nonspecific and the nature of response. When advised by the airline, the public relations bureau will provide general information about the threat.

Specific information may be obtained from the carrier involved and the Los Angeles Police Department, which is responsible for any bomb search. News media access to public areas will be at the discretion of the executive director or his designee and all applicable airport and safety regulations will apply.

● OVER THE WATER AIR ACCIDENTS

In over-the-water air accidents, the Los Angeles County Sheriff's Department Information Bureau will provide media transportation via boat to the accident scene. Primary contacts for accident information will be the airline, Los Angeles County Sheriff's Information Bureau, and Fire Department, Department of Beaches and Harbors; Los Angeles City Fire Department, and the U.S. Coast Guard.

● ALERT 22 AND ALERT 33

Emergencies are described as:

ALERT 22—An unsafe flight condition in which an aircraft emergency may occur

ALERT 33—An aircraft incident appears imminent or has occurred

ALERT I—A possible over-the-water aircraft emergency

ALERT II—An aircraft accident has occurred offshore

A public relations representative will provide the following information:

1. Airline involved
2. Time of the incident
3. Expected time of arrival
4. Reason given for the alert

Specific information may be obtained from the airline involved and the fire or police agency handling the response.

● AIRFIELD EMERGENCY

During an airfield emergency such as an aircraft accident or fire, news media covering the incident should report to Airport Security Post 2 located on the frontage road west of Sepulveda Boulevard just north of the Sepulveda tunnel. All other entrances will be closed. The news media will be advised if a decision is made to use another access point.

A public relations representative will meet the news media at Post 2, or designated access point, to check credentials and issue press armbands.

A restricted area will be established at the scene of the emergency. *Under no circumstances will the news media or any other personnel not involved in life-saving or firefighting operations be permitted inside the security lines until all rescue operations have been completed. These security lines will be established in the best interest of news coverage insofar as rescue operations permit.* Photographs and videotapes may be taken in or from any area to which news media with press armbands have been permitted access.

Based on national airport security measures, *no news organization's remote TV vans and radio cars will be allowed on the airfield. All crews and equipment will transfer to Department of Airports vehicles.*

A shuttle system will be operating to transport news media to the scene as permitted by the agency in charge of the incident. The Department of Airports strongly discourages use of press pools. Coverage will be limited to a pool only at the specific direction of the agency in charge.

The Department of Airports recognizes and understands the importance of interviewing the victim(s) of a crash, natural disaster, hijacking, or hostage taking incident. However, the department's first responsibility is to the victim(s) and their right to privacy. Credentialed news media will not be arbitrarily denied access to the victim(s), but must understand that some victims are reluctant to be interviewed or photographed and the department will support their decision. News media should be aware that access to the victim(s) may be subject to approval by the airline involved, the Federal Aviation Administration (FAA), the Federal Bureau of Investigation (FBI), and the National Transportation Safety Board (NTSB).

News media will not resist, obstruct, oppose, or interfere with any law enforcement officer in the lawful execution of his or her duties.

The news media is not exempt from any federal, state, or local law, and if arrested will be handled in the same manner as any violator.

Department of Airports police personnel who experience difficulty with members of the news media will make a full report of the circumstances to the airport's chief of police. If no laws were broken and additional follow-up is necessary, action will be taken by the department's director of public relations.

● AIRCRAFT HIJACKING, SABOTAGE, OR HOSTAGE-TAKING INCIDENT

The Los Angeles Department of Airports police will respond initially to aircraft hijacking, hostage taking and sabotage incidents. The Federal Aviation Administration has jurisdiction over such incidents when the incident occurs in flight. The Federal Bureau of Investigation has jurisdiction over aircraft hijacking, hostage taking, and sabotage incidents when the incident occurs on board an aircraft on the ground. Once jurisdiction has been established, the Department of Airports and all other agencies provide support to the agency with primary jurisdiction only as requested by that agency.

The FAA, FBI, or other lead agency in the incident will be the primary source of information about the circumstances of the incident and the process to resolve it.

The department has established a hijacking center at its construction and maintenance yard, 7411 World Way West. The news media should assemble at this location unless an alternate site has been designated. Various agencies involved in the incident will have representatives there and telephones will be activated for use by the news media.

● HAZARDOUS MATERIALS

Any material—solid, liquid, or vapor—that can cause harm to life or the environment is a hazardous material. The wide variety of hazardous materials, their different forms, and potential harm, require that persons exercise extreme caution when making efforts to identify and control a hazardous materials emergency. Some materials are particularly dangerous and can permeate and permanently contaminate much of what they contact. Contact on the skin, clothing, or inhalation of even small amounts of these substances can cause illness, loss of consciousness, or death.

The Los Angeles Fire Department establishes the command post and assumes command of such an incident, marshals all necessary resources, and takes actions necessary to stabilize the situation. The Los Angeles County

Health Department will monitor the area for any hazard and clear the area for use. Media will be admitted under escort when these agencies have determined it is safe to do so.

Airport police shall keep all unauthorized personnel out of the contaminated area. Information about the incident is provided by the Los Angeles Fire Department. The Los Angeles County Health Department is the secondary source of information.

● STRUCTURAL FIRES

Structural fires at the airport are the responsibility of the Los Angeles City Fire Department. It will assume command of the response. Information about the cause and progress of fire suppression will be provided by the fire department. LAX public relations will have a secondary role providing information about the cause and the incident's impact on flight operations at the airport.

● NATURAL DISASTERS

In the event of a major earthquake, it is likely the mayor would declare an emergency and the emergency operations control center in city hall would be activated. When such a declaration is made, all disaster activities of city departments would be controlled from the operations center.

Information about fire suppression at the airport is the responsibility of the Los Angeles Fire Department. Individual airlines will provide information about the disaster's effect on their operations. Public relations will provide information about damage to structures, roadways, runways, and its impact on airport operations.

● ACCESS TO PASSENGER TERMINALS

The news media is accorded access to public areas in the passenger terminals, except for portions of the Tom Bradley International Terminal past passenger-screening checkpoints. Access to airline-controlled areas that are nonpublic, on the airline ramp, or beyond screening in the case of the Tom Bradley International Terminal, will be under airline escort. In all cases the news media will undergo passenger screening of their person and equipment.

Use of limited parking curbside at the terminals is discretionary on the part of the Department of Airports. News crews, especially those with electronic news gathering equipment, may park curbside between terminals or in metered parking provided free for up to eight hours by the department. When filming at the airport notify public relations.

● MEDIA PARKING AT LAX

Effective February 1, 1989, members of the news media on assignment at Los Angeles International Airport will be provided up to eight hours of courtesy parking under the following conditions:

1. Vehicles must be parked at a meter in metered parking lots only.
2. The media representative must display on the dashboard of the vehicle a photocopy of their current and valid press credential issued by the Los Angeles Police Department or Los Angeles County Sheriff's Department. This ID must be clearly visible from outside of the vehicle.
3. The Department of Airports asks for the news organization's cooperation to prevent misuse of this privilege for personal business.
4. This procedure replaces all previous courtesy parking procedures. Previously issued and/or utilized IDs are now invalid for airport parking.

(*Note:*) As in the past, parking of minicam vehicles curbside for on-the-spot coverage of breaking stories may be permitted on a case-by-case basis for limited periods. Advance permission should be requested by contacting Department of Airports public relations bureau, at (213) 646-5260.

Generally speaking, the news media enjoys access to the same areas as does the public—ticketing lobbies, sidewalks, waiting areas, and concourses. Areas beyond the security checkpoint are open to the news media after news representatives and their equipment undergo the security check at the screening checkpoint. These areas are open to the news media without any prior notice to the public relations bureau or any other bureau at the airport.

● AIRFIELD EMERGENCY

In the event of an emergency, media should meet at the Southside Command Post. Airport public relations staff will accommodate media to the extent possible from this location. Media arriving at any other location may experience delays.

● AFTER-HOURS MEDIA ASSISTANCE

After normal office hours (8:30 A.M. to 5:00 P.M., Monday through Friday) media should leave messages with the Ontario communications center, 714-988-2700, which in turn will contact the Ontario public relations manager. If the public relations manager is unavailable, the captain of the safety officers may respond to the press and provide information.

● EARTHQUAKE

In the event of a major earthquake, the public relations staff will handle all media requests from the public relations office or the airport tour guide office at the base of the air traffic control tower.

Finally, past experience at Ontario has shown that many news incidents or events are unpredictable, and so it is best to let the experience and judgment of the public relations bureau determine procedure in situations that have no precedent.

Part VI

Addenda

Forms

● **POTENTIAL CRISES LISTING**

Rate your organization on scale of one through ten—ten being most likely—as to likelihood of a crisis in the following areas:

Security concerns _____

Product recall _____

Product ban _____

Employee problems (this could range from union strife to sexual harassment suits) _____

Community concerns (is the planned plant expansion met with resistance?) _____

Pollution and environmental concerns _____

Pending lawsuits _____

Regulatory changes _____

Plant closings _____

Layoffs _____

Supplier problems _____

Production problem _____

Financial concerns (debt rating drops, stock price swings, poor

earnings) _____

Merger/Takeover _____

Death/Serious illness of CEO (or other key executive)

activist protests _____

● EVALUATION SHEET

For each public and crisis, list the appropriate message and channel of communication with the person(s) responsible.

PUBLICS	MESSAGES	CHANNELS OF COMMUNICATION	INDIVIDUAL(S) RESPONSIBLE
Customers			
Business community			
Neighbors			
Competitors			
Financial community			
Government/Legislature			
Clients			
FCC consultants			
Energy commission			
Media			
Vendors			
Families			
Partners			
Stockholders			
Legal group			
PRSA groupings			

● MESSAGE DEVELOPMENT SHEET

Write out three key messages about your organization that you want communicated during a crisis.

1. _____
_____
_____
_____
_____
_____
_____

2. _____
_____
_____
_____
_____
_____
_____

3. _____
_____
_____
_____
_____
_____
_____

● POTENTIAL PROBLEMS WORKSHEET

List potential problems and the ways they may occur, then note how severe each could be or how they could escalate.

	PROBLEM/ISSUE	WAYS PROBLEM MAY OCCUR	SEVERITY/ ESCALATION POTENTIAL
1.	_____	_____	_____
2.	_____	_____	_____
3.	_____	_____	_____
4.	_____	_____	_____
5.	_____	_____	_____
6.	_____	_____	_____
7.	_____	_____	_____
8.	_____	_____	_____
9.	_____	_____	_____
10.	_____	_____	_____
11.	_____	_____	_____
12.	_____	_____	_____
13.	_____	_____	_____
14.	_____	_____	_____
15.	_____	_____	_____
16.	_____	_____	_____
17.	_____	_____	_____
18.	_____	_____	_____
19.	_____	_____	_____
20.	_____	_____	_____

● CRISIS TEAM DEVELOPMENT SHEET

Part I. Planning

Fill in all that apply for planning stage.

Position or Department	Name
1. CEO	_____
2. Public relations	_____
3. Sales	_____
4. Marketing	_____
5. Research & Development	_____
6. Security	_____
7. Personnel/Psychologist	_____
8. Legal	_____
9. Finance	_____
10. Manufacturing	_____
Product 1. _____	_____
Product 2. _____	_____
Product 3. _____	_____
Product 4. _____	_____
Product 5. _____	_____
11. Other _____	_____
12. Other _____	_____

Part II. Crisis Communications Action Team

FUNCTIONAL ASSIGNMENT	POSITION	NAME	TELEPHONE
1. Leader			
2. Spokesperson			
3. Backup spokesperson			
4. On-site coordinator			
5. Legal			
6. Physical arrangements			
7. Press statements			

● **TELEPHONE/MAIL LOG**

DATE	TIME	INDIVIDUAL	COMMENT	ADDRESS OR TELEPHONE	NEEDS CALL BACK

● CHECKLISTS

Who will be assigned to the site coordination? _____

Who is on your team? _____

Who is the spokesperson? _____

Who will back them up? _____

Who will develop the plan? _____

Who will distribute it? _____

How will it be updated? _____

When will drills occur? _____

List some scenarios. _____

_____

_____

Where is your command post going to be? _____

Where will the media center be? _____

Do these rooms contain the following, as appropriate?

_____ accessible tables and chairs

_____ trash receptacles

_____ ashtrays

_____ paper

_____ pencils and pens

_____ copies of the crisis plan and team members

_____ sufficient electrical outlets

_____ the capacity to be secured

_____ radio and television capabilities

_____ nametags

_____ clocks

_____ restroom/shower facilities nearby to freshen up

_____ refreshments

_____ fax machines

_____ a direct phone line

List your key media contacts.

RADIO/TV/NEWSPAPERS	CONTACT	TELEPHONE	FAX

● KNOW YOUR ORGANIZATION

Write or copy below your company's mission statement for easy reference.

● COMPANY AND INDUSTRY ANALYSIS

Also, to help you as you learn more about your organization, list key business points, as suggested.

Strengths

Weaknesses

Opportunities

Threats

Products

Customers

Key Vendors

Plant and Office Locations

Years in Operation

Key Personnel (Attach or include biographies as appropriate)

Resources

For further information and reading on crisis communications, I recommend the following resources:

IABC Communication World
A compilation of writings, cases, and plans.

Bulldog Reporter Crisis Communication Handbook
A compilation of short articles by experts in the field.

Public Relations Society of American (PRSA)
PRSA provides seminars on a regular basis. Check with your local chapter for listings and dates.

University courses and classes
Many local colleges and universities offer one-day courses or semester classes focusing on crisis communications.

Local public relations businesses and organizations

Public Relations Journal

Notes

1. James G. Gray Jr., *Managing the Corporate Image* (Westport, Conn.: Quorum Books, 1986), 25–26.

2. Gerald C. Meyers and John Holusha, "Crisis Susceptibility Audit Summary." *When It Hits the Fan: Managing the Nine Crises of Business* (Boston: Houghton Mifflin Company, 1986).

3. Dieudonnée ten Berge, *The First 24 Hours* (Oxford: Basil Blackwell Ltd., 1990), 45.

4. Ibid., 46.

5. Norman R. Nager, *Public Relations Management by Objective* (New York: Longman, 1984), 329–335.

6. Steven Fink, *Crisis Management: Planning for the Inevitable* (New York: Anacom, 1986), 95.

7. Ibid., 98.

8. Ibid., 96–100.

9. Marion K. Pinsdorf, *Communicating When Your Company is Under Siege* (Lexington, Mass.: Lexington Books, 1987), 27.

10. Martin J. Smith, "Losing the Lackluster," *The Orange County Register*, 1 May 1991, E1.

11. Ibid.

12. Steven Fink, "Prepare for Crisis, It's Part of Business," *The New York Times*, 30 April 1989, D1.

185

13. David Steinberg, "A Plan in Action," *PR Newswire,* (no date): 10.

14. James Wilson, "Managing Communication in a Crisis: An Expert's View," *IABC Communication World,* December 1985, 13–16.

15. Martha Ray, "Presumed Guilty: Managing When Your Company's Name is Mud," *Working Woman,* November 1991, 31.

16. Kemeny Commission's account of the incident taken from Steven Fink's book, *Crisis Management: Planning for the Inevitable* (New York: Anacom, 1986), 110.

17. Steven Fink, *Crisis Management: Planning for the Inevitable* (New York: Anacom, 1986), 110.

18. James G. Gray Jr., *Managing the Corporate Image* (Westport, Conn.: Quorum Books, 1986), 27.

19. Albert J. Tortorella, "Crisis Communications: If It Had a Precedent, It Wouldn't Be a Crisis," *IABC Communication World,* June 1989.

20. Bruce Allar, "John R. Hall Chairman & CEO, Ashland Oil, Inc./Leadership Profile Series," *Sky Magazine,* July 1990, 37–39.

21. Norman Sklarewitz, *Public Relations Journal* (May 1991): 34–36.

22. The manual divides emergencies into five categories: Trade, an emergency such as a strike or delayed sailing; Business page, or unfavorable press related to such items as financial reports or sale of the company; Shipboard, such as natural disasters (hurricane) or accident; Media, like a bomb or other threat that could cause sinking; and International, for events involving terrorists or other attacks.

23. Mary Connelly, "Iacocca Battles to Salvage Minivan's Reputation," *Automotive News,* 4 February 1991, 1, 37.

24. Mary Connelly, "Chrysler: Problems are 'Old News,'" *Automotive News,* 4 February 1991, 37.

25. Mary Connelly, "Iacocca Cries Foul to Dealers," *Automotive News,* 4 February 1991, 37.

26. Ibid., p. 37.

27. Gerald Meyers and John Holusha, *When It Hits the Fan: Managing the Nine Crises of Business* (Boston: Houghton Mifflin Company, 1986), 62.

28. Case based on information provided in article by George M. Morris, president and chief executive officer of Financial Shares Corporation. Morris, George M., "Bankers Use Public Relations as Survival Strategy," *Public Relations Journal* (September 1991): 7–13.

29. Diane Thomas, Public Information Officer, Santa Ana Unified School District. Interview by author. Santa Ana, California, January 1992.

30. Pinsdorf, 97.

Bibliography

Allar, Bruce. "John R. Hall, Chairman & CEO, Ashland Oil, Inc./Leadership Profile Series." *Sky Magazine* (July 1990): 34–36.

Benn, Alec. *The 23 Most Common Mistakes in Public Relations.* New York: Amacom American Management Association, 1982.

Birkby, Robert C. *Boy Scout Handbook.* Irving, Texas, 1990.

Connelly, Mary. "Chrysler: Problems are 'Old News.'" *Automotive News* (4 February 1991): 37.

———. "*Consumer Reports* Cites Snag in A604 Ultradrive Gearbox." *Automotive News* (4 February 1991): 1–37.

———. "Iacocca Cries Foul to Dealers." *Automotive News* (4 February 1991): 37.

Dunkle, Marie K. "Crisis Communications, Formula for Risk Reduction." *Contingency Journal* (July-September 1990): 35.

Feder, Barnaby J. "P.R. Mistakes Seen in Breast-Implant Case." *The New York Times*, 29 January 1992, C1.

Fink, Steven. *Crisis Management, Planning for the Inevitable.* New York: Amacom, 1986.

Fisher, Lynn and William Briggs, Ed.D. "Communication with Employees During a Time of Tragedy." *IABC Communication World* (February 1989).

Gray, James G. Jr. *Managing the Corporate Image: the Key to Public Trust.* Westport, Conn.: Quorum Books, 1986.

Harrison, E. Bruce, APR. "Assessing the Damage." *Public Relations Journal* (October 1989): 43.

Holusha, John. "Exxon's Public-Relations Problem." *The New York Times*, 21 April 1989, D1.

Jackson, Patrick. *Public Relations Journal* (April 1985): 28.

McGrath, George. "Maintain an Ongoing Investor Relations Crisis Plan." *IABC Communication World* (March 1988).

Meyers, Gerald C., and John Holusha. *When It Hits the Fan: Managing the Nine Crises of Business*. Boston: Houghton Mifflin Company, 1986.

Mitroff, Ian I. "Crises Find Our Heads in the Sand." *Los Angeles Times*, 31 March 1989, 7.

Morris, George M. "Bankers Use Public Relations as Survival Strategy." *Public Relations Journal* (September 1991): 7–13.

Nager, Norman R. and T. Harrell Allen. *Public Relations Management by Objective*. New York: Longman, 1984.

Parrish, Michael. "Spill: Officials Ignored Cost Estimates." *Los Angeles Times*, 8 October 1991, A14.

Phillips, Charles S. *Secrets of Successful Public Relations*. Englewood Cliffs, N.J.: Prentice-Hall, 1985.

Pinsdorf, Marion K. *Communicating When Your Company is Under Siege*. Lexington Books, 1987.

Ray, Martha. "Presumed Guilty: Managing When Your Company's Name is Mud." *Working Woman* (November 1991): 31.

Sauerhaft, Stan and Chris Atkins. *Image Wars—Protecting Your Company When There's No Place to Hide*. New York: John Wiley & Sons, 1988.

Sklarewitz, Norman. "Cruise Company Handles Crisis by the Book." *Public Relations Journal* (May 1991): 34–36.

Smith, Martin J. "Losing the Lackluster." *The Orange County Register*, 1 May 1991, E1.

Steinberg, David. "A Plan in Action." *Public Relations Newswire* (no date): 10.

Stephenson, Donald. "Worth Repeating." *IABC Communication World* (August 1985).

ten Berge, Dieudonnée. *The First 24 Hours*. Oxford: Basil Blackwell Ltd., 1990.

Tortorella, Albert. "Crisis Communications: If It Had a Precedent, It Wouldn't Be a Crisis." *IABC Communication World* (June 1989): 42–43.

Werner, Lawrence, APR. *Public Relations Journal* (August 1990): 30–31.

Wilson, James. "Managing Communication in a Crisis: An Expert's View." *IABC Communication World* (December 1985): 13–16.

Winner, Paul. *Effective PR Management: A Guide to Corporate Survival*. Condon, N.J.: Kogan Page Ltd., 1987.

Index

NOTRE-DAME
DE PARIS

by Richard and Clara Winston

and the Editors
of the Newsweek Book Division

NEWSWEEK, New York

NEWSWEEK BOOK DIVISION

JOSEPH L. GARDNER   *Editor*

Janet Czarnetzki   *Art Director*
Edwin D. Bayrd, Jr.   *Associate Editor*
Laurie P. Phillips   *Picture Editor*
Eva Galan   *Assistant Editor*
Lynne H. Brown   *Copy Editor*
Russell Ash   *European Correspondent*

S. ARTHUR DEMBNER   *Publisher*

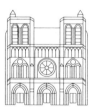

WONDERS OF MAN

MILTON GENDEL   *Consulting Editor*

Contents

A silver and gilded copper reliquary known as the right arm of Saint Louis, the thirteenth-century King of France.

A nineteenth-century plan by Viollet-le-Duc shows Notre-Dame's western façade as it might have looked with the spires originally intended to crown the towers.

Introduction

The "aged queen of French cathedrals," Victor Hugo called Notre-Dame de Paris in 1831. And to the famous novelist, the historic church was indeed ancient: nearly seven hundred years had passed since Bishop Maurice de Sully decided that the capital of France needed a cathedral worthy of its emerging preeminence. "Every face, every stone of the venerable monument," continued Hugo, "is a page not only of the history of the country, but also of the history of science and art." For this reason, the authors of the following narrative have selected Notre-Dame — neither the oldest, the largest, nor even the most beautiful Gothic cathedral — as the stage on which to present their dramatic review of a millennium of French history.

It was at Notre-Dame that the Crusades were preached, Te Deums sung for victories, funerals conducted for the noble and royal dead. Mary Queen of Scots was married there, Napoleon crowned, Joan of Arc beatified. Charles de Gaulle came to the cathedral to celebrate the liberation of Paris from the Nazis in 1944, and twenty-six years later the great of the world assembled to mourn the passing of France's man of the mid-century. Far more than a house of worship, the cathedral of Paris has stood at the very center of French and indeed all European history since the age of faith in which it was erected.

Two hundred years in the building, Notre-Dame was never really completed according to the scheme of its original designers. By the fifteenth century the cathedral was already considered outdated; to men of the dawning Renaissance it was but a grotesque symbol of the barbarian past, a hulking, gloomy pile to which the epithet "Gothic" was contemptuously affixed. Later, baroque additions would destroy much of the original harmony, all in the name of modernization. By the time of Hugo, it took a good deal of imagination and perhaps self-deception to appreciate the grandeur of the abused shrine.

Then, an inspired and dedicated architect of the mid-nineteenth century, Eugène Emmanuel Viollet-le-Duc, began the painstaking work of restoration; and only in the present decade, with the cleansing of all Parisian monuments, has the cathedral been revealed in its pristine elegance. To reverent believers, students of history, even idly curious tourists, Notre-Dame de Paris is now, more than ever, the supremely beautiful sight in what is widely regarded as the world's supremely beautiful city.

THE EDITORS

NOTRE-DAME
IN HISTORY

Notre-Dame, we call her, although so many of the cathedrals of France bear the same name: Our Lady. There are Notre-Dame of Rouen, Notre-Dame of Chartres, Notre-Dame of Amiens, Notre-Dame of Strasbourg, and a host of others. But the cathedral of Paris is *the* Notre-Dame. She is neither the tallest, nor the biggest, nor the most typical of the great Gothic churches of France. Yet she remains the cathedral of cathedrals, the epitome of the Gothic, the symbol of Paris and therefore of France. Eight centuries of French life have left their mark upon her stones. For eight hundred years the history of France, brilliant and somber, tumultuous and contemplative, has unfolded in her shadow. Most of the great men and women of France have stepped through her portals, and many of them lie buried beneath her pavement.

The visitor who today approaches the cathedral from the great plaza opened by Baron Haussmann in the nineteenth century has a view of the western façade that was denied to previous generations. Formerly, buildings clustered closely around the cathedral, as they still do on the north, where they are separated from the walls and buttresses only by the width of the rue du Cloître Notre-Dame. Something has been gained, something lost, by the creation of the vast open square in front. Distance diminishes size but provides a greater sense of the graciousness of the whole.

From a vantage point near the ugly bronze statue of Charlemagne and his paladins, the essential harmony of the cathedral can be felt, and its complexity also. The vertical and horizontal elements appear to be in perfect balance. The strong upward thrust of the buttresses that divide the façade into three parts, the pointed arches of the portals, the looping series of arcades, and the four soaring, narrow bays of the towers contrast with the horizontal bands of the Gallery of Kings, the Great Gallery, and the tier of the rose window. But the towers themselves, masculine in their strength, do not appear so very tall. For the sense of height, and the full medieval effect, it is necessary to approach closer, to stand on the parvis — that forecourt which takes its name from the medieval French word for Paradise. The word suggests the faith with which the cathedral was built — for was not the Church a way to Paradise.

In the center of the parvis is a slab from which all distances are measured to the remotest frontiers of France. That slab may serve as a symbol both of the intense centralization of France and of the central place of this cathedral in the country's life. We might add: and in the life of the world as well. For the tourist buses and cabs draw up incessantly, disgorging travelers from all over the world. But the Japanese in kimonos and clicking clogs, the Germans in *Lederhosen,* the Americans in their jeans, the guides with their flocks of bored or attentive listeners, need not disturb us. The parvis would have been similarly crowded with pilgrims, worshipers, and sight-seers throughout the cathedral's history.

Standing close to the iron railing, the visitor must tear his eyes away from the central portal with its dramatic — not to say melodramatic — portrayal in stone of the Last Judgment. He must look up to the imposing row of sculptured figures that stretches across the façade, and higher still to the magnificent rose and the sky framed between the north and the south towers.

On Sacred Ground

Then the sheer force of that wonderful façade will fill him with awe — as it was meant to do. From this position the towers look their full height of 226 feet. The builders originally planned spires for these towers, but clearly there was no need. As the towers stand, substantial and restrained, they express a confident rather than a perfervid faith.

The near-whiteness of the stone comes as a surprise to a visitor who has not been in Paris for a few years. In the afternoon sunlight the façade looks dazzlingly bright, rather than the uniform sooty black that he remembers. In the interval, much of Paris has been similarly transformed, for the late President de Gaulle and André Malraux, his Minister of Culture, launched a program of cleaning the city's monuments. There were protests; some feared that cleaning would pit and weaken the ancient stone. Others argued that the blackness of age enhanced the architecture. In fact, much experimentation was needed before the most effective and least harmful method of cleansing was discovered: neither chemicals nor sandblasting but forceful jets of pure water.

The process is a slow one, and in mid-1970 had not yet been completed. In a modern industrial city, soot flakes down perpetually from the sky, and streaks of gray and black had already begun to taint the newly washed limestone blocks. If one walked around to the small park at the rear of the cathedral and looked at the south side of the apse, he could have seen scaffolding still in place, although no workmen were visible. The lingering sootiness of the walls appeared even darker against the fresh look elsewhere.

The visitor in 1970 may have been taken aback by the scaffolding. He had come to see a great work of art, and found parts of it looking like a construction site. But the men and women of the twelfth and thirteenth centuries, who contributed their sous (or rather deniers then) and sometimes their labor to raising a testament to their faith, would have found the scaffolding a familiar sight. In our time it is made of steel pipes that are somewhat thinner than the round wooden posts lashed together with ropes that were used throughout the Middle Ages. And planking covers the crossbars; the medieval carpenter would have used hurdles — mats made of woven twigs. But the patterns of braces and uprights are still the same, seven and eight centuries later. Then, as now, it would often have been deserted. For it is wrong to imagine that the shouts of artisans, the clang of chisels, and the clatter of drays bringing loads of stone, lime, sand, and wood went on incessantly for more than two hundred years. The great cathedrals like Notre-Dame were under construction for centuries; but major building campaigns alternated with long spells of inactivity. Not that fervor diminished during those early centuries, but funds dwindled. Construction necessarily slowed or came to a standstill for long periods while the bishops and cathedral chapters replenished their treasuries.

An enormous part of the wealth of France was dedicated to the Virgin and the saints from the middle of the eleventh to the middle of the fourteenth centuries. Millions of tons of stone were quarried to erect eighty cathedrals, some five hundred large churches, and countless smaller parish churches. The fever for building seems to have taken possession of Western man during the very centuries in which the fever for going on

Artistic representation of the gods — whether in appeasement or glorification — is as old as man's earliest civilizations. In Paris the medieval sculptors who decorated Notre-Dame were the heirs of a tradition dating from the Roman era — as can be seen by the three fragments at right of a Gallo-Roman votive pillar uncovered beneath the apse of the cathedral in 1711.

pilgrimages and going on crusades had likewise seized him. If it seems incredible that a primitive economy and social structure could sustain these varied enterprises — perhaps the time has come to revise our notions of how primitive the organization of medieval life was.

The wealth that was poured into the making of Notre-Dame de Paris derived from two sources: the position of Paris as the seat of a steadily growing royal power, as the residence of the Capetian kings who had replaced the Carolingian line toward the end of the tenth century; and the natural fertility of the Île-de-France.

Île-de-France sounds strange to the modern ear. But in the Middle Ages regions largely surrounded by rivers were regarded as islands. The exact territory comprising the Île-de-France fluctuated with political changes; but in the broad sense it was the area surrounded by the Seine, the Oise, the Aisne, the Ourcq, and the Marne. On the whole it was a level land of deep soil, wide marshes, broad fertile plains, and dense forests. Surprisingly large remnants of those forests still stand today in the green belts surrounding Paris. The slow-flowing, navigable rivers made transport easy even before Julius Caesar came, saw, conquered, and built his straight Roman roads. Here was country predestined by geography to become a center of civilization. And the great beds of granite and limestone dispersed among the low hills of the region assured ample supplies of building materials as soon as the inhabitants should outgrow huts of wattle and daub.

Caesar's lieutenant Labienus found the Gallic tribes called Parisii established in a small settlement on an island in the Seine: the true island that is now called the Île de la Cité. To the Roman eye, the military im-

portance of the place was self-evident, and Labienus promptly began the first of the many sieges of Paris. The Gauls burned their wooden bridges to the mainland, but Roman technology made light of rivers. Labienus succeeded in crossing the Seine twice during the campaign. He easily routed the undisciplined Gauls — and the history of the Roman city of Lutetia began. The Romans fixed their permanent camp on the Left Bank, quarried stone from Mount Lutetia — as Mont-Sainte-Geneviève was then called — and in the course of the centuries of the Pax Romana provided a theater, an amphitheater, an aqueduct, baths, temples, and other public buildings. Remains of the ancient Roman *thermae* can still be seen in the Cluny Museum, which has incorporated the ruins of these baths into its structure.

Roman expansion of the city to the Left Bank did not detract from the importance of the Île de la Cité. There, protected in a later era by a Roman wall, stood the palace of the prefect, the law court, and the temple of Jupiter. It was only natural that the Romans should build this temple to the chief of their gods at the eastern end of the island. For the spot was already hallowed by a Druid shrine. With a similar impulse, the Christians erected their first basilica where Jove's altar had been overthrown. Sanctity persists, though the names of the gods change. Notre-Dame stands upon ground that has been sacred from remote antiquity.

In 1711 workmen engaged in digging a burial vault for the archbishops of Paris came upon the remains of the Gallo-Roman wall some six feet below the pavement. They also found nine blocks of stone bearing inscriptions and reliefs. These have been identified as

parts of a votive pier erected in Roman times. The finds now stand, appropriately enough, within the somewhat funereal solemnity of the Roman baths in Cluny Museum. One of the stones bears an inscription indicating that it was dedicated in the reign of the Emperor Tiberius (A.D. 14–37) by the shipowners of Paris. It is interesting to note that seventy-odd years after Caesar's conquest these wealthy native guildsmen proudly ignore the Roman name of Lutetia and refer to themselves as *nautae Parisiaci,* Parisian shipmen. The name of the city survived the Roman intrusion, just as the guild survived the vicissitudes of history for more than a thousand years.

The carving on the Roman stones, much blurred by time and long burial in the earth, is in a style that can best be described as "provincial classic." The gods in man's image — Jupiter, Vulcan, and the Gallic Esus (a Celtic parallel to Hercules) — are sculpted conventionally. More skill and passion seem to have been lavished on the fourth side of one stone, where a bull and three cranes are represented — creatures associated with the ancient cult of the Great Mother, which preceded the worship of male gods. Thus early in the history of the Île de la Cité the goddess in one of her many guises had her devotees.

The Romans were tolerant. They recognized the general identity, despite many local variations, of the great body of mythology and ritual that stretched from the mountains of Hindustan to the shores of the Atlantic Ocean. Hence they readily adopted barbarian gods, including them within their own pantheon or allowing the "natives" to continue worshiping them. If the Gauls chose to call Hercules Esus, that was their affair, so long as they paid their taxes with regularity and obeyed the laws of their Roman governors.

But when a religion claimed exclusiveness and universality, as did that of the Christians, Roman tolerance reached its limits. Persecution followed; the preachers of the new religion were crucified, thrown to lions, roasted on gridirons, broken on the rack, and beheaded. But the Romans discovered to their dismay that a faith founded on a martyrdom was only nourished by the blood of martyrs. Christianity spread. It reached from the slave quarters to the highest ranks of Roman society; and eventually, early in the fourth century, the Emperor Constantine conquered in the sign of the cross. But long before that official acceptance, Gaul had been proselytized. By the third century Christian worship was being practiced in the catacombs of Paris, and during the brief reign of the Emperor Decius (249–251) the first Bishop of Paris was tortured and executed. His name was Dionysius or, to give it the French form, Denis.

Virtually no historical facts are known about Saint Denis, but legend has been all the more active on his behalf. With his companions, Rusticus and Eleutherius, he preached the Gospel incessantly, making countless converts, until the patience of the Romans wore thin. They must in fact have been exceedingly patient, for he continued to evangelize until the age of ninety, when he was put under arrest. Despite ferocious tortures, Saint Denis refused to deny his faith. Finally he was taken to the temple of Mars and Mercury on Montmartre and there beheaded. Whereupon, according to the *Golden Legend,* "the body of Saynte Denys reysed hymselfe up and bare his hede beetwene his armes,

as the angels ledde hym two leghes fro the place which is sayd the hille of the martyrs unto the place where he now resteth by his election and the purveance of god. And there was heard so grete and swete a melodye of angels that many that herd it byleuyd in oure lorde."

The spot where Saint Denis was tortured, on the eastern end of the Île de la Cité, ultimately became a pilgrimage station and the site of a priory called Saint-Denis-du-Pas. For the religion the bishop had preached continued its conquering course unchecked by the invasion of the German tribe of Franks, who subsequently gave the country its name. Their fierce and treacherous warrior-king Clovis, who in the fifth century founded the French monarchy by murdering his neighbors, converted to Christianity under the pressure of policy and the persuasions of his wife, Clotilda. He made Paris his capital, founded the church of Sainte-Geneviève, and established a dynasty that lasted until the middle of the eighth century. Under his descendants, the city of Paris throve. Many of these Merovingians — as they were called after a possibly mythical ancestor of Clovis — proved to be as bloodthirsty as the founder of the kingdom. But some of them were cultivated, and all of them were pious. They followed Clovis's example in becoming benefactors of the Church.

By the latter part of the sixth century at least two large churches, and probably several smaller ones, stood on the Île de la Cité. Together, the two chief churches constituted the cathedral — which meant the episcopal church where the bishop had his seat, or *cathedra*. One was dedicated to the first Christian martyr, Saint Stephen; the other was already called the church of Our Lady: Notre-Dame. French archaeologists and his-

torians have recently discovered how extremely common was the practice of building two separate concathedrals (as well as a separate baptistery) during the so-called Dark Ages. The necessity for this practice arose out of the nature of early Christianity as a mystery religion. Large numbers of new converts were attached to the Church but had not yet received baptism. In fact, since baptism washed away all sins, a prudent believer often postponed it throughout his life. Like the Emperor Constantine, many believers were baptized only on their deathbeds — when there was little likelihood that they could commit new sins. Until baptism, the convert was known as a catechumen, a Greek word meaning "one who is under instruction."

Early Christian liturgy, which is still preserved in the liturgy of the Eastern Orthodox Church, was divided into two parts, one for the catechumens and one for the baptized believers. After the sermon and prayer, and before Consecration, the order was given: "Catechumens, go out!" Only after the catechumens had all left and the initiates were among themselves would the secret Creed be recited and the communion bread and wine be distributed.

The architecture of churches reflected this division. The narthex, usually a colonnaded porch in front of the nave of a basilica, was originally built so that catechumens could participate in the first part of the service and then depart without disturbing the rest of the congregation. But as conversions increased and Christianity spread, the narthex alone proved inadequate. It became the practice to build two separate churches: one for the initiates and one for the unbaptized faithful. Such "double cathedrals" have been iden-

tified throughout France and deep into northern Italy. Like so many similar pairs, the two on the Île de la Cité were dedicated to Saint Stephen and to the Virgin. North of these churches of Saint-Etienne and Notre-Dame there stood, from the fourth century on, the episcopal baptistery of Saint-Jean-le-Rond.

Little remains of these two early — but surely not earliest — churches on the Île de la Cité. Their foundations lie beneath or have become part of the substructures of later Merovingian churches found under the pavement and the parvis of Notre-Dame in the course of Viollet-le-Duc's excavations and reconstruction work during the nineteenth century. The walls must have been enormously thick, composed of pebbles and rough-cut quarry stones held together by cement. A form of coursing was achieved by alternating layers of flat bricks taken from ruined buildings of Roman times. These walls were plastered and painted in floral and foliage designs, red against a white background.

The Merovingian churches of Saint-Etienne and Notre-Dame were by no means small, although they would be dwarfed by the present cathedral. From the evidence of the foundations, Merovingian Saint-Etienne must have been about 170 feet long and perhaps 70 feet wide. This compares favorably with the basilica of Tours, built over the tomb of Saint Martin, which according to Gregory of Tours was 160 feet long, 60 feet wide, and 45 feet high. Undoubtedly, Saint-Etienne would have had a timbered roof, the great beams painted in brilliant colors — for the Franks loved deep reds, blues, and golds. The floor was bright with mosaic, the columns of black and white marble. Probably this marble had been lifted from older Roman ruins. The abstract painted motifs against the white plaster walls must have shown up brilliantly in the light of many windows. For the Merovingians brought as much light as possible into their churches — Gregory of Tours mentions that the basilica built over the tomb of Saint Martin was illuminated by no less than fifty-two windows and eight doors.

With the rise of the practice of infant baptism and the conversion of entire peoples to Christianity, the distinction between catechumens and the baptized had fallen into oblivion. The original reason for the existence of the two separate churches disappeared. It seems likely, though our sources are vague on the question, that the smaller church of Notre-Dame continued to be associated with the inner circle of initiates and thus remained more properly the site of the bishop's *cathedra*. But Saint-Etienne was more capacious. The Bishop of Paris functioned there when he wished to perform some important ceremony before a great concourse of people. Nevertheless, a feeling seems to have lingered among the Parisians that the church of Notre-Dame was the bishop's true seat.

That feeling triumphed after the disasters of the ninth century, for it coincided with the increasing fervor for the Virgin throughout the Western world. But for a time during that turbulent ninth century it seemed as if neither Christian civilization nor any Christian churches in France would survive the onslaught of the pagan Northmen. The broad, navigable rivers of France were like an open invitation to these fierce sea rovers, who were then entering upon their great period of expansion. The dragon-prowed Viking ships were the best in the world at the time, equally at home on the wild wastes of the mid-Atlantic and the tranquil rivers of Europe.

Beginning in 841, the Northmen repeatedly swept up those rivers, looting, burning, imposing tribute. Few dared oppose them. The very sight of the black ships inspired terror. France, weakened by fratricidal wars among the descendants of Charlemagne, could not put up effective resistance. Monks huddled in their walled monasteries praying, "Deliver us from the fury of the Northmen." A contemporary wrote: "And so among us the sword of barbarian men rages, unsheathed from the scabbard of the Lord! And we, wretched creatures, live as though paralyzed, not only among the hideous evils done by savages, but as well among the wars fought without pity between our own peoples, amid sedition and fraud."

Bishops, abbots, counts, dukes, and kings all paid heavy tribute to persuade the invaders to withdraw or to ransom important prisoners. But after a brief respite the pirates would always return, demanding still more silver and gold. By the middle of the century the Vikings had ravaged Poitiers, Tours, Blois, Orléans, Bayeux, Beauvais, Chartres, and many lesser places. Paris, too, was not spared. One hundred twenty Viking ships under a Danish chief named Ragnar Lodbrok sailed up the Seine in 845. King Charles the Bald awaited them with an army where the river makes a great loop to the north outside the city — for he was determined to protect his royal abbey of Saint-Denis. But his soldiers fled in terror when the Northmen callously hanged a band of captives to trees outside the walls of Saint-Denis. Then, not bothering to lay siege to the abbey this time, the Vikings moved on to Paris

and captured the city on Easter Eve. It was a mournful Easter for the Parisians. The enemy looted the monasteries and churches, slew monks and priests, and agreed to withdraw only when Charles paid them seven thousand pounds of silver.

Eleven years later another band of Vikings appeared on the Seine. On December 28, 856, Paris fell once more, and this time the churches were burned. Only Saint-Etienne, Saint-Denis-du-Pas, and Saint-Germain-des-Prés were spared — on payment of enormous bribes. Notre-Dame was evidently badly damaged, but it was probably not wholly destroyed; the Northmen were too busy looting and taking slaves to waste their time breaking down massive stone walls.

In spite of grievous sufferings and losses, the citizens of Paris were still wealthy — the monk Abbo complains of their pride, their love of purple and gold garments, and their belts studded with gems. He also reproaches them for their devotion to "the foul charms of Venus." Nevertheless, the Parisians were also devoted to the Virgin. They set to work simultaneously strengthening the defenses of their city and rebuilding Notre-Dame. In hopes of protection from pirates, they dedicated their city to Mary — a sign of the rising cult of the Virgin that was to dominate later centuries. Evidently, they performed prodigies of labor. By 868 they had sufficiently completed the work on the new cathedral to transfer to it the relics that had formerly been housed in the aging church of Saint-Etienne. One of the most precious of these relics was a nail from the True Cross, presented to Charlemagne by the Patriarch of Jerusalem sixty-nine years earlier.

Thereafter, Saint-Etienne, which had probably also

suffered some damage from the Vikings, gradually lost its status as con-cathedral. The bishop's seat stayed in Notre-Dame. Unfortunately, we have no contemporary descriptions of this rebuilt cathedral of Notre-Dame, and not a stone remains to tell us what it looked like.

The Parisians had acted with rare courage in building even while the Northmen were returning again and again to attack the city. They displayed equal courage in defense, for after the pillaging of 856 Paris did not fall again. Toward the end of the century it withstood a four-year siege, and by its heroic resistance saved the rest of France from Viking conquest.

The region around the mouth of the Seine was beyond saving. The Northmen had entrenched themselves too solidly there; and since there was little left to rob where so many of them had passed, they settled down to make use of the true wealth of the region, the land itself. Early in the tenth century Charles the Simple made the best of a bad bargain by granting to Rollo the Northman what he already held: the territory at the estuary of the Seine. In return, Rollo agreed to live at peace with the French, become the vassal of Charles, and accept Christianity.

Thus Rollo the Raider became Duke of Normandy, and the wild Northmen turned into the shrewd, hard-headed, commercial-minded Normans. Within a century they had abandoned Old Norse for the language of the people they ruled. And they ruled well. While they proved troublesome as vassals of the King of France, often growing more powerful than their overlord, they gave Normandy better government than could be found in most parts of Europe. The French-speaking Normans remained as bellicose and enterprising as

their forebears; but they had learned to value permanent possession rather than piracy. In the next two centuries they more than doubled the size of their original grant in Normandy. And on their foreign adventures, they tried to hold what they seized.

These dukes of Normandy were a rough lot, domineering, treacherous, and ruthless. But in the eyes of their contemporaries they more than made up for these qualities by their piety. They adopted the Christian religion of their subjects with the zeal of converts. And although they had a reputation for being closefisted, they were always generous in their benefactions to the Church. Moreover, they threw their influence into the struggle for religious reform, which began at about the same time that they settled in Normandy. The traditional date for the cession of Normandy to Rollo is 911; the monastery of Cluny, which became the great focus of the monastic revival, was founded in 910.

In those troubled times the monasteries offered employment and security, a measure of peace in this world, and salvation in the next. No wonder men flocked to them. The new monastic orders, in particular the Cluniac and Cistercian, expanded at a fantastic pace. Each monastery needed at least a chapel; the great ones aspired to churches of a size that rivaled or exceeded the cathedrals of the cities. Well endowed by the dukes and their vassals, receiving the revenues from tracts of rich land scattered all over France and England, garnering additional wealth from their own labors in restoring wasteland to productivity, the monks had the means to build. And they built.

They were sharing the passion of the age. It is true that in many places throughout Europe older churches

had been damaged or destroyed by the raids of Vikings, Saracens, and Magyars. But as we have seen from the example of Notre-Dame in Paris, these were quickly rebuilt, even before the invaders had been beaten back or converted. With more stable times, however, came something else: a new impulse of hope, a desire to glorify God in the works of man. Contemporaries were conscious of this new spirit. The chronicler Raoul Glaber, writing of the period after 1030, put it into famous words:

> All over the world, and especially in Italy and France, people began to rebuild their churches. Most of these were well constructed and in no need of alterations. But all Christian countries were rivaling each other to see which should have the most beautiful temples. It seemed as if the world was shaking itself and casting off its old rags, was putting on here, there, and everywhere the pure white robe of churches.

In Normandy, many of the great new temples were abbey churches: Mont-Saint-Michel, Fécamp, Saint-Ouen at Rouen, Saint-Etienne and La Trinité at Caen. But the secular clergy could not long lag behind the monastics, and at Coutances, Bayeux, and Evreux the bishops likewise began building on a scale unprecedented in the history of Christian Europe. This fever for building was accompanied by an outburst of architectural creativity, by endless experimentation, ever-growing sophistication, and a passionate absorption in both the engineering techniques and the artistic expressiveness of construction. The scale of building activity rapidly produced a large corps of professional, highly skilled architects who traveled from place to place, often accompanied by itinerant masons and car-

penters. In effect, the demand created something not too different from the modern construction company.

The new architectural style that resulted from unceasing experimentation during the eleventh and twelfth centuries is known as Romanesque. The term itself was invented by a Norman archaeologist and originally applied to the whole architecture between Roman times and medieval Gothic. In the sense that the word means "like Roman," it is a misnomer; but then "Gothic" is likewise a misnomer, for Gothic art had nothing to do with the Goths. It suffices that both words by now have the sanction of tradition.

The cruciform shape of the Romanesque churches passed on into the Gothic. There is the long nave crossed toward the eastern end by a transept and terminated by the rounded apse inherited from the Roman basilica. Some Romanesque churches provided an apse on the west as well as one on the east; and quite often, as at Vézelay, there is a huge narthex, although the original reason for this covered porch had long since disappeared.

Romanesque's characteristic two towers of the western façade, and the use of sculpture around doors and arcades, were also to be perpetuated in the later Gothic churches. So also, above all, was the use of stone vaulting to close in the nave, in place of the wooden ceilings that had previously spanned the void. The narrower side aisles had been vaulted in stone earlier, but stone vaulting over the great naves represented an act of daring on the part of the builders, and it was testimony to their increasing skill and confidence.

The earliest vaults were semicircular barrel vaults, which gave a tunnel-like and rather monotonous look to a long nave. Erecting such vaults likewise required large amounts of scaffolding and centering (wooden arch supports) during construction. A device at once aesthetic and practical solved this difficulty. At regular intervals the builders introduced what are called transverse arches, running across beneath the barrel vault from pier to pier. The banded effect of the transverse arches relieved the monotony, and at the same time simplified construction; for the scaffolding could be shifted from bay to bay after each transverse arch and its accompanying section of vaulting had been placed.

As the skills of the masons advanced, dressed stone replaced the rubble and mortar used in the earliest Romanesque churches. The easily cut limestone of Normandy and the Île-de-France facilitated this practice. At the same time experimentation in vaulting continued. Over square bays, barrel vaults intersecting at right angles were tried again for the first time since Roman days. Some masons learned to strengthen these "groined vaults" by ribs along the groins, that is, at the lines where the two vaults met. A significant step toward the Gothic vault had been taken.

It has often been said that the stone vaulting that characterizes Romanesque architecture sprang from the desire to build fireproof churches — after so many Merovingian and Carolingian basilicas had been damaged or destroyed by fire during the barbarian raids of the ninth and tenth centuries. But this practical argument seems rather faulty, since wood continued to be used in the tie beams, struts, and rafters that supported the roofs over the vaulting. Moreover, since the roofs were invariably built before the vaulting, many years passed — during which the church was often in contin-

uous use — before the all-stone interior was achieved. And fires continued to ravage stone-vaulted Romanesque churches after the barbarian raids had ceased. Vézelay, Chartres, Reims, Amiens, Beauvais, Canterbury — to name only some of the most famous cathedrals — suffered serious fires in the eleventh and twelfth centuries. In fact, the contemporary description of the burning of Canterbury cathedral in 1174 suggests that vaulted churches may have been subject to greater fire hazards than were earlier churches. At Canterbury sparks from burning cottages outside the gates of the cathedral were carried by the wind between the joints of the lead sheets that covered the roof. There they smoldered undetected until the whole roof was ablaze and the great tie beams came crashing down into the choir, setting fire to the monks' wooden seats. No one had noticed smoke because the fire burned so long between the elaborately painted vaulted ceiling and the roof above it.

It is more likely that the stone vaulting of the Romanesque church sprang from aesthetic and religious impulses rather than practical needs. It bespoke an ambition to build on a more magnificent scale than hitherto, a desire for glorious earthly works to express the glory of God. That spirit accompanied the upsurge in economic and political life, the rapid growth of towns and monastic orders, the increase in population, the widening of horizons that came with the Crusades, and the new concentrations of power in the Capetian dynasty in France, the Norman and Angevin dynasties in Normandy and England, the Hohenstaufen dynasty in Germany and Italy. The same spirit continued on into the Gothic era. As Frederick Artz has succinctly

The abbey church of La Madeleine at Vézelay in central France is a superb example of the transition from Romanesque to Gothic architecture. The Romanesque nave, with its striking alternation of colored stonework, is topped by semicircular barrel vaults. Decorated pier clusters support the massive rounded arches of the nave arcade. In the much brighter Gothic choir beyond, the pointed vaults and arches characteristic of the newer style predominate.

put it in *The Mind of the Middle Ages:* "Like the great monuments of later Roman and Byzantine architecture, huge Romanesque and Gothic churches seem built not to the measure of man and this world, but to the measure of infinity and eternity."

The origin of Romanesque architecture is a vexing question. Certainly, influences from as far east as Armenia played some part in its development. The Norman conquest of Sicily, which coincided with the Norman conquest of England, added a dynamic element to the existing Arab and Byzantine cultures of southern Italy. A century after the Norman invasion of Sicily, the cross-fertilization of Byzantine, Arab, and Norman cultures would produce the marvelous cathedral of Monreale, with its Arab apse, Byzantine mosaics, Norman capitals, and North Italian bronze doors. The skills of Greek and Arab laborers, combined with the wealth and energy of the Norman king, made this great Romanesque cathedral the product of a single impulse. Begun ten years after Notre-Dame de Paris, it was completed within the incredibly short span of eight years — while the cathedral of Paris was two hundred years in the building.

But for all that the Romanesque led the way to the Gothic, and for all the many resemblances, there is no mistaking the two styles. The Romanesque system of vaulting influenced the whole appearance of the church, and everything else flowed from that: the massiveness, solidity, dimness, the sense of power and earthbound foursquareness.

The barrel vault exerts a continuous lateral thrust along its whole length. It therefore required thick walls pierced by few openings to sustain this outward pressure. With a beamed ceiling, the thrust had been directly downward. In addition, wood is far less heavy than stone. Hence it had been easier for the builders of Merovingian and Carolingian churches to leave large openings in the walls for windows. Romanesque vaulting introduced a new harmony, consistency, and grandeur by its use of stone throughout the interior; but the churches were dark. This "dim religious light" also corresponded with the intentions of the builders; it coincided with the growing mystical spirit of the tenth to the twelfth centuries. But in the more optimistic and worldly times of the late twelfth and thirteenth centuries, when travel and the Crusades had opened so many windows on the world, builders regarded the darkness as a defect. The history of the Gothic may in a sense be regarded as an architectural striving to recapture the light that had been lost in the previous centuries. In the second quarter of the twelfth century that striving was put directly into words and stone by Abbot Suger of Saint-Denis.

II   The Cathedral Crusade

For half a millennium the abbey of Saint-Denis had enjoyed the patronage of the Frankish kings. They had bestowed upon it vineyards, orchards, town and country estates, villages, forests, until it became the wealthiest abbey in France. When their royal progresses took them to the vicinity of Paris, the kings stayed at the abbey rather than in the city. And most of them made arrangements for their mortal remains to be laid to rest at Saint-Denis. "Mother of churches and crown of the realm," contemporaries called it. The abbey's prestige bothered the bishops of nearby Paris, but there seemed very little they could do about it.

One of the worst thorns in the side of the bishops of Paris, spiritual heads of a great city dedicated to commerce, was the Fair of Saint-Denis. Founded by the Merovingian ruler Dagobert I in the seventh century, the fair was held annually in October and lasted for a full four weeks. Here Venetian, Syrian, and Jewish merchants chaffered with Gascons, Lombards, Saxons, and Greeks, exchanging English wool and fleeces, Flemish cloth and hides, for silks, spices, pearls, and perfumes. And the monks of Saint-Denis reaped a handsome profit from renting booths.

For four hundred years the fair, which also drew throngs of pilgrims to the relics of Saint-Denis, proved to be an admirable source of revenue. It was so profitable that in the middle of the eleventh century the monks sought and obtained permission from King Henry I to establish an additional fair and religious feast during the summer. This became the famous Lendit, which specialized in cloth, leather, parchment, fur, and horses. The bishops of Paris eyed its success jealously; and in 1109, taking advantage of a temporary

coolness between the king and Abbot Adam of Saint-Denis, they persuaded Louis VI, the Fat, to allow them to establish a second Lendit in honor of a fragment of the True Cross that had recently been acquired by Notre-Dame de Paris. The question of the two Lendits made one more chapter in the five-hundred-year-old rivalry between the see of Paris and the abbey of Saint-Denis.

Saint-Denis was indignant over this "outer Lendit," as the new fair at Paris was called. When Louis's boyhood friend Suger became Abbot of Saint-Denis in 1122, he promptly used his influence to recapture sole rights to the Lendit for his abbey. In 1124 Louis revoked the privilege that Notre-Dame had enjoyed for only fifteen years. He granted Saint-Denis both the right to hold the fair and its site in the plain between Paris and the abbey. This was an outstanding victory for the new abbot. In addition to the considerable material benefits for the abbey, the new privilege strengthened the claims of Saint-Denis to religious primacy in France.

Abbot Suger, one of the most remarkable men in an age rich in eminent personalities, was a living demonstration that the Church was the chief avenue of social mobility in the twelfth century. The gifted son of poor parents, probably peasants, he was born around 1082. Sent to the abbey for education at the age of ten, he was thrown in with Prince Louis, the future King of France, who was attending the abbey school at the same time. Louis and Suger became fast friends for life.

Suger grew to maturity in a Church throbbing with excitement and racked by dissension over the reformist movement of Pope Gregory VII, which was carried

into the monasteries by Suger's contemporary Bernard of Clairvaux. Throughout Suger's boyhood, every pilgrim had brought stirring news of the gathering armies of the First Crusade. When he was barely seventeen, his heart leaped at the good tidings that the Holy City had been recovered from the infidel. The Crusade, coming as it did in his most impressionable years, was never far from his mind. All his life he longed to take up the cross himself, but his duties and his vocation kept him at home. Instead, he embarked upon what has often been called "the cathedral crusade."

Suger took his monastic vows at the age of twenty-four, and soon distinguished himself by his intelligence, diplomacy, and capacity for work. Abbot Adam sent him on frequent missions to Rome and elsewhere on the affairs of both the abbey and the king. By the time Adam died, it was a foregone conclusion that Suger would succeed him and inherit also the Abbot of Saint-Denis's traditional role as chief adviser to the king. In that capacity, Suger quickly became the king's mainstay in domestic and foreign policy.

Suger himself relates that even while he was still a pupil in the school of Saint-Denis, he had longed to rebuild the ancient, dilapidated abbey and abbey church. The existing Carolingian church was nearly four hundred years old. In addition to its state of disrepair, the old church was too small for the crowds that thronged into it on feast days to pray before the bones of Saint Denis, Saint Rusticus, and Saint Eleutherius, a nail of the True Cross, what then passed for the Crown of Thorns (later King Louis IX, Saint Louis, would bring the "true" Crown of Thorns to Notre-Dame), and many other relics. Suger himself has

vividly described the crush of the crowd:

Often on feast days the crowds as they moved in opposite directions . . . prevented those attempting to enter from entering and also drove out those who had already entered. . . . No one among the countless thousands of people could move a foot because of their very density; no one, because of their very congestion, could do anything but stand like a marble statue, benumbed, or as a last resort, scream. The distress of the women, however, was intolerable; squeezed by the mass of strong men as in a wine-press, they exhibited bloodless faces as in imagined death, cried out horribly as though in labor.

From the moment he took office as abbot, Suger set about reorganizing the mismanaged affairs of the abbey, increasing its revenues, and systematically setting aside part of the increase as a building fund. Suger had that breadth of knowledge, grasp of the whole, and capacity for detail which are among the characteristics of genius. Despite his humble origins, he negotiated with popes and kings on a plane of equality; but he also saw to it that his peasants obtained improved plowshares. Under his guidance, the weak French monarchy increased its power. Simultaneously, the abbey and its many possessions throve.

In Suger's mind, the fortunes of the abbey and the fortunes of France were virtually identical. He demonstrated that conviction in the literary labors of his later years, for he divided his time between writing a life of Louis VI and a history of his own administration of Saint-Denis, with special emphasis on the building of his church. Thus we are fortunate in having an account of the spiritual motives and the practical problems of

church building from the pen of a man who conceived and directed the work. Suger controlled every phase of the building, choosing the stone from the quarries, going into the forests to find the trees for the tie beams that supported the roof, consulting with his architects on questions of design and the order of construction.

There were no real precedents for the kind of church that Suger wanted to build. The Crusaders, whose tales he eagerly listened to, had returned with descriptions of the resplendent churches of Constantinople, above all Hagia Sophia with its fabulous domes. Not that Suger thought of erecting domes; that would have been too violent a break with the tradition of the churches he had seen, and the techniques would probably have been beyond the capacities of his architects. But he wanted a similar effect of height and magnificence; he wanted vast spaces so that there would be room for all, and ample light to show to best effect the gold, gems, marble, and porphyry with which he hoped to fill his new church. For Suger loved brightness, glitter, light. And out of that love, combined with the mystique of royalty, the exaltation of mystical theology, and the long history of experimentation by the builders of Romanesque cathedrals and abbey churches, a new style was born, an architecture dominated by height and light: the Gothic.

To Suger light was more than illumination. It was metaphysical being, an emanation of divinity, of all things closest to God because least material. Light was spirit, intelligence, understanding; and the more men understood, the closer they came to God — provided they had faith. *Fides quaerens intellectum,* faith is always seeking understanding, wrote Anselm of Canter-

bury, whom Suger in his youth had undoubtedly met.

The metaphysics of light was closely bound up with Saint-Denis itself. It had been elaborated by that mysterious personality known as Dionysius the Pseudo-Areopagite. This was a fifth-century Syrian philosopher who for obscure reasons pretended to be the same person as the Dionysius of Athens who is mentioned in the Scriptures as a convert and follower of Saint Paul in the first century. His books, *On the Divine Names, On the Celestial Hierarchy, On Mystic Theology,* were avidly read by such men as Suger. And at Saint-Denis it was held as an article of faith that the scriptural Dionysius, the Syrian philosopher, and the Saint Denis who had carried his head in his hands from Montmartre to the site of the abbey in the third century, were one and the same person! A former abbot of Saint-Denis who wrote a biography of Saint Denis had declared all three identical, and how could anyone be so bold as to challenge a tradition that was three hundred years old?

Peter Abelard, the great philosopher and tragic lover, did undertake to challenge the tradition. After his affair with Héloïse came to its terrible denouement — Abelard's emasculation by her uncle's henchmen — Abelard took refuge in Saint-Denis. But that brilliant and passionate man aroused dissension wherever he went. At Saint-Denis he set about proving from texts that the Syrian philosopher had not been Saint Denis, the apostle of France. Saint-Denis angrily expelled the contentious philosopher, and Abelard took refuge in a solitary hut near Troyes — where students from all over Europe came flocking to hear his provocative lectures. But that is another story.

33

Suger's preparations for building his church took many years. He announced his intentions in 1125, but did not begin construction until 1137, the year that Louis VI died and was succeeded by Louis VII. Masons, sculptors, glassmakers, and other craftsmen had to be imported from Normandy and the south, or trained on the site, for there was not much of a building tradition in the Île-de-France at that time. Moreover, and this was the perennial problem of medieval builders, as far as possible the old church had to continue in use while the new one was rising. A church was as vital to men of the twelfth century as bread and wine, and even more vital to a community of monks. Consequently Suger tried to preserve as much as he could of the old Carolingian church. He left the nave intact, tore down the western apse of the twin-apsed church, and built a façade with three portals and two towers, like the Abbey of Saint-Etienne at Caen. Behind the façade he erected a three-aisled narthex, and then a new nave to link up with the old Carolingian nave. This work proceeded with fabulous speed; it was well advanced by 1140. Then Suger abruptly stopped work on the upper parts of the façade towers and embarked on the building of the choir. With that choir, it has been said, Gothic architecture began.

The choir was covered by a cross-ribbed vault, and pointed arches were used throughout — emphasizing that verticality which we have come to associate with the Gothic. Surrounding the choir was a double ambulatory with nine radiating chapels whose outer walls were reduced to mere skeletons by a pair of tall windows in each. "The entire sanctuary is thus pervaded by a wonderful and continuous light entering through

the most sacred windows," Suger wrote enthusiastically.

"Sacred windows" may give us pause unless we understand that for the first time in architectural history Suger had filled his windows completely with stained glass. Such glass was not unknown; indeed, France seems to have been the country of its origin. But we know little about its history; few fragments of early glass have survived, and before Suger's time we have only occasional records of donations of stained glass. Suger, however, was the first to install such glass on a large scale, employing it as a form of painting with light to depict sacred subjects. And for subjects he selected those scenes from Scripture that conformed with the Pseudo-Areopagite's theology. Thus Moses appeared veiled before the people of Israel as the universe is obscured from men's understanding until they are permeated by the Divine Light. "Bright is the noble edifice that is pervaded by the new light," Suger wrote — and by "new light" he meant both his stained glass and Christ.

Miracles abound in Suger's own account of the building of Saint-Denis. It was a miracle that he had found exactly the right stone at the Pontoise quarry, a miracle that the forest contained exactly the number of trees he needed for his roof, a miracle that he secured the gems he needed to ornament the huge crucifix he set up in the choir. A collection of hyacinths, sapphires, rubies, emeralds, and topazes only recently amassed by King Henry I of England found its way by devious means into Suger's hands. "We paid four hundred pounds for the lot, though they were worth much more," he wrote with unmistakable self-satisfaction. But the greatest miracle of all was the preservation of

his unfinished choir during a storm of unprecedented violence. Suger's account of it is so important because one phrase suggests that in the building of Saint-Denis he had taken a tremendous leap toward mature Gothic architecture.

The roof of the choir had been completed and the vaulting begun. One day Bishop Geoffrey of Chartres was celebrating mass in the partly finished church. (The bishop was a frequent visitor, himself engaged in rebuilding his church and therefore interested in Suger's work. In fact, he borrowed sculptors from Suger and lent the abbot some of his workmen in return.) Suddenly a violent storm arose. Houses, stone towers, and wooden bulwarks around Saint-Denis were blown down by the force of the wind. Rain descended in torrents and the wind howled ferociously. Bishop Geoffrey at the altar, looking up at what the abbot called "principal arches," saw them "miserably trembling and swaying hither and thither." Suger's account continues:

The Bishop, alarmed by the strong vibration of these arches and the roofing, frequently extended his blessing hand in the direction of that part and urgently held toward it . . . the arm of the aged St. Simeon [a relic]; so that he escaped disaster . . . by the grace of God and the merit of the Saints. Thus the storm, while it brought calamitous ruin in many places to buildings thought to be firm, was unable to damage these isolated and newly made arches, tottering in mid-air, because it was repulsed by the power of God.

There has been some controversy over what precisely Suger meant by "principal arches." One scholar has recently suggested that the abbot was speaking of the arches of flying buttresses. But it is possible that he was

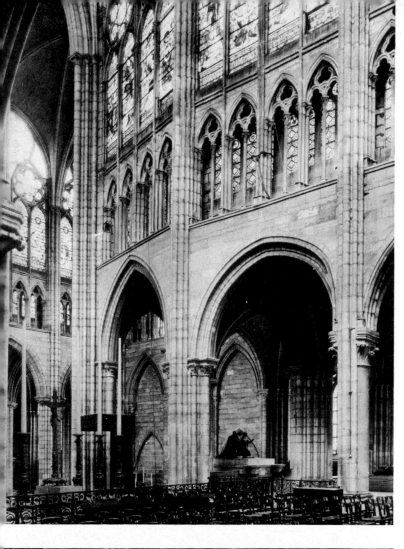

referring to the ribs, standing alone under the roof before the webbing had been spread between them. This would be further evidence of the way in which Gothic vaulting was constructed and a confirmation of Otto von Simson's concise verdict that Saint-Denis "was certainly the first Gothic edifice completed."

By 1144 Suger was ready for the consecration of his choir. He set the date for June 11, three days before the opening of the Lendit, so that visitors to the fair could attend. The celebration was a notable event. Young King Louis VII came with his beautiful, forceful, and newly wed queen, Eleanor of Aquitaine. The counts and nobles could not be numbered. Saint Bernard was present and Archbishop Theobald of Canterbury came from England. In all, there were nineteen bishops and archbishops simultaneously celebrating mass.

Suger's high altar glittered with gold; he had encased it in golden panels on all sides and covered it with gold as well "so that the whole altar would appear golden all the way around." For the Eucharist he had provided golden pouring vessels and golden vials. The clerics in their brilliant vestments, the royal pair and the nobles in their flashing silks, the crosses studded with gems, the many-colored light pouring down through the stained-glass windows, provided the populace with a foretaste of Heaven. And the populace was indeed represented; according to Suger himself, all of Paris came to Saint-Denis that day to see the new church and to gape at the throng of notables. With his keen sense of the theatrical, Suger arranged his bishops in two groups of nine in the choir and crypt, to correspond with the nine chapels around the choir and the

Suger's proud description of his altar — "forty-two marks of gold, a multifarious wealth of precious gems, jacinths, rubies, sapphires, emeralds and topazes, and an array of large pearls" — was still applicable in the fifteenth century when the panel at left was painted. It shows the high altar of Saint-Denis fittingly surmounted by the cross of Saint Eloi, patron of goldsmiths. Suger appears prostrate at the feet of the Virgin (right) in a stained-glass window from his abbey church — a modest stance that would have pleased his friend and mentor, Saint Bernard. Shunning all luxury and worldliness, Bernard presumed to teach the Devil himself (right below).

nine tiers of angels of whom Dionysius the Pseudo-Areopagite spoke in his *On the Celestial Hierarchy*. The King of France and his following thus provided the visible representation on earth of the angelic order in Heaven.

Saint Bernard was hardly pleased by such display, for which he had in the past rebuked his friend Suger. The other prelates must have had divided emotions; they praised Suger's accomplishment, but their admiration was tinged with envy and the ambition to emulate him. The royal approval suggested, moreover, that what was wanted in France were cathedrals like Suger's Saint-Denis. It was scarcely accidental that after the bishops returned home there began an explosion of building throughout France. Work began at Sens almost immediately, then at Senlis, Noyon, Laon, and finally at Paris — all within twenty years of the consecration of Saint-Denis.

There is no evidence that young Maurice de Sully, future Bishop of Paris, was present at the consecration of Saint-Denis. But it seems likely that he was in attendance that day, for he was a member of the Chapter of Notre-Dame at the time and would almost certainly have accompanied his bishop to the grand ceremony.

The chapter was the organization of priests and other officials responsible for the maintenance of a cathedral, for its services, charities, and school. Created originally to assist the bishop, the chapter as often as not spent much of its time contending with him. Its members belonged to the secular as opposed to the regular, or monastic, clergy; but in the eighth century the bishops imposed upon them almost monastic "canonical" regulations — hence the name canons. Gradually the rules governing their community life were relaxed, and ultimately they became a powerful corporation of individuals with revenues of their own. Their relationship with the bishop varied widely. In some places they elected him from their own ranks; in some places they were subservient to him; in others, independent of him. The dean of a chapter was often nearly as powerful as a bishop; the chancellor was virtual secretary of the diocese; the treasurer controlled the finances of the cathedral and sometimes of the diocese as well. The chapter usually had charge of the cathedral school and was always responsible for the "fabric" — by which was meant the actual physical structure of the cathedral.

The Chapter of Notre-Dame occupied a large cloister consisting of some forty houses north of what is now the rue du Cloître Notre-Dame. It had an income of some 80,000 livres, maintained a library and a famous singing school, and was steadily growing in independence and power. In the twelfth century, however, it had not yet freed itself completely from the bishop's control, and a strong bishop could repress if not suppress the canons' taste for wine, women, a groaning board, and gambling. (In fact, not until 1335 did the long struggle come to an end when the bishop at last abandoned all claims to jurisdiction over the dean, the chapter as a body, or any of the canons as individuals.)

Maurice de Sully, like Suger of humble stock, came to Paris from Sully-sur-Loire around 1137, to study in the cathedral school. He probably heard lectures by the greatest teachers of the age, Hugh of St. Victor and Peter Abelard, and rubbed elbows with fellow students who were to be the great ecclesiastics of his own generation, John of Salisbury and Thomas Becket. Like Suger, he was the same age as his young sovereign, Louis VII, who was also educated at the cloister of Notre-Dame. Maurice soon distinguished himself by the eloquence of his preaching, the orthodoxy of his theology, and his skill in scholastic debate — venturing to oppose even the famous author of the *Sentences*, Peter Lombard. A subdeacon by 1147, Maurice rose swiftly in the hierarchy of the Chapter of Notre-Dame. In 1159 he became archdeacon shortly after none other than Peter Lombard was elected bishop.

Archdeacons were notorious in this period. As financial and administrative officers of the diocese, they were regarded as rapacious canon lawyers who lined their own sleeves (in the twelfth century men often carried money in their sleeves) by incessant exactions. "Whether an archdeacon can possibly attain salvation" was said to be a standard debating proposition in the schools. But the archdeacon also had a good chance to succeed to the episcopal seat, for the chapter tended to regard him as one of their own. If he were elected bishop, he might help his chapter for a time — until the needs of his new dignity forced him to turn to battle with his own archdeacon over revenues and prerogatives.

Maurice did not remain archdeacon long enough to imperil his salvation. Bishop Peter Lombard died in 1160. The chapter found itself unable to choose between two candidates: Maurice and Peter the Glutton, so named for his habit of devouring scholastic texts. King Louis intervened to procure the election of Maurice who, on October 12, 1160, was consecrated the seventy-fourth Bishop of Paris. Three years later, the cornerstone of Notre-Dame de Paris was laid.

Given the conditions of the time, the decision to

build a new cathedral was inevitable. Work had started on such smaller Gothic churches as Saint-Germain-des-Prés, Saint-Martin-des-Champs, and Saint-Pierre, the last at Montmartre near the supposed site of the decapitation of Saint Denis. Moreover, Paris itself had expanded mightily under the long and essentially prosperous reign of Louis VII. From the hill of Montmartre a contemporary traveler looking down upon the "turreted city surrounded by great walls" could think he was beholding Rome itself. The walls were the ancient Roman walls of the Cité, the turrets those of the Royal Palace and the Grant Chastelet, which guarded the Grant Pont. But the city had already spilled out over both banks of the Seine; a wooden palisade protected the right-bank area opposite the Île de la Cité. On this same right bank, across from what is now the Île Saint-Louis, lay the stronghold of the Knights Templar, the Temple. The Temple at this time was a financial as well as religious enterprise; it was the nearest thing to a central bank that Europe possessed. In its shadow many fine suburban houses were rising outside the stockade, for this populous city could no longer be confined within walls.

Thousands of students of many nations swarmed in the crowded streets and jammed into high-priced lodgings — sometimes as many as eighteen to a room. Vast quantities of food and wine were brought by boat up the Seine from Normandy and down the Seine from Champagne and Burgundy to be unloaded at the Chastelet and the Grève — for boats could not easily pass through the stone arches of the Grant Pont. A busy commercial mart, Paris was also a political and religious center of increasing importance. Louis VI and Louis

VII had strengthened the French monarchy, subdued rebellious vassals, and established firm ties with the papacy. Foreign dignitaries came frequently to Paris to negotiate with the king. Thomas Becket, Henry II of England, Pope Alexander III, Rainald of Dassel, simultaneously Archbishop of Cologne and Chancellor of Frederick Barbarossa's Holy Roman Empire — such eminent men acknowledged the growing importance of Capetian France by seeking the friendship of King Louis VII.

Louis himself was a pious and modest man, given to deprecating his worldly possessions. He once remarked to an Englishman: "Your master the King of England lacks nothing; he possesses men, horses, gold and silk, gems, fruits, wild beasts and all things else. We in France have nothing except bread and wine and joy." But Louis's new Bishop of Paris had more of Suger's temperament. He understood that prestige must be visible. Paris, the greatest city in France, could not lag behind such small towns as Senlis, Noyon, and Sens, and such abbeys as Saint-Denis. Paris must have a cathedral worthy of a capital.

Statues representing the king and the bishop, as well as the powerful Dean of the Chapter of Notre-Dame, can be seen to this day on the Portal of Saint Anne, the south portal of the western façade. The sculptors set to work right at the beginning of construction, carving capitals for the columns and statues for the portals — although these statues would not be inserted in their places for some forty years. The oldest part of the Portal of Saint Anne — it was rebuilt in the thirteenth century — is the tympanum, the curved triangular space under the arch. In its center the Virgin sits

Among the students who flocked to the capital in the twelfth century was Maurice de Sully, represented at right by his official seal. As Bishop of Paris, Maurice began the construction of Notre-Dame. The bas-reliefs at left from Saint Stephen's portal are thought to represent scenes from the life of Parisian scholars.

majestically on a square, ornamented throne, enclosed within turrets like a miniature cathedral. She sits with a certain hieratic stiffness, the Child on her lap, and both gaze straight ahead, as if unaware of the adoring angels to either side. Beyond the angel on her left (our right), identified by his crown and regal look, Louis VII humbly kneels. On her right Maurice de Sully asserts his ecclesiastical prerogative. He stands proudly, his crook over his right shoulder, a small and stocky man who looks more conscious of his power than does the king of his, perhaps because Maurice had traveled a longer way than Louis to achieve it.

Tucked into the corner of the tympanum to the left of Maurice, his back bowed to conform to the curve of the arch and the habit of the scribe, in his hand a book in which he seems to be making an entry, sits a man who has been identified as Barbedor, Dean of the Chapter. He is a young man with a face rather like Maurice's, except that he is beardless. Barbedor deserves his place on the façade of the cathedral. Chaplain and confessor to Louis VII, he was the direct intermediary between king and bishop. He also served for sixteen years as dean, and in that capacity supervised much of the construction. What is more, he devoted a large part of his personal wealth to furthering the work. It was he who compensated owners whose houses had to be razed and he who furnished the funds for the stained glass of the choir.

Like Suger, Maurice evidently spent the first few years of his episcopate putting his house in order, increasing revenues, accumulating a building fund, and preparing the site. A whole row of buildings on the île de la Cité was demolished so that a new street could

be cut — the rue Neuve Notre-Dame — extending from the old church of Saint-Etienne to the highway that ran to the Petit Pont. Thus the cartloads of materials could be brought directly to the old church, which was used as a workshop. Due penance would be made for this desecration by dedicating the portal on the south façade of the new cathedral to Saint Stephen.

By that time, halfway through the third quarter of the twelfth century, so many cathedrals were rising that a vast corps of skilled workmen was available. Notre-Dame de Paris, like the other great cathedrals of the Middle Ages, was built by professional workers tightly organized in guilds, their wages established by law or by hard bargaining between the guild masters and the cathedral chapters, their practices carefully regulated by the traditions and rules of the guilds. Teams of such workmen moved from city to city, from site to site, as a particular cathedral reached the stage that called for their special skills. Contracts with these itinerant construction companies were carefully drawn up, specifying even such details as the ruling that mortarmen were to be exempt from the onerous obligation of night-watch.

Before any work could begin, the stone had to be found. Millions of tons of stone were quarried in the île-de-France during the cathedral-building centuries — more, it has been said, than during the whole history of ancient Egypt. Fortunately, beautiful stone of varying degrees of hardness underlay much of the country-side around Paris. Most of the stone for Notre-Dame came from quarries on the Butte Saint-Jacques, from Bagneux, Arcueil, and Montrouge. The quarrymen, unlike the other workmen, tended to be residents of

the area who spent their lives amid choking clouds of stone dust. Since transportation was expensive, they cut the blocks roughly to shape in the quarry — there was little point in carting tons of waste material to the building site.

The quarryman had to know stone intimately. Working with primitive equipment, without benefit of explosives or mechanical saws, he had to find the lines of cleavage in the beds, to follow the grain of the stone. As a rule, he chose the softer varieties wherever their use would do no harm, as in the sculptures and facings. But for bearing surfaces, for the drums of columns and overhanging cornices, he had at his disposal the firm, hard stone called cliquart. No doubt the pay scales varied for the different types of stone, since the workmen were paid piecework by the block rather than by the hour.

From the quarry the stone had to be transported in oxcarts or on barges to the site. An oxcart could carry perhaps one ton — and thousands of tons of stone were needed. No wonder that the sculptors of Laon cathedral placed statues of oxen at the corners of their towers, in tribute to the patient beasts.

Sometimes men took the place of the oxen. This "cult of the carts" has given rise to the legend of whole populations rushing to aid in the work. The cult is first recorded at Chartres in 1144, when nobles and common folk harnessed themselves to the carts and dragged them to the cathedral site. Whenever they stopped to rest, they bewailed their sins, and when they arrived at Chartres they flung themselves to the ground and begged the priests to scourge them. From Chartres returning pilgrims spread the cult to Rouen and then

45

"Nowhere have I seen a tower like that of Laon," declared the medieval mason Villard de Honnecourt, whose whimsical sketch appears at right. The statues that perch precariously upon the towers honor the oxen whose labor helped build the great cathedrals of France.

throughout Normandy and France, wherever churches to the Virgin Mary were being built.

Such outbursts of popular enthusiasm remind us of the spirit that underlay the building of the cathedrals — a spirit that made possible the enormous financial sacrifices on the part of the common people, the clergy, and the nobles alike. But these episodes were infrequent and occurred mostly at the beginning of construction. Had they happened more often, the draymen and bargemen, who depended on the work for their daily wages, would have put a stop to such volunteer labor. Indeed, there is a story in one of the *chansons de geste* of a penitent nobleman who served in a cathedral workshop for almost nothing, out of a desire to atone for his sins. The other workmen regarded him as a scab, to use the modern term; they attacked him and beat him to death.

At the masons' lodge the stone was dressed to its final shape. The stonecutters carefully marked each block or cylinder to show where it was to be placed on the wall, column, or arch. In addition to these "position marks," they chiseled their personal marks — rarely letters of the alphabet, more often symbols: combinations of triangles, crosses, arrows, zigzag bars. These masons' marks were the equivalent of signatures; they ensured that when the week's work was totaled there would be no disputes over how many blocks each man had delivered. But the marks also served as an expression of the medieval mason's pride in his work. A father handed his mark on to his son. If a son worked on the same job with his father, he would add a small additional stroke to distinguish his own mark. By examining marks, archaeologists have been able to trace the travels of the itinerant masons from cathedral to cathedral across France.

The workshops also employed large numbers of smiths. Stone blunts iron tools swiftly, and the smiths were kept constantly busy forging or sharpening the hammers, picks, chisels, points, punches, claw chisels, drags, saws, and drills with which the masons worked. In addition, smiths made the chains that were used both for hoists and sometimes for strengthening walls and the nippers that gripped the stones — instruments rather like giant ice tongs, which were held closed by the stones' own weight. At the height of their activity the cathedral workshops were an inferno of noise: carts rumbling, masons' hammers pounding, smiths' anvils clanging, workmen shouting orders to their helpers from high up on the scaffolding or the walls.

The simplest form of stoneworking consisted of making the rough blocks that were used with rubble and mortar to fill the interior of walls and buttresses to the required thickness. Such work could safely be left to apprentices. The smoothly finished blocks of larger sizes for the facings of the cathedral — as well as the drums for the columns, the cylinders for colonnettes, the wedge-shaped voussoirs that formed the arches, and the complexly faceted keystones — required the experience and talent of the trained journeyman. The lacelike tracery of windows, the intricacies of capitals, the multiple planes and curves of moldings, were necessarily reserved for the master mason. Medieval writers did not differentiate between masons and sculptors; but it is clear that the men who carved the madonnas, patriarchs, saints, kings, and gargoyles that adorned the cathedrals knew themselves to be artists, even though they only occasionally signed their work. With the growth and spread of the Gothic style, these sculptors became more daring, more realistic, and more obtrusive. They literally covered the cathedrals with their works; there are twelve hundred sculptures in Notre-Dame de Paris, some three thousand at Reims.

The masons' lodges, originally simple workshops, in time developed into a kind of clubhouse, where the masons lived and offered hospitality to traveling members of the guild. The lodges acquired libraries of works on architecture and geometry, set up schools for teaching apprentices the mysteries of the crafts, and jealously guarded the rights of the masons.

One of the great discoveries of the medieval mason was of the extraordinary strength of a thin-shelled web with double curvature. The web is the area of a vault between the stone ribs, and in many cathedrals it is made of an extremely thin mixture of rubble stone and mortar. The ribs supported this structure during the slow setting period of medieval mortars. But it has been observed that sometimes, because of bombings or other accidents, the ribs of vaults will fall and the vaults will nevertheless hold. This fact has given rise to much controversy on the function of medieval rib-vaulting. Some writers on the Gothic have gone so far as to assert that the ribs were purely decorative. It has remained for modern builders in concrete, who rediscovered the extraordinary strength of thin curved shells — an eggshell is an example of the principle — to explain the puzzle. There is no doubt that the ribs strengthen the Gothic vault. But the effect of doubly curved, thin-shelled webbing added an extra element of strength and security. The vault webs of Notre-Dame are only six inches in thickness. Yet, they have held firm for eight hundred years!

The carpenters, of course, were as important as the masons. The lives of the workmen depended upon their care in lashing together the scaffolding poles. They built the ramps up which materials were carried and set up the shoring that held walls in position. They chose, hewed, and installed the tie beams, plates, and rafters of the roofs, binding the members together with mortise-and-tenon joints, through which wooden pegs were driven. Carpenters also had to be engineers, for they built and maintained the "great wheel," which was installed on a platform under the roof and used for hoisting stone and other heavy materials into place. These wheel-windlasses were operated by manpower, sometimes in the form of a treadmill, but they afforded considerable mechanical advantage.

The greatest call upon the skills of the carpenters came in the construction of the falsework or centering, the complex curving frames that supported arches during construction. Unless the centering had the proper curvature, the stone arch would not hold when the wooden support was removed. Moreover, the process of "striking" or "decentering" called for delicate judgment. If the wooden frame was removed too soon, while the mortar was still green, the arch might collapse. But leaving the centering in place too long was also dangerous. For if the mortar had set so hard that it had lost all plasticity, when the centering was removed and the building settled, the vault might crack open. The medieval carpenters seem to have devised ingenious methods of removing wedges a little at a time, so that the arches could settle gradually as the mortar hardened. Still, it must have been a tense moment for carpenters, masons, and the master of the work alike each time the falsework was finally removed.

The master of the work, *magister operis,* sometimes called master mason or master builder, combined the roles of architect, general contractor, and chief foreman. He was on the site every day directing operations, but he also drew up the plans, made models of the projected building, organized the order of construction, and negotiated with the canons, the bishop, or the abbot. Carrying his *virga,* the measuring rod, he went about the works in elegant robes, with his gloves in his hands but not on them. These gloves were a sign that he had sprung from the guild of masons but that he now worked with his head rather than his hands.

Surviving contracts with masters of the work indicate that they were well paid and much sought after. In addition to a daily fee, they received an allowance for clothing, free food and lodging, and could eat with the monks or canons if they liked. On the other hand, they were not subject to the restrictions imposed upon monks and, sometimes, on canons. Their food allowance was one and a half times that of a monk, and on fast days they dined in the kitchen — which presumably meant that they need not keep the fast.

The masters were learned men, not untutored practical geniuses. They attended the monastic schools until they acquired a reading, writing, and speaking knowledge of Latin. Then followed years of apprenticeship to a stonemason and more years as a journeyman mason, during which they wandered over Europe studying buildings and acquiring those secrets of geometry, design, and engineering that were closely guarded in the lodges. Eventually came promotion to the honored rank of master mason. Not all master masons became workmasters, of course; only those who had genius as well as practical competence were called upon to design and build the cathedrals. Their accomplishments are the testimony to their genius. Though the word architect was seldom used in the medieval period, these men were certainly great architects.

Unfortunately, we do not know the name of the first master of the work at Notre-Dame, although a certain "Richard the mason" witnessed a cathedral document in 1164 and the names of some of the later great masters have been preserved. But it is clear, from the very fabric of the cathedral that now stands before us, that Bishop Maurice de Sully made an inspired choice. When he was ready for the laying of the cornerstone of the choir in 1163, he had at his disposal an architect whose ability matched the bishop's vision.

III   A Bible in Stone

From the point of view of Louis VII of France, the year 1163 seemed an excellent time to embark on the building of a new cathedral for his capital. Twenty-six years before, when Abbot Suger began his reconstruction of Saint-Denis, Louis had been a mere child still under the abbot's tutelage. He had just brought home his high-spirited, fifteen-year-old bride, Eleanor, heiress of Aquitaine and Poitou. On his arrival in Paris, he found his father, Louis the Fat, newly dead and himself King of the Franks at the age of seventeen. He had spent the next years in struggles with rebellious vassals, in fruitless efforts to subdue his wife, and in endless prayers to Heaven to grant him a male heir to succeed him on the throne.

Louis blamed his ill luck in fathering only daughters upon the terrible sin he had committed at Vitry on the Marne, during his war with the Count of Champagne, the most redoubtable of his vassals. Leading his army in person, Louis had set fire to Vitry. The populace had fled to the sanctuary of the church, but that too caught fire. More than a thousand men, women, and children were found burned to death in the charred ruins. For a while Louis bore the reproaches of Bernard of Clairvaux, but in the long run he could scarcely endure his own contrition. Waking and sleeping, he heard the cries of the victims, the roar of the flames. He fell into such a deep depression that for a time his physicians feared for his life.

It was partly in penance for the horror of Vitry that Louis took the cross seven years later. Abbot Suger, with many misgivings, consented to act as regent of France during the king's absence on the Second Crusade. But although Saint Bernard himself had blessed the Crusade, God in his inscrutable wisdom evidently had not. Deceived by the Byzantines, ambushed by the Turks, beset by hunger, thirst, and plague, the vast army of Franks, Flemings, Poitevins, Aquitanians, and Germans dissolved into a disorderly rabble. Franks quarreled with Germans, Louis's men with Eleanor's men; and the king and queen had their private disputes as well. Eleanor threatened divorce, and Louis had to lead her back to Europe a virtual captive.

When they reached Italy after a harrowing voyage, Pope Eugenius III tried to restore harmony to the young royal pair. He went so far as to bed them down together in his own palace, on a couch spread with brocades, and talk to them like a father to his children. But the reconciliation was brief, and three years later the pair separated for good — in those days grounds of consanguinity could always be found when politics or pique required royal divorces. Louis kept their daughters, but he had to swallow the bitter pill of returning to Eleanor her lands of Poitou and Aquitaine. The pill tasted even worse when these lands immediately fell to his most formidable rival Henry Plantagenet, the Duke of Normandy, who promptly married Eleanor. Two years later Eleanor wore a crown once more, for her new husband became King Henry II of England. Moreover, Eleanor gave Henry what she had denied Louis: a son. And more male heirs followed. A dismayed Louis could not know that Henry Plantagenet would have little joy of his sons when they were grown to manhood.

Louis hurriedly married Constance of Castile. She died in 1160, leaving him with two more daughters to add to the two he already had by Eleanor. Terrified

by the prospect of extinction of the Capetian line, Louis entered his third marriage less than a month after Constance's death. His choice fell upon Alix of Champagne; the marriage had the additional merit of settling his old quarrel with the counts of Champagne.

By 1163, when he attended the dedication of Notre-Dame cathedral, Louis's years of travail seemed over. The adroit diplomacy of Thomas Becket, Henry II's chancellor, had at last settled the intermittent war between France and England on the borders of Normandy and Aquitaine. Becket had partly reconciled the two kings and effected a marital alliance between them by betrothing Henry's son Henry to Princess Marguerite, the daughter of Louis and Constance. By then Henry of England's attention was focused on his growing quarrel with his former chancellor, for he had unwisely made Thomas Becket Archbishop of Canterbury. The new archbishop became an obstinate defender of the rights of the Church against the Crown. On the other side of Louis's kingdom, Emperor Frederick Barbarossa was engaged in a similar struggle against the Church, and he had carried it so far as to drive Pope Alexander III into exile and set up an antipope. Thus Louis, ruler of a small country hemmed in by hungry and aggressive neighbors, could for the time being breathe easier. His antagonists were preoccupied, and Louis, in the prime of life, could turn his attention to the arts of peace, which by temperament he preferred.

In a perilous middle position, France relied on her traditional religious orthodoxy. Louis therefore welcomed the exiled pope to France. The close alliance between France and the papacy went back more than four hundred years, and Louis VII, like his predeces-sors, took pride in the epithet "most Christian King." If France could not brandish the mightiest sword in Europe, she could nevertheless lead the way in the battles of the Lord. Already Louis felt that he was winning all the campaigns in the cathedral crusade, and he gave generously to help Maurice de Sully build a church worthy of his capital city.

The king's largesse, however, could not sustain so vast a project. Funds had to be raised from every possible source. Maurice de Sully, like the other great episcopal and abbatial builders of the time, employed all the usual methods for raising money. Human vanity was exploited: the right to be buried inside the cathedral was sold before a donor's decease and even before there was a cathedral to be buried in. For the sake of a plaque testifying to their donation, the faithful gave the profits of a fishpond or a mill or a barge or a ferry. The guilds of shoemakers, fishermen, glassmakers, iron-mongers, and whatnot were invited to make contributions. Appeals were repeatedly made to nobles and wealthy merchants. Maurice personally persuaded a notorious usurer to offer a large sum to the building fund in order to win remission of his sins.

But the most effective method of raising money was the dispatch of missions. A party of canons, headed by the most eloquent members of the chapter, was provided with papal bulls, letters of recommendation from king and bishop, and some of the cathedral's more precious relics. Then it was sent out on collection tours, which might extend from the nearby parishes to points as distant as Hungary, Sicily, Scotland, and Scandinavia. The dispatch of these envoys became a fund-raising ceremony in itself, with the clergy and

Processions such as the one in the fifteenth-century miniature at left were a familiar sight in medieval France, where sacred relics were carried through the city streets in order to raise money to erect cathedrals. The mania for building that swept the nation is illustrated in the 1448 illumination at right. Twelve churches — including the four in the intricate ornamental border — in honor of the twelve apostles are seen at various stages of completion.

populace forming processions and accompanying the missionaries to the gates of the city to speed them on their way.

One method of raising funds was quick, easy, and efficient, but unfortunately it was destined ultimately to undermine the moral integrity and unity of the Church. That method was the granting of indulgences in return for a pilgrimage to a church and an offering to its saints. An indulgence was supposedly only a pardon to a contrite sinner, which would relieve him of the temporal punishment for his sin; but it was widely understood to be a general remission of sins. Pope Urban II granted the first plenary indulgence to the soldiers of the First Crusade — and thus started a flood that the Church could not check. Soon "pardoners" were going about everywhere in Europe offering indulgences for trivial sums. The pardoners pocketed their commissions, the building funds of the cathedral chapters swelled, but the coinage of spiritual redemption inevitably became debased. By the time of the Reformation, the sale of indulgences had corrupted the sellers and become one of the central issues of the reformers. In a sense, the Church foundered on the rocks upon which the cathedrals grew.

Considering the competition, it is astonishing that these methods worked at all. For the whole of France was building cathedrals, and Italy, Germany, England, Bohemia, and even faraway Hungary were also entering the race. Yet for two hundred years the missionaries and the pardoners went from city to city, from fair to fair, throughout Europe, and those who had just given generously to build their own church somehow found it possible to give again for a distant cathedral

they could never hope to see — such was the love of Heaven, the fear of Hell and, it must be added, the relative prosperity of Western Europe in the twelfth and thirteenth centuries.

Everywhere, moreover, the novel Gothic style, begun by Suger at Saint-Denis and continued by Maurice at Notre-Dame de Paris, triumphantly displaced the Romanesque. At Senlis, Laon, Lisieux, Chartres, Meaux, Angers, Noyon, Poitiers, Soissons, and many smaller places a perpetual cloud of stone and mortar dust overhung the towns as the builders learned from, imitated, and strove to outdo one another.

At Paris the work proceeded steadily, at a reasonable pace. Maurice de Sully was a solid, deliberate man, not one to outrun his resources by a feverish initial campaign that would then lapse for years while new funds were frantically collected. Once the cornerstone was laid — perhaps by Pope Alexander in person — and the elaborate dedication ceremonies completed, Maurice matched outgo to income and employed just enough workmen to keep the cathedral growing briskly but not wastefully. The foundations were dug thirty feet deep and filled with the hard stone of Montrouge to take the enormous weight that would be raised upon them.

The chancel — choir and apse — was built first. For here the priests officiated, here the high altar must stand. Once the chancel was built, the church could function. As Maurice conceived them, choir and apse would be big enough and grand enough for the celebration of royal weddings, funerals, and victories even before the completion of the nave. By itself, in fact, the chancel formed a sizable church, 170 feet long and 157 feet wide, with the vaulting of the choir rising to

the unprecedented height of more than 100 feet. Four tiers of windows — sapphire, ruby, topaz, and emerald — poured jeweled light into the sanctuary. Auxiliary altars were ranged against the curving outer wall of the apse, and the ambulatory, the wide passageway that swept around the eastern perimeter of the building, was to be double-aisled.

Such a plan had already been attempted at Saint-Denis. But the immense scale of the new Notre-Dame multiplied the technical difficulties. The vaults were higher and the spans wider than had so far been conquered by the new building style. Yet Maurice de Sully and his architect were aiming for impressive vistas, not to be spoiled by a multiplicity of supporting members.

The problem was ingeniously solved by the spacing of the pillars, and by combining simple transverse arches with a system of triangular ribbing. The resultant design was a triumph of both aesthetics and practicality. It would be imitated again and again in subsequent churches; but the clarity, grace, and noble perspectives of the apse at Notre-Dame de Paris have remained overwhelming. Yet this portion of the church was built in less than twenty years. More important, it set the dominant motif for the remainder of the cathedral, even though building continued well into the fourteenth century.

When we stand in the apse today, we should be aware of a number of later changes. To be sure, the basic structure has not been tampered with, and all of the columns are still those innocent round ones that art historians have labeled Transitional. The builders left behind the massive piers of the Romanesque but had

not yet learned to disguise the girth of their supports by the flutings, the crimpings, the host of tricks with form that we immediately identify as Gothic. These columns reveal at once how they were made. Twelve or thirteen uniform solid drums of hard stone are laid one above the other. Each column rests sturdily on a square base. Each is topped by a capital that is evidently meant to echo the Corinthian mode. But the classical acanthus leaves are simplified, almost rusticated. The same sort of columns were to be continued throughout the nave, but there they would be supplemented by a more typically Gothic pier, made up of a cluster of colonnettes.

It almost seemed that beginning the construction of Notre-Dame had regained the favor of Heaven for the Capetian dynasty. Two years after the laying of the cornerstone, all the bells in Paris burst forth in peals of joy, and the citizens rushed into the streets with torches and candles, creating such a sudden blaze of light that the whole city seemed afire. Alix of Champagne had borne Louis VII the male heir he had prayed for through three marriages and twenty-eight years as ruler of France. Gerald of Wales, who was then a student in Paris, vividly described the excitement that ran through the city at the birth of Philip Augustus:

> The author of this work, being in the city, and then a young man in the twentieth year of his age, immediately leaped to the window from the couch on which he had stretched himself and fallen into his first sleep; and looking out, he saw two very poor old women in the street bearing torches . . . and exulting with joy. . . . And when he had inquired of them the cause of such commotion and exultation, one of them imme-

diately looked up at him and replied: "We have now a king given us by God, by whom disgrace and loss, punishment and grievous shame, confusion and sorrow in abundance, shall come upon your king."

Throughout the boyhood of Philip Augustus, Louis was engaged in an almost continuous struggle with his most powerful vassal, King Henry of England. Despite the disparity in wealth and power between the tiny Capetian monarchy and the vast Plantagenet empire, Louis managed to hold his own. Whenever he was driven to retreat by military force, he would remind Henry of his oath of vassalage — for Louis was technically Henry's overlord for his Continental lands. And Henry, a scrupulous observer of the feudal code by conviction and necessity — for he did not want to be a bad example to his own restive vassals and sons — invariably granted the requested truce.

Louis, to give him due credit, also tried to be scrupulous, but he lacked his rival's will and resources. In 1174, taking advantage of Henry's preoccupation with the revolt of his eldest son — which Louis himself had fomented — the French king invaded Normandy. He raised one of the largest armies that had been seen in Europe for many years and laid siege to the formidable city of Rouen. So large was their army that the French were able to split into three groups and thus divide the watch into three eight-hour periods. Finally a continuous, full-scale assault was launched. But instead of fighting without respite, the citizens of the populous city similarly apportioned their numbers and manned the walls in three shifts.

After many days of unremitting battle, the feast-day of Saint Lawrence arrived. Louis, who had a special

veneration for the martyr, ordered a day's truce, which his heralds ceremonially announced. The citizens of Rouen accepted gladly; there were gay celebrations of the holiday, and a tournament was held outside the city in full view of the French troops. The sight was too much for the besiegers. Louis's allies and counselors came to him and urged him to take advantage of this priceless opportunity to steal up to the walls with scaling ladders and take the city by surprise assault.

"Far be it from me to sully my royal honor with so foul a stain," Louis at first replied. But he was soon overborne by the arguments of his nobles. At last he consented. Word was spread throughout the army by whispers, and the advance began.

Fortunately for the citizens, some clerks in a tower who were passing the time — perhaps with forbidden dice — happened to look out the window and noticed the preparations. They immediately began to ring Ruvell, the great bell of Rouen, summoning the defenders to the walls. Hearing the clangorous warning, the besieging army rushed forward, mounted ladders already in place, and were shouting in triumph at the summit of the wall — when they were counterattacked by the soldiers who had been playing at battle outside the walls. A violent struggle ensued; the defenders of Rouen won, and the besieging army that had violated the truce withdrew with heavy losses. Shortly afterward, King Henry came to the relief of the city. Ashamed that he had been lured into breaking his word, Louis no longer had the heart to continue the fight. He and his vast army retreated with, as the chronicler put it, "no other reward but dishonor for such great labor."

Louis VII did not quite live to see the choir and apse of Notre-Dame completed. An old man before he reached sixty, he arranged for the coronation of his heir at Reims but was himself unable to attend the ceremony. After a lingering illness, he died in the beloved shadow of the new cathedral, in the very Cloister of Notre-Dame where he had been raised as a child. His contemporary William of Newburgh praised him as "a man of fervent devotion toward God and singular mildness toward his subjects, and also one who highly reverenced men in holy orders." But, William added, "he was rather more simple than became a monarch, and in some of his actions he most clearly expressed the truth of the Apostle's words, 'Evil communications corrupt good manners.' Indeed, by putting undue trust in the counsels of certain nobles who cared too little for what is honorable and just, he frequently sullied his otherwise admirable character."

To his son Philip Augustus, Louis left the conquest and absorption of the Angevin possessions on the Continent. His own greatest monument was the ring of noble churches and cathedrals in and around Paris. Saint-Denis, Sens, Vézelay, Noyon, Senlis, Laon, Reims, Châlons-sur-Marne, Mantes — almost as many magnificent churches were begun or reconstructed during his reign as there were towns and abbeys in the royal domain.

In these cathedrals a new kind of music was replacing the Gregorian plain chant whose powerful, straightforward recitative had seemed the musical reflection of the foursquare, massive Romanesque churches. The new polyphonic style, more rhythmical and more complex, full of surprises like the nascent Gothic, had

its origin at Notre-Dame de Paris. Leoninus and Perotinus, two composers of genius, made Paris the center of the musical world. Leoninus in his *Magnus Liber* provided enough two-voiced music to cover the whole round of the ecclesiastical year. Perotinus, suiting his compositions to the acoustic demands of the new choir of Notre-Dame, rewrote many of Leoninus's organums by adding more voices and interweaving them into intricate melodies.

With pomp and circumstance, the high altar of Notre-Dame was consecrated in 1182. Assisted by Maurice de Sully, the papal legate, Henri de Château-Marçay, mixed holy water and chrism and inscribed the requisite seven crosses upon the altar. Then the altar was washed, wiped, and rubbed once more with oil of catechumens and chrism. The incense was blessed, and a grain of incense was placed in each of the corners of the altar and at its center. Then, once more, came the scraping and cleansing, sprinkling of the altar cloth and ornaments with holy water, and censing of the altar. Only then could the first mass be celebrated at the new altar.

It was a high honor for Maurice de Sully to have the papal legate present at this important ceremony. It was a higher honor still, three years later, for him to have Heraclius, the Patriarch of Jerusalem, officiate in his new choir. To men of this era of Crusades, the patriarch was the greatest ecclesiastic in the world next to the pope. Heraclius, however, had not come in triumph but as a supplicant. The plight of the Latin Kingdom of Jerusalem, established by the victorious Europeans of the First Crusade, had grown pitiable; the Saracen armies, united at long last under the able rule of Saladin, were rapidly conquering one Christian outpost after another. Heraclius pleaded with Philip Augustus to undertake a new Crusade before the Holy City itself fell to the Moslems. But the shrewd young King of France responded with evasions; he was more interested in stirring up the sons of Henry II of England to renewed revolt against their father. The patriarch then went on to England to offer Henry II the keys to Jerusalem and the crown of the Latin Kingdom of Jerusalem itself if he would bring an army to save the jewel of Christendom. Henry provided money and some soldiers, but he too had no intention of leaving his own lands unguarded while the predatory King of France and his own still more predatory sons remained at home.

Two years later, in 1187, the inevitable but incredible tidings came: the "enemies of God" had taken Jerusalem. What was more, they had captured the True Cross and had almost wiped out the Latin Kingdom. Only the cities of Tyre, Antioch, and Tripoli remained in Christian hands. The entire Christian world mourned in despair for a time — and then began to burn with a new crusading fever. Even such wary and self-interested monarchs as Henry II and Philip Augustus were caught up in the universal passion. For the time being they buried their disputes and agreed to take the cross. But even while preparations for the new Crusade were going forward, Philip Augustus connived with Richard Coeur de Lion to launch a new attack upon the aging King Henry. Suddenly Richard and Philip became the best of friends; with their combined forces they overwhelmed the unprepared English king, harried him until he fell ill from exhaustion and humiliation, and

forced him to a surrender that broke his spirit. On July 6, 1189, Henry II, one of the greatest of English monarchs, died muttering to himself: "Shame, shame, shame on a conquered king." The leadership of the new Crusade was left in the hands of Philip Augustus of France and Richard Coeur de Lion, the new King of England.

The friendship between Philip Augustus and Richard died promptly with Henry II, for Richard inherited the Plantagenet interests and his father's conflicts with the Franks. The quarrels between the two young sovereigns, begun on the Continent and continued in Sicily, came to a head in the swollen and terrible encampment at Acre in the Holy Land. There, laying siege to the Saracens in the formidable walled city of Acre, besieged in their turn by Saladin's encircling army, a vast host of Crusaders suffered and died of famine, pestilence, and the unbearable heat. The arrival of Philip Augustus and Richard with fresh arms, food, and soldiers turned the tide. Acre was taken by storm, despite the Greek fire and burning pitch that poured down from the ramparts. But although Austrians, Franks, Germans, Normans, Provençals, Englishmen, and even Scandinavians from the recently converted realms of the far north participated in the assault, the credit for the capture of Acre went to Richard Coeur de Lion. He dominated the army of the Third Crusade with his flamboyant personality and conspicuous wealth — he had taxed England till it bled to equip his army, and on the way to the Holy Land he had replenished his treasury by taking Cyprus and selling it to the Templars. Both King Richard and King Philip Augustus fell ill with the quartan fever

that was ravaging the Crusaders. Richard stayed on, but Philip, wracked by disease, gnawed by envy and suspicion, decided to return home less than a month after the fall of Acre. Before Philip left, Richard made him swear a solemn oath that he would observe the Truce of God and protect the lands of the King of England as if they were his own.

The crusading fervor began to melt away after the taking of Acre and the departure of Philip Augustus. Although Richard stayed on for more than a year, reconquering the coast of Palestine and acquiring such a reputation that his very name struck terror in the hearts of the Saracens, he did not succeed in regaining Jerusalem. Eventually, in September 1192, he hastily made peace with Saladin — who died six months later — and in October set out for Europe. He had come within sight of Jerusalem, but he had failed in the Crusade's chief objective: to recapture the Holy City. At least, however, under the terms of the new peace treaty, Christian pilgrims would be able to visit the Holy Places unhindered.

Richard had reason to hasten home, for the affairs of his kingdom were in disorder. His barons were restive, his brother John was intriguing against him, and Philip Augustus — violating his oath — was attacking Richard's lands in Normandy. Had it not been for the imperiousness and good sense of Richard's mother, Eleanor of Aquitaine, his whole realm would have fallen apart in this crisis.

Richard set sail over perilous autumnal seas, in a time of unusual gales, and had the ill luck to suffer shipwreck on the coast of Istria. Trying to make his way home overland, he fell into the hands of Duke

Judging from the spirited joust at left between the helmeted Richard Coeur de Lion and the fierce, blue-faced Saladin, the Third Crusade was an enterprise consistent with the rules of chivalric warfare. In truth, the grim scene below of Richard massacring his Saracen hostages in the Holy Land is much closer to reality. From his balcony at left, Richard complacently observes the gruesome spectacle. Headless corpses are piled up beneath a platform on which two blindfolded men are about to be beheaded. Others await their turn, while soldiers lead the next victims to the ladder.

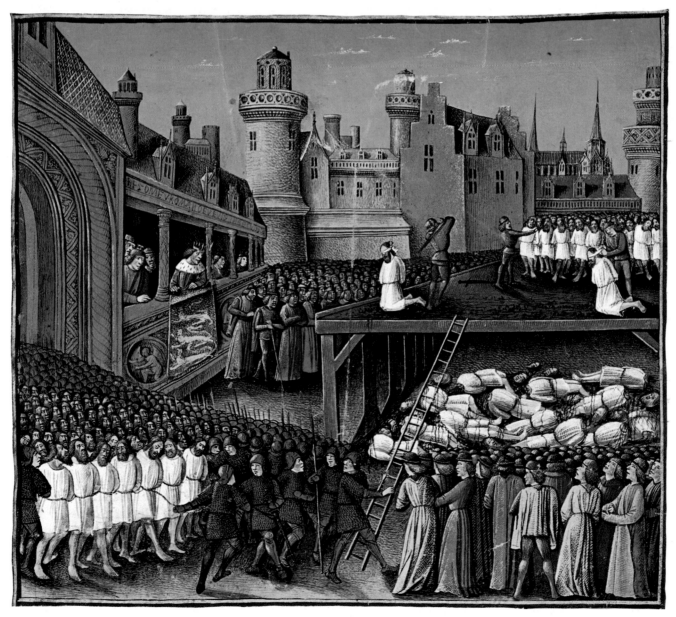

Leopold of Austria. Leopold turned him over, at a price, to his overlord, Emperor Henry of Hohenstaufen, who had succeeded Frederick Barbarossa. For two years thereafter Richard remained the most famous captive in the world, while his enormous ransom was being raised. Philip Augustus, defying both the pope and public opinion, exerted all his diplomacy to keep the King of England a prisoner as long as possible so he could pursue his war for recovery of the Angevin lands. All went well for the French until "the devil was loosed." Then Richard, free at last, rapidly threw Philip back on the defensive. By the closing year of the twelfth century Richard was beginning to threaten the Île-de-France itself, when an arrow loosed in a petty quarrel with one of his vassals put a sudden end to the brilliant and sometimes unsavory career of Richard Coeur de Lion.

These stirring events — in the Holy Land and in Europe — inevitably slowed the work of building Notre-Dame de Paris, if only because the driving spirit behind it, Maurice de Sully, was so much preoccupied during the years of peril and warfare. Maurice served Philip Augustus much as Suger had served the king's father. Although Bishop Maurice does not appear ever to have become quite so important in the affairs of the realm as Suger had been, it is significant that Philip Augustus, before leaving for the Third Crusade, appointed Maurice one of the executors of his will. The Crusade and the subsequent war with England strained the resources of France. It became harder to raise funds for building after so much treasure had been poured into equipping the men who died in the disease-ridden squalor of the camp at Acre.

Nevertheless, Maurice had guarded his own revenues well. Early in his episcopate he completed his noble episcopal palace, which occupied the area between the new cathedral and the Seine. And throughout his long tenure as Bishop of Paris, work on the cathedral never ceased. By the time Maurice died in 1196, the great nave was substantially finished. As his last act of faith toward the cathedral he loved, Maurice provided in his will the sum of one hundred livres for the expenses of roofing. He left an equal amount to the "poor clerks" of the cathedral of Paris — for he himself had once, long ago, been just such a poor clerk, living on the charity of earlier bequests.

The nave of Notre-Dame de Paris benefited by the advances in the techniques of Gothic architecture that were being made all over France at this time. Outside, to support his 110-foot-high vaulting, the master of the work threw up a series of flying buttresses — perhaps for the first time, perhaps in imitation of what had been done at Saint-Denis and in smaller churches around the Île-de-France (the question of priority is in dispute and perhaps can never be definitely settled). The sexpartite vaults — crossed ogives with a supplementary arch passing through their keystones — seemed to fling themselves toward Heaven, as if to reproduce in stone the soaring ambitions of Philip Augustus.

The double aisles of the choir continue through the nave, but there is a remarkable difference in the supporting columns. In the choir, these are uniform round shafts on square bases. In the long nave, the same scheme is followed in the central vessel. But the effect of a monotonous parade of pillars all exactly alike is broken by the inspired treatment of the central line

of columns separating the two aisles. Here simple shafts alternate with pillars surrounded by colonnettes that add both strength and grace. The changing rhythm of these columns is one of the greatest charms of the nave at Notre-Dame, for the colonnettes impose a vertical movement that contrasts beautifully with the horizontal feeling of the simple shafts, whose successive circular drums are plainly visible.

The capitals of the columns in the nave, as compared with those of the choir, illustrate the completed transition from Romanesque to Gothic. The floral patterns are still stylized, but there is a greater approach to realism, a greater fineness in the depiction of each leaf. Indeed, in spite of its vast size, fineness is the dominant characteristic of this nave. The structural members are thinner, leaner, less massive than those of the choir. The builders by then had acquired confidence in *opus francigenum,* or "French work," as Gothic architecture was generally called throughout Europe. They had a better understanding of the strength of colonnettes and pointed arches, and they had added to their already considerable arsenal of structural reassurances the vital device of the flying buttress.

With flying buttresses to support the upper parts of the nave, tribunes above the aisles were not strictly necessary. They were built nevertheless, for the sake of additional strength and consistency with the choir, and are among the most beautiful aspects of Notre-Dame de Paris. Wide, well-lighted, they are vaulted by simple crossed ogives that run down to engaged columns, between which the arcades are additionally supported by graceful, slender pilasters. Some of the capitals in these tribunes display long, narrow recurved leaves — first

examples of the crockets that were later to become so popular in Gothic architecture and that were used lavishly on the façade of Notre-Dame.

Under Maurice de Sully's successor, work on the façade began immediately after completion of the nave. As chance would have it, the new Bishop of Paris was named Eudes de Sully and came from the same town of Sully-sur-Loire as had Maurice. But there was no kinship between them, and in fact the two men were as different as pauper and prince. Eudes de Sully was a noble, related to many of the great secular and ecclesiastical lords of France and England. Indeed, Philip Augustus was his cousin; and Eudes de Sully as bishop had the rare courage to "obey God rather than man," as the biblical phrase so current at the time had it. What that meant in practice was that he opposed his king and obeyed the pope, who had placed the French realm under interdict to punish Philip for repudiating his second wife. In quarrels with the papacy, kings expected support from their own bishops. But Eudes de Sully immediately stopped services in the cathedral of Paris and enforced the interdict throughout his diocese.

But although his relations with Philip were often strained, as Maurice's had scarcely ever been, Eudes de Sully had one great advantage over his predecessor that redounded to the benefit of Notre-Dame: he was independently wealthy. He was also willing to devote his large means to the embellishment of his cathedral. The result was that the original design of the western façade was reconceived on a more ambitious scale — so much more ambitious that the façade ultimately took more years to build than had the choir and nave

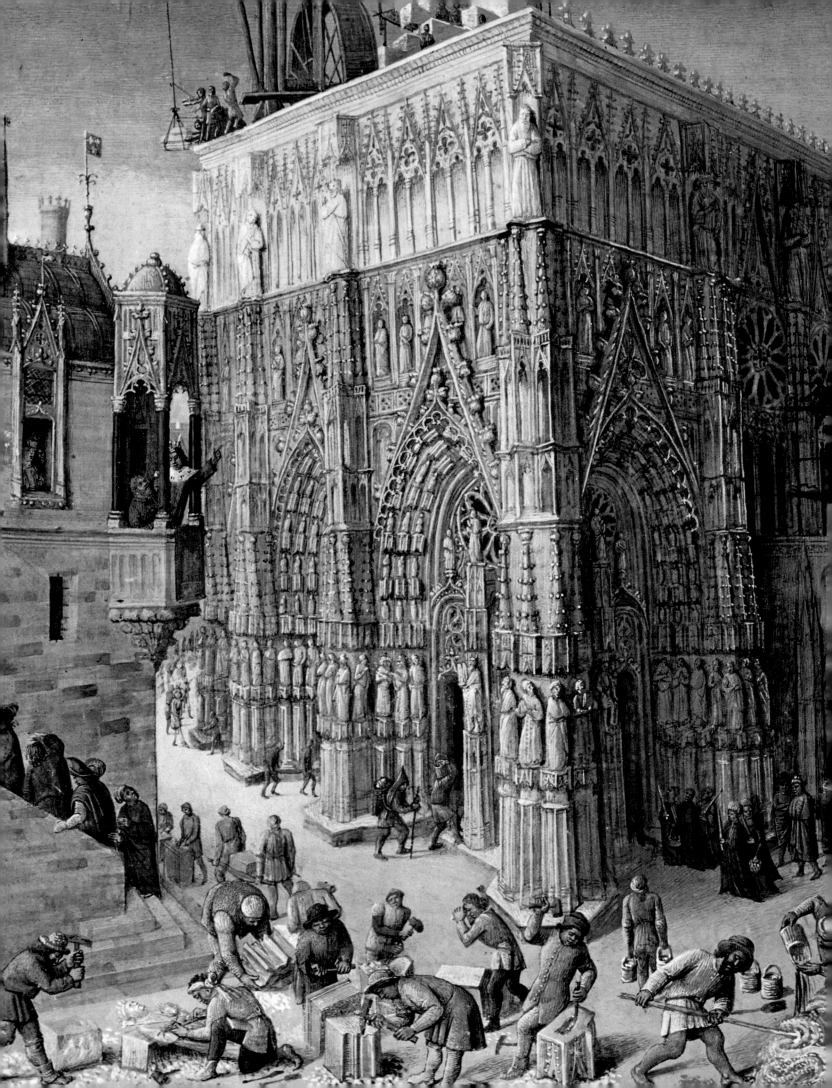

together.

It was during the first twenty-five years of the thirteenth century that the grandiose western façade was erected as far as the stage of the great rose. The magnificence of the façade harked back to Norman ancestors, particularly Saint-Etienne and La Trinité at Caen with their schemes of three portals and two towers. It is even possible that the ancient Christian basilicas of Syria influenced the design of the Paris façade — Crusaders and pilgrims would have seen these many times. Saint-Denis, Senlis, Noyon, Laon, and other churches of the Île-de-France likewise served as models. But for perfection of balance, harmony of parts, and beauty of detail, the western façade of Notre-Dame de Paris equals or surpasses all.

The three great portals, each set between a pair of buttresses, all differ somewhat in height and width as well as in sculptural subjects. The central portal, higher and wider than the other two, has suffered the most damage from time and man — those two great enemies of architectural monuments of which, Victor Hugo remarked, man is the worse. In 1771 the architect Jacques Soufflot destroyed the beauty of the portal by enlarging it so that processions with canopies could pass through. The nineteenth-century restoration permits us to see the portal in its original shape, but much of the sculpture is the work of Eugène Emmanuel Viollet-le-Duc and his pupils.

The subject, traditional for cathedrals, gives the central portal its name: the Portal of the Last Judgment. At the summit of the tympanum a majestic Christ sits in judgment upon the sinful and the good, whose souls arc being weighed by Saint Michael in the upper lintel.

Two angels beside Christ hold the nails, lance, and cross (those sacred relics that the chivalry of France were trying to wrest from Saladin at the time the original sculptures were carved). A little lower than the angels, Mary and Saint John kneel before Christ to pray that mercy be shown to the human race. On the left side of the upper lintel, under Christ's upraised right hand, the saved rise to Heaven; on the right, the damned are being dragged down to Hell. The crowned souls of the just are being guided to Paradise by a lovely angel; a savage demon tugs at a long rope dragging the sinners downward. In the covings to the left of the tympanum Heaven and all its angels, patriarchs, saints, virgins, and doctors of the Church, are displayed; while on the right are chaos, horror, the ugly twisting and writhing shapes of Hell and all its demons.

Viollet-le-Duc's restorations on the pier, pillars, splays, and bases of the great central portal were as true to the originals as he could make them in the nineteenth century. A mere list of the subjects suggests the complexity of this religious art: Christ as teacher, the Liberal Arts, the Wise and Foolish Virgins, the Apostles, the Virtues and the Vices — a large segment of Christian doctrine and Christian history was incorporated into this one great portal.

Yet the central portal, with its wealth of sculpture, is only one of three. The Portal of Saint Anne, to the right, contains the oldest sculptures in the cathedral, as has already been noted. The lintels of this portal show scenes from the New Testament: the Annunciation, the Visitation, the Nativity, King Herod and the Magi, Saint Joachim and Saint Anne, and so on.

63

FACADE   OCCIDENTALE

The statues below the lintel are reconstructions from the workshop of Viollet-le-Duc.

The left portal, the Portal of the Virgin, is distinguished from the others by the gable above the tympanum. As the whole church was consecrated to the Virgin, so also was one entire portal of the façade. Here was the place for those scenes recorded in the Apocrypha, which so stirred the imaginations of men in the twelfth and thirteenth centuries: the death, assumption, and coronation of the Mother of God. It is worth remarking that during those centuries, in which the Virgin was venerated with unprecedented fervor, two women wielded unprecedented political power in Europe: Eleanor of Aquitaine and her granddaughter, Blanche of Castile, the mother of Saint Louis of France.

The thirteenth-century tympanum of the Portal of the Virgin shows Mary's burial and assumption. Below this scene sit three kings of Judah, to emphasize Mary's royal ancestry, and three prophets, to recall the Old Testament prophecies of the coming to earth of Jesus Christ.

To the thirteenth-century mind, the Virgin provided the link between human lowliness and divine majesty. She had also incorporated into herself the goddesses of the ancient world, those seasonal goddesses like Ceres and Proserpine. Hence it was only natural that the pier should show in bas-relief the changing seasons and the ages of man, that the pillars should depict the months and their labors. A Bible in stone, a calendar in stone: the medieval cathedral tried, like the medieval summa, to be an epitome of all the knowledge that was needed for life and salvation.

Above the three portals, running across the entire façade, the builders of Notre-Dame created the Gallery of Kings. Here twenty-eight kings of Israel looked out over the Île de la Cité. The statues we now see are restorations, for in the French Revolution antiroyalist Paris saw the twenty-eight as kings of France, not Israel, and took them down. But if they misinterpreted the letter of the religious iconography, can it be said that they misinterpreted the spirit? The statues of the gallery may have depicted the kings of Israel, not France; but the sculptors had indeed been glorifying the only monarchy they knew. In the Gallery of Kings they were undoubtedly proclaiming their pride in the triumphs of the French monarchy, which had grown so notably in power and prestige during the first quarter of the thirteenth century.

On the western façade of Notre-Dame, symbolic statuary groupings of astonishing artistry tell the story of the New Testament in stone. At left is a close-up of the main portal, devoted to the Last Judgment. The majestic figure of Christ, presiding over the separation of the blessed from the damned, dominates the tympanum; another, more compassionate Christ, occupies the central pier. A detail from the upper lintel (below, near left) shows Saint Michael and Satan weighing souls, as an angel and a demon crouch beneath the scales of justice. The twisted bodies suffering the tortures of hell (below, at far left) are from the right-hand voussoirs of the portal. At right is the upper portion of the famed Portal of the Virgin. The tympanum depicts Mary's coronation; the upper lintel, her dormition in the presence of Christ, two angels, and the twelve apostles; and in the lower lintel are the seated figures of the three prophets and the three kings of Judea. Below is a detail of the stylized flourishes that form the grillwork of the Virgin's door. Spanning the entire width of the façade above the portals is the Gallery of Kings — a detail appears at right below. The twenty-eight statues of the kings of Israel, set in niched arches, are nineteenth-century works commissioned by Viollet-le-Duc to replace the originals, which were destroyed during the French Revolution.

IV

While Maurice and Eudes de Sully had been devoting their talents and solicitude to Notre-Dame cathedral and the quarter around it, King Philip Augustus provided a setting for the majestic monument by improving the capital. The story goes that he was standing at his window one day when a cart, churning the muddy street below him, sent such foul odors to the king's nostrils that he forthwith ordered the streets of Paris to be paved. The work began at once, but like cathedral-building, it could not be completed in a day or a year. In fact, it continued steadily for 150 years. The quarrymen of the Île-de-France were kept fully employed on this and many other projects during the forty-three years of Philip's reign. The king erected a great wall, eight feet thick, strengthened by some five hundred towers, around the city. He built Les Halles to shelter the market traditionally held on the spot. The Louvre, too, was begun in Philip's reign.

Along with the fortification and embellishment of the capital, Philip Augustus pursued a vigorously expansionist foreign policy that abruptly altered the balance of power in Europe. With Richard Coeur de Lion out of the way and luckless John Lackland on the English throne, Philip rapidly conquered Normandy and most of the other Plantagenet possessions on the Continent. He completed this conquest, significantly, in the same year that Eleanor of Aquitaine — who had remained the *grande dame* of England past her eightieth year — died and was laid to rest beside her husband, Henry II, in Fontevrault Abbey.

That same year, 1204, there were Frenchmen in the streets of Constantinople, gathering "booty so great that none could tell you the end of it: gold and silver, and vessels and precious stones, and samite, and cloth of silk, and robes of vair and gray, and ermine, and every choicest thing found upon the earth. . . . Never since the world was created had so much booty been won in any city."

Those Frenchmen were part of the army of the Fourth Crusade, which like the third had set out to retake Jerusalem. It ended by capturing the Christian city of Constantinople and overrunning a sizable portion of the Byzantine Empire for the benefit of Venice. The Latin Empire, which the Crusaders established in Byzantium, ruled over a sullen populace. Threatened from without by the Moslems, it lasted for only half a century. But during that time French interests, bound together by intricate familial ties and feudal relationships, extended from the English Channel across Europe and through the Adriatic and the Aegean seas to the shores of the Black Sea.

Such conquests were temporary, however, and did not directly affect the growth of the royal domain and the increasing power of a centralized monarchy in France. Another misdirected crusade, no less motivated by lust for booty, had a more lasting effect upon the fortunes of the French people and the ultimate destiny of France. That was the Albigensian Crusade, one of the more somber chapters in the history of France. It was named after the city of Albi in southern France, which for a time was the center of the Catharist heresy.

The general intellectual awakening of the twelfth century, the renewal of contacts between Christendom and the outside world, and the growing secular influence of the papacy had stimulated severe criticism of the Church both from within and from without. Some

Against Heathen and Heretic

of the most fervent and orthodox churchmen of the age, like Saint Bernard, denounced the venality and luxurious tastes of many ecclesiastics with a fury that almost matched that of the heretics. Reforms were initiated, but the need for reform remained perennial. The new orders of monks, such as the Cluniacs and Cistercians, began in simplicity and austerity but eventually succumbed to the temptations of wealth and display. The higher prelates were also powerful secular lords with expensive tastes and interests that compromised their religious mission. The Crusades themselves involved the Church in so much political maneuvering, in so many concessions to expediency, that they undermined the spirituality of the papacy even as they strengthened its secular authority.

It is against this background that the rise of heresy in northern Italy and southern France must be viewed. Heretics by definition are those who find themselves on the losing side in disputes over dogma and church policy. Protestantism ceased to be a heresy and became a separate church because it won a few battles. The people of Languedoc were not so fortunate; history therefore speaks of them as "heretics." But in fact they came very close to setting up an independent church of their own before they went down to defeat in a bloody and merciless war.

The Catharist or Albigensian church originated from two principal strands: from reformist movements within Catholicism, such as that of the Waldensians, also called "the poor men of Lyons" (who preached doctrines not unlike those later taken up by the Franciscans); and from ancient Manichean beliefs which had lingered in the Balkans, northern Italy,

southern France, and Spain. The Manicheans held that this world was the creation of the power of evil, which they saw as engaged in a perpetual struggle with the power of good. Priests and the whole organization of the official church were, in their view, but instruments of evil. Absolute pacifism, near or total vegetarianism, abstinence, and continence were among their tenets. The Catharist preachers needed only to point to the corrupt lives of many members of the clergy for their arguments to be convincing to the laity. And those preachers themselves were so fanatically ascetic — to the point, so it was alleged, of sometimes voluntarily starving themselves to death in order to escape this evil world — that their example won them countless followers in a region noted for its luxury and easy living.

It was difficult to found a church upon such doctrines, but the Cathars (the word comes from Greek, meaning "the Pure") succeeded by certain compromises that made room for the salvation of ordinary humanity. The leaders or bishops freed themselves from evil by becoming *perfecti*, leading lives of utmost purity. They in turn could pass on salvation to the faithful by a laying on of hands called the *consolamentum*, or consolation, which would usually be administered to the layman just before death. This, in a way, was a reversion to the primitive Christian practice of deathbed baptism.

The new doctrine began winning many adherents around the middle of the twelfth century. By the beginning of the thirteenth century it had become so widespread in the countryside around Albi, and in much of southern France all the way to the Pyrenees and beyond, that Catholic churchmen became seri-

ously alarmed. When papal legates and missionaries failed to sway the heretics, Pope Innocent III called for a crusade against these fellow Christians. The immediate pretext was the assassination of a papal legate by one of the officers of the Count of Toulouse.

The war that began in 1208 was marked by unprecedented cruelty. The northern French barons under the leadership of Simon de Montfort deliberately embarked on a policy of sheer terrorism, as a contemporary noted:

> The nobles of France, clergy and laity, princes and marquises, agreed among themselves that whenever a château they invested refused to surrender and had to be taken by force, the inhabitants were to be put to the sword and slain; thinking that afterwards no man would dare to stand out against them by reason of the fear that would go abroad when it was seen what they had already done.

One consequence of this policy was the terrible slaughter at Béziers, in which the entire population of the city was killed. It was here that the Cistercian abbot Arnald-Amalric, queried on how to distinguish Catholics from heretics, is supposed to have said: "Slay them all; God will take care of his own." Whether or not these words were ever spoken, they express the spirit in which the war was conducted. And as a further consequence, heretics and Catholics united to defend their land against the invader.

The Albigensian Crusade developed into a protracted war of conquest on the one side, a stubborn territorial defense on the other. It continued for more than a generation, until the rich and prosperous civilization of Languedoc lay shattered, its cities burned, its vines uprooted, its flourishing commerce ruined, its independence gone. Butchered by ruthless mercenaries, fanatical knights, and the agents of the newly created Inquisition, the heretics were exterminated. The smoke of burning faggots and flesh rose above the whole Midi. Only a few heretics escaped into the mountains of Savoy and Piedmont — where their persecution continued down to the nineteenth century.

It soon became clear that the real object of the war was annexation by the French crown of the powerful county of Toulouse. That aim was undeviatingly pursued by Philip Augustus until his death in 1223, by his son Louis VIII, and after his death three years later by Blanche of Castile, who governed France during the minority of her son Louis IX, the future Saint Louis. The counts of Toulouse, Raymond VI and Raymond VII, attempted to preserve their independence by asserting their Catholic orthodoxy while defending their Catharist subjects. They turned and twisted, sometimes hunting or pretending to hunt heretics, sometimes summoning their heretic vassals to join them in the defense of their country. Ultimately it proved impossible for the counts to walk the diplomatic and theological tightrope. Although Count Raymond VII held Toulouse against overwhelming odds, the devastation of the countryside and the frequent betrayals by his Catholic clergy ultimately forced him to capitulate. He agreed to a humiliating treaty, yielding his independence in return for peace and a lifting of the ban of excommunication that had been imposed upon him. On April 12, 1229, the defeated Count of Toulouse came to Notre-Dame de Paris to be reconciled to the Church.

The decorously draped stone figure at left, from Eleanor of Aquitaine's tomb in Fontevrault Abbey, belies the vigor and passion of the woman who had been queen of both France and England. As an impediment to monarchical authority, Eleanor's native province was rivaled only by its neighbor Toulouse. The thirteenth-century bas-relief below depicts the crown's savage campaign to subdue that rebellious region. Against overwhelming odds, the inhabitants (on the right) desperately maneuver a catapult in an effort to scale the palisade that separates them from their besiegers.

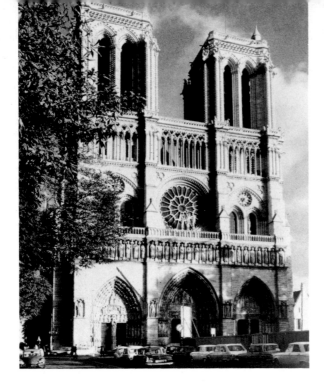

All around the parvis outside the bright new façade of Notre-Dame seats had been erected for the dignitaries. The ladies, nobles, and prelates were decked out in their most brilliant robes. Queen Mother Blanche and fourteen-year-old King Louis sat side-by-side on thrones, flanked by bishops and barons. In their presence, Raymond VII signed the act of surrender. Then he was stripped to his shirt and breeches, a cord was placed around his neck, and he was dragged down the whole length of the nave to the high altar. There, to complete his shame, he knelt and was scourged by the cardinal-legate of the pope. After that humiliation — surely one of the most dramatic of the many stirring scenes that were to take place in Notre-Dame de Paris over the centuries — the count was held prisoner in the Louvre for another six months.

Raymond survived to emerge from prison and lead other fruitless rebellions perhaps only because the queen mother and the royal party needed him as a possible counterpoise to other powerful barons. Blanche of Castile — a foreigner, exceedingly if not excessively devoted to the Church, more ready to listen to the advice of her Spanish retainers than her French counselors — had inherited the beauty, the presence, and the iron will of her grandmother Eleanor of Aquitaine. These qualities enabled her, in a time of unending feudal plots and counterplots, to maintain her position and save the kingship for her son. She taught him well, and she made him a judicious king, concerned for the welfare of his humblest subjects. Unfortunately, she also imbued him with such intense piety that he led the nation on two more disastrous Crusades.

By the time Louis IX became King of France, the rose window of the western façade of Notre-Dame had been completed. This magnificent wheel of stone, like a huge halo around the head of the Virgin whose statue poises on the balustrade in front of it, is one of the miracles of thirteenth-century architecture. The rose is thirty-two feet in diameter — the largest of its kind when it was erected — and the builders confronted the triple problem of sustaining the immense pressure of the surrounding stone upon so large a gap in the wall, of dividing the space into approximately equal areas, and of providing room enough for the glass, so that the window would serve its function of admitting a flood of colored light to the interior.

They solved these problems ingeniously by arranging slender colonnettes like the spokes of a wheel all around the central oculus. These spokes run to a second circle of trefoiled arches on which rests a second series of colonnettes. But here, in between each radius, an additional colonnette to the outer rim has been inserted. The elegant result is approximately equal division of the space and tremendous strength in the whole structure. Functionalism alone, however, was never the aim of the medieval builder; and the effect of this rose is one of singular harmony, restfulness, and confidence. The loveliness of the stone tracery is enhanced by the sturdy semicircular arches, ornamented with innumerable crockets that surround the upper half of the window. These arches again rest on columns that recapitulate the theme of the window itself. So also do the slender columns of the bays between the buttresses to either side of the rose. The wheel theme also is recapitulated in the two blind roses in the tympanum of each bay; the crockets of the semicircular arch are

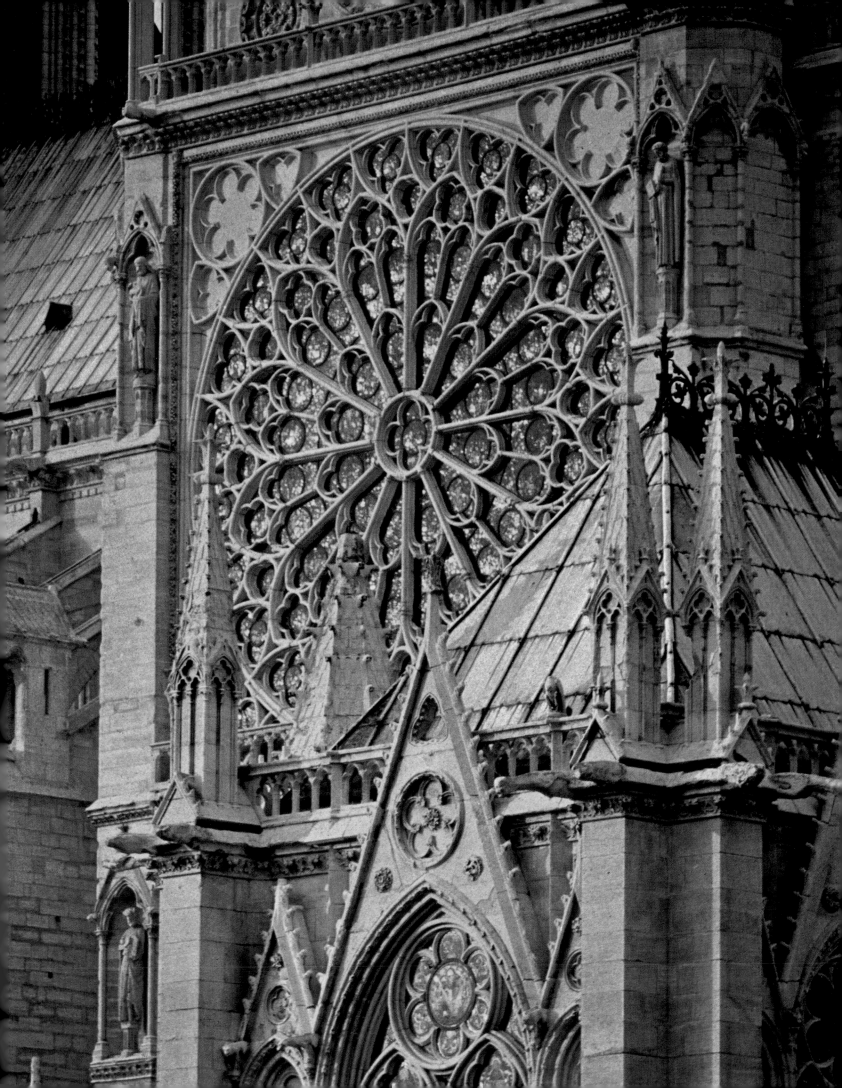

repeated in the cornice that extends across the entire façade above the rose.

Seen from the interior, the western rose is somewhat disappointing. A good third of it is obscured by organ pipes that were installed there in the eighteenth century. And all the original glass has vanished; what we now see are nineteenth-century restorations. Although they are good work, they remain only a dim simulacrum of the thirteenth-century glass. One realizes that fully if one stands at the crossing of the transept and looks up at the rose of the northern façade. Here, in the glorious rose window built by Jean de Chelles around 1250, the gemlike glass — blue, red, green, brown, and yellow, but predominantly blue — is almost all of the thirteenth century.

Without binoculars, the subjects depicted on the northern rose are difficult to make out from the ground, but the colors, and the light that falls through them onto the church floor, are breathtaking. Mary is in the center of the wheel, of course; in the circles around her are the kings and prophets of the Old Testament. The window is larger than the western rose and contains proportionately more stone to glass; but it looks no heavier. The whole enormous structure rests upon the frail clerestory windows below it, but the lacelike tracery and the small trefoiled roses in the corners distribute the weight so perfectly that no sagging or cracking has appeared in seven centuries.

The southern rose, unfortunately, did not fare so well, perhaps because exposure to the sun weakened it more than the others, perhaps because normal maintenance was neglected on this side. At any rate, this rose began to buckle in the sixteenth century. An eighteenth-century reconstruction made matters worse, and the whole façade crumbled. In the nineteenth century Viollet-le-Duc decided that the trouble lay in the inadequate buttressing. He therefore reinforced the buttresses and rebuilt the entire wall, creating a new southern rose in the original style. Here is our chance to judge his merits as a restorer. The glass, predominantly red in keeping with tradition, is deceptively good. The expert may recognize it as nineteenth-century, but the overwhelmed lay observer is not likely to question its authenticity.

The stone tracery follows the same pattern as that of the other roses. It casts an interesting light on the reverse "progress" in architecture. For Viollet-le-Duc, with all the resources of nineteenth-century engineering science behind him, found it necessary to make his stone framework thicker and therefore somewhat clumsier than that of the medieval roses. Yet it is scarcely surprising that he could not compete with the thirteenth-century builders. For by the reign of Louis IX the new Gothic style had become the native language of France's architects. They were completely at home in it, had been working in the style for generations, son learning from father, apprentice from master, and had developed a boldness and assurance that enabled them to use stone almost as we use steel today. The passion for more and more light, ever leaner supports, had seized them all. Notre-Dame was brand-new, as cathedrals went, but to these thirteenth-century master builders it already looked antiquated, outmoded. And so, even before the structure was complete, they began modernizing it.

Around 1230 the original buttresses were replaced

Notre-Dame's flying buttresses arc effortlessly in space, creating a dramatic impact that tends to obscure their crucial structural role in counteracting the thrusts of the stone vaulting.
  Overleaf:
The multicolored panes of the rose window in the north transept (left) have illuminated the interior of Notre-Dame since the thirteenth century. The south rose (right) was completely rebuilt by Viollet-le-Duc in the nineteenth century. He reproduced the pink and crimson tones for which this window was always famed.

by the immense scapular arches that give Notre-Dame its characteristic appearance. Along with this operation, lateral chapels were installed along both sides of the nave to take advantage of the space between the upright buttresses. More light was sought by increasing the amount of glass in the clerestory. During the thirteenth century much of the wall between the buttresses was removed and the opening was almost entirely filled with glass: a procession of twin lancet windows each surmounted by a miniature rose. Shortly afterward, the thirteenth-century north and south roses, which had been about eighteen feet in diameter, were also removed. Because of the installation of the lateral chapels, the transept façades were no longer in line with the rest of the structure. New façades were now built and the present vast roses — perhaps twice the diameter of the old ones — were installed in the north and south façades. But the traditional color scheme was kept: the north rose predominantly blue, the south an exquisite pink developed especially in the Paris glass workshops.

Colored glass had become a decisive element of the new architecture. The row upon row of immense, multicolored windows glowing within the dusk of lofty vaults made these thirteenth-century cathedrals like no buildings known before or since. The Middle Ages loved glittering things, shiny materials, strong colors, as we may see by the vast stores of jeweled, enameled, gilded objects kept today in museums or church treasuries. Yet colored glass outdid all other works of art in brilliance. The great Norman-Sicilian churches sheathed their walls in mosaic. The Romanesque churches had been brightened with wall paintings. In

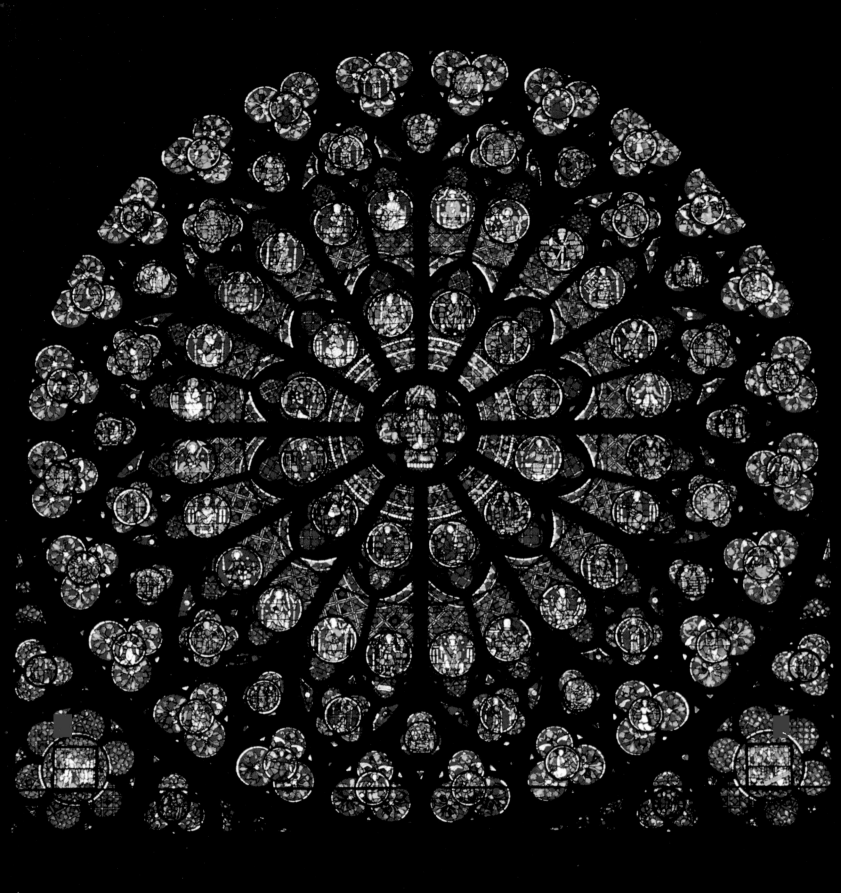

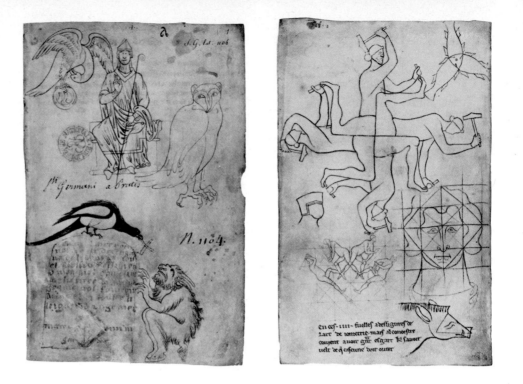

Those medieval artisans who used Villard de Honnecourt's Sketchbook *as a manual of instruction benefited from the master mason's wide-ranging curiosity. As these pages indicate, architectural renderings and geometrical devices were mingled haphazardly with drawings of human, bird, and animal figures.*

Italy, the possibilities of colored marble — white, green, pink, and black — gave churches a suave richness. But neither mosaic nor paintings nor marble could begin to equal the jeweled intensity of French stained glass. As sunlight struck the outside of the church from any direction or at any angle, the interior was emblazoned with shimmering veils of colored light. Even on dark days the windows fulfilled their expository function, telling stories from the Old and New Testaments, celebrating saints and heroes, and commemorating the benefactors of the church — those members of the royal house or of the local nobility and the prosperous guildsmen who contributed generously to the window fund.

With each of the many windows further subdivided into panels, medallions, circlets, and niches, the stained glass formed a vast picture book which could repay a lifetime of study. But seen all together, the glass was overwhelming. Thanks to it, the inside of the church became miraculous, supernatural, the nearest approximation man could make on earth of the divine city promised to the faithful after death. When stained-glass windows filled entire bays of the clerestory, the cathedrals of the thirteenth century proclaimed the underlying principles of creation and were a visible sign of the power and perfection of the Creator.

But even as we admire these miracles, we must remember that the windows were made by men. The skills involved had reached a high degree of development. Color was infused into the molten glass itself — cobalt yielding the vast range of blues; iron oxide with added gold, the ruby reds; silver oxides, the yellows. But the same additives would also, in lesser or greater proportions, at higher or lower temperatures, produce

purples or greens. The glassmakers commanded an astonishing number of these chemical tricks, secrets never written down and lost in subsequent centuries. Only in the middle of the nineteenth century, under the inspiration of Viollet-le-Duc, did the new scientific chemists laboriously analyze the composition of the glass and reconstruct the manner of its making. It then became evident that the very accidental nature of the process, the impurities of the ingredients, the lack of uniformity in each sheet of glass — which might be wavy, thick or thin, full of blisters and bubbles — had a great deal to do with the liveliness of the final effect. Glass made according to tested formulae and under controlled temperatures turned out to be a sorry imitation of the real thing. And then the lead armatures in which the panes of glass were set like so many jewels were also subject to infinite variations of coarseness and fineness, curvature or flatness. The soldering of the joints could be done neatly or roughly, and this too influenced the effect.

Before the final assembly, the colored glass was trimmed to size either by heating or cutting with a diamond, and it was then painted with the requisite details. Folds were painted into the garments, features upon faces, leaves upon trees. This was essentially an enameling process, utilizing a mixture of cullet (scrap glass), copper, and so-called Greek sapphire, dissolved in a vehicle of wine or urine. The second baking of the glass again produced surprises and idiosyncrasies, which became the despair of later scientific ages when they attempted to match the effects.

A small corps of artists was responsible for the designs. The stamp of certain masters can be seen in the

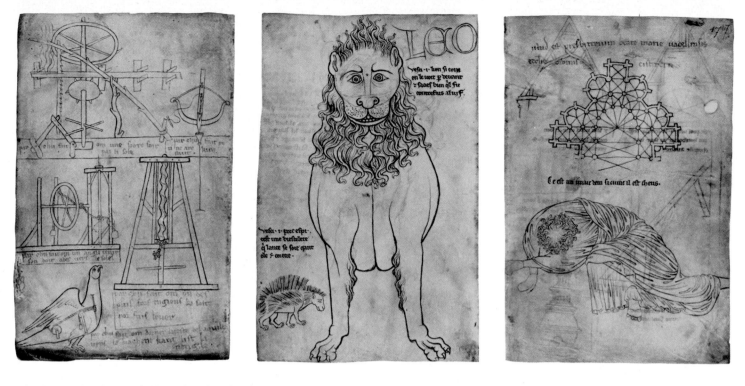

windows of a host of churches in the Île-de-France and beyond. Perhaps only a few workshops turned out all the stained glass. These shops had to be situated close to the raw materials — river sand was needed for the glass itself and forests to provide ample charcoal for the smelting. Chartres had the most notable workshop of all. Its glass was greatly in demand and exported as far as Canterbury in England. But there is reason to believe that the Chartres workshop employed Parisian artisans. For Paris, as the royal city, was the most active center of the decorative arts and attracted the finest craftsmen. Illuminators of manuscripts provided the king and court with psalters and books of hours; weavers of tapestries made vestments and altar cloths; goldsmiths and jewelers fashioned the reliquaries that were growing ever more elaborate.

It remained for the saintly King Louis — who washed the feet of beggars, submitted to frequent flagellation, attended mass twice daily, and thought he was doing his friends a favor by presenting them with hair shirts — to create the most elaborate reliquary of all. Louis heard that the Latin emperor in Constantinople was willing to sell the Crown of Thorns, the most precious relic in his possession. Mostly out of piety, but partly with the political aim of strengthening the Latin Empire, Louis agreed to the purchase — and raised part of the sum by a special tax on the Jews of Paris. But while the emperor was in France accepting King Louis's offer, his uncle in Constantinople had pawned the relic to a Venetian businessman. The Crown of Thorns, nevertheless, was redeemed for the vast sum of 177,300 livres and brought to Paris enclosed in three caskets like an Egyptian mummy, one of wood, one of silver,

and one of gold. With the whole population of Paris watching, the king and his brother, barefoot and in tunics, carried the precious burden into the cathedral of Notre-Dame.

The king wanted the relic near him, however, and soon he had it moved from Notre-Dame to the chapel of Saint Nicholas, within the palace. But when still more relics began arriving from Constantinople — a piece of the True Cross, the blade of the Holy Lance, the Holy Sponge — it became obvious that the old chapel was not splendid enough to house so many sacred objects. It was torn down, and within seven years — from 1241 to 1248 — the Sainte-Chapelle was built, its walls virtually all of blue and red glass. In the upper chapel Louis himself would frequently show the relics to the assembled notables.

Louis IX lavished donations upon the poor, upon the Hôtel Dieu, the chief hospital of Paris, and of course upon Notre-Dame de Paris. He managed to keep peace among his barons and with the sovereigns of Europe by sheer force of moral authority. But although his reign was peaceful at home, on the whole, his piety led him to embark upon terribly costly adventures *outre-mer*. In 1244, when he was in his thirtieth year, Louis fell so gravely ill that the ladies in attendance upon him disputed whether to draw the sheet over his face, for some thought him already dead. But he recovered, and as soon as he regained the power of speech he vowed that he would go on a Crusade. Horrified, his mother, Blanche, begged him not to go, and she even persuaded the pope to release the king from his vow. But Louis had rigid notions of honor. After lengthy preparations — which included transforming Aigues-

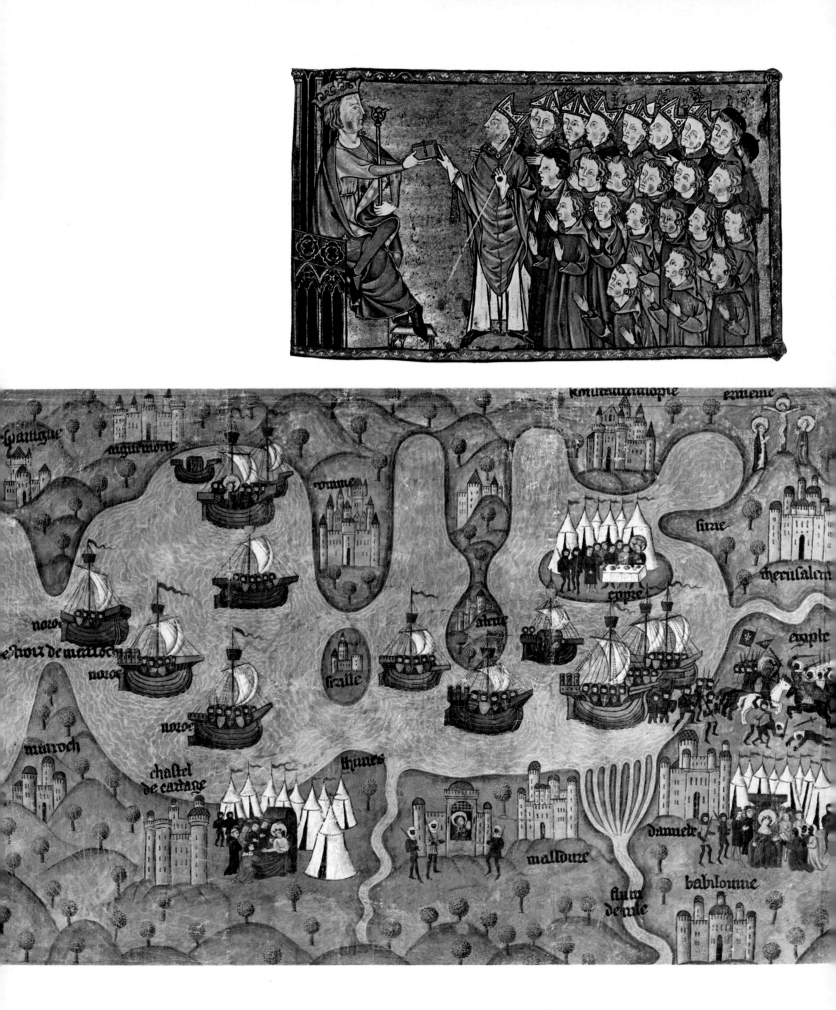

Mortes into a port from which the expedition could sail — Louis embarked in 1248.

The aim of the Seventh Crusade was the conquest of Egypt, regarded as the key to the Holy Land. All began auspiciously with the capture of Damietta, but plague and heat took their toll of the Crusaders as usual. The campaign ended with the capture of Louis himself. Threatened with torture by the Saracens, Louis calmly replied that he was their prisoner and they could do as they wished with him. The Sultan of Egypt, impressed by his demeanor, agreed to ransom him for a million gold bezants (500,000 livres). Louis consented to pay the sum for his men; since it was beneath a king's dignity to barter himself for coin, he would surrender Damietta in return for his own release. "When the sultan heard this he said: 'By my faith, this Frank is large-hearted not to have bargained over so great a sum! Now go and tell him that I will deduct a hundred thousand livres from the ransom.'"

Louis was large-hearted in almost all his dealings. While lingering in the Holy Land for four years after his release from captivity, he fortified the cities of Caesarea, Jaffa, and Sayette at his own expense. After his return to France, he voluntarily restored to Henry III of England some of the lands that Philip Augustus had won. He endowed abbeys, almshouses, and hospitals everywhere in France, built lodgings for the blind near Paris, and created the first home for women who were euphemistically called *Filles-Dieu*, in which he placed "a great multitude of women who, through poverty, had lapsed into the sin of incontinence."

In spite of his piety, Louis was by no means priest-ridden. He restrained the greed and ambition of his bishops and archbishops, often rebuffing them as his grandfather Philip Augustus had done. At one time the ecclesiastics complained that sentences of excommunication were no longer effective. They asked the king to employ his secular power to sustain these sentences. Louis promptly replied that he would gladly do so — if they gave him the right to judge whether the sentences were just. The churchmen answered that they could not allow this, since they alone were supposed to judge in spiritual matters. In that case, the king retorted, he could not help them. For if their sentences were unjust, as they sometimes proved to be (and he gave examples), he would be acting "contrary to God and against right."

The fact was that, in spite of his mild disposition, Louis succeeded in pushing forward the policy initiated by his great-grandfather Louis VII and so notably continued by Philip Augustus. That is, he extended the sway of the French monarchy to the point that it became more powerful than any single noble or coalition of vassals. Under Louis, France acquired a true central government and at least the beginnings of a real civil service. The king's court, the *curia regis,* began dividing into government departments; the king's household was developing into a bureaucracy. The importance of Paris increased as the government reached out to all corners of the land through the king's *enquêteurs,* emissaries from the court who traveled about the country acting on the complaints of citizens and inquiring into the conduct of local administrators. In effect, Louis was reinstating in France the system of *missi dominici* that had held Charlemagne's empire together more than four centuries earlier.

In a lintel from the north façade (near right), the Virgin flees Egypt on a donkey. Her coronation scene appears in the tympanum of the Red Portal (far right). And within the cathedral (center), a graceful and ethereal Mary holds the Infant in her arms.

One of the most signal developments of the age of Saint Louis was an inadvertent by-product of his character and his rule. This was the rise of that complex code of behavior known as chivalry. The ideal of the courteous knight, protector of widows and orphans, defender of God and his liege lord, a man skilled in song and verse, adept at games and storytelling, consumed with passion for a lady he could never hope to possess — this ideal knight never existed outside the romances. Nevertheless, such notions made their way from Languedoc to northern France along with returning soldiers and impoverished troubadours. Saint Louis himself, though guilty of discourtesies toward his wife, was widely regarded as the paragon of the knightly ideal. Despite his concern for the poor, he maintained a proper princely state at table and in the appurtenances of his court. He was gentle with his subjects, honorable in his dealings with friend and foe alike, and would not break his plighted word even when it had been given to an "enemy of God." His example, and the long period of domestic peace during his reign, fostered the social arts that were bound up with the notion of chivalry.

Whether the actual status of women improved under the influence of chivalry is a much-debated question. As in earlier, ruder times, heiresses continued to be virtually bought and sold for economic reasons. But women often governed feudal estates while the men were away on the Crusades; and such strong women as Blanche of Castile and Louis's queen, Marguerite of Provence, must have provided an example to the less fortunate members of their sex. And there seems little doubt that the fervent devotion to the Virgin Mary reflected at least some changes in the social structure. For at the same time Mary began to be adored like a human as well as a divine queen.

The new humanization of the Virgin is expressed in the charming statue of her that stands on the pier of the portal in the northern façade. Here the treatment is far more realistic than the august, hieratic Mary of the western façade. The Queen of Heaven stands leaning slightly to the right, looking at her son (the statue of the infant Jesus has not survived) with a singularly human tenderness. In the lintel of the same portal there is another Virgin Mary, equally humanized. The subject is the Nativity; ox and ass warm the Babe with their breath. Mary lies raised on one elbow, head cupped in her hand, wearing the dreamy expression of any mother meditating on her son's future.

There are still more Marys on the portal of the north façade. In the second tier of the tympanum the Heavenly Queen appears at last, the Mary of miracles, interceding for the deacon Theophilus, who has sold his soul to the devil in return for worldly goods and honors. Stricken by remorse and terror, Theophilus prays fervently to the Virgin, whereupon she snatches from Satan the pact signed in blood.

Yet another Virgin may be seen over the small door that enters the third bay of the choir, a short distance farther down the rue du Cloître Notre-Dame. Known as the Red Portal, from its painted doors, it provided a convenient entrance from the cloister for members of the chapter. In the tympanum an angel is placing a crown upon Mary's head, while Jesus blesses his mother; this is a repetition of the scene on the western façade. But our interest focuses upon the two kneeling

figures who represent the donors of the Red Portal: Louis IX and Queen Marguerite.

These statues may have been carved long before they were placed above the door some time between 1265 and 1267. For they show a youthful and handsome royal pair, when in fact Louis was by this time past fifty and nearing the end of his life. In 1270, so weak he could neither walk nor ride, he embarked on a new Crusade, the Eighth Crusade. As on the Seventh Crusade, he let himself be diverted from the true object: the Holy City. His brother, Charles of Anjou, persuaded him to attack Tunis. Summer heat and plague destroyed his army, and Louis himself died on August 25, 1270. His bones, returned to France, were carried to Notre-Dame in solemn procession and then buried at Saint-Denis.

Some of Louis's most loyal vassals did not accompany him on that last Crusade. A new spirit was in the air, an antagonism toward the Church, which had urged men on to wasteful foreign adventures or subverted the very meaning of crusading by "commuting" the crusaders' vows to allow them to attack fellow-Christians. Popular disgust with the futility of the cause to which Louis had sacrificed his riches and his health was vividly expressed by one of the foremost writers of the age, the trouvère Rutebeuf. A gifted forerunner of François Villon, Rutebeuf was essentially a poet of the people. He did not mince words in his attacks on the friars or in his condemnation of crusading:

> Am I to leave my wife and children, all my goods and inheritance, to go and conquer a foreign land which will give me nothing in return? I can worship God

just as well in Paris as in Jerusalem. . . . All you people, great and small, who go on pilgrimage to the Promised Land, ought to become very holy there; so how does it happen that the ones who come back are mostly bandits?

Twenty-one years after the death of King Louis IX, the last Christian possession in Palestine was lost. The great age of the Crusades was over, and the age of the Church's hegemony was fast fading. At the beginning of the thirteenth century Pope Innocent III had wielded a virtual dictatorship over the secular rulers of Europe. During the sixty years after Innocent's death the Church seemed to be consolidating its gains on all fronts. The Inquisition had wiped out heresy; the new Dominican and Franciscan orders exercised close control over dangerous thinking in theology. Thomas Aquinas and the other great scholastics, many of them associated with the University of Paris, diverted the potentially dangerous philosophy of Aristotle and the new trend toward scientific thinking into channels of orthodoxy. The Church had demonstrated its capacity to collect vast sums for buildings, for Crusades, for an enormous administrative apparatus, and for wars conducted by the papacy itself. All over Europe its possessions, tithes, and exactions had increased enormously.

But in the very process of acquiring such power the Church set in motion countervailing forces, both within itself and among the peoples it dominated. A growing middle class with a rising sense of national consciousness resented what it regarded as taxation for the benefit of a foreign power, with the ensuing drain of capital toward Rome. The feudal nobility had largely infiltrated the higher ranks of the clergy and had brought with it into the Church its family concerns and secular habits. The kings, who on the whole had successfully established central governments that overrode provincial interests — this was especially true for France and England — would no longer brook interference in domestic affairs from churchmen at home or popes in Rome.

The brewing conflict came to a head at the beginning of the fourteenth century, during the reigns of Philip the Fair in France and Edward I in England. Both monarchs needed money for their wars against each other; both resorted to taxation of the Church and confiscation of the funds and property of monastic orders. When Pope Boniface VIII protested and restated the ancient papal claims to supremacy over secular rulers, Philip the Fair ordered him arrested. The physical attack on the pope in his palace at Anagni in central Italy horrified Europe — and also marked a break in the long tradition of cordial relations between France and the papacy. The aging pontiff was soon released, but the shock brought him to his grave.

In the confused maneuverings that followed Boniface's death and the brief reign of an interim pope, Philip the Fair succeeded in dominating the College of Cardinals. A French archbishop was elected and took office as Clement V in 1305, but he did not dare to proceed to Rome. He established his curia at Avignon — and thus began what was later called the Babylonian Captivity of the Church.

Avignon was technically situated in the Holy Roman Empire, but French language, culture, and influence prevailed there, and for the next seventy years the papacy was largely subservient to the rulers of France. In Avignon, to be sure, the popes were safe from the unpredictable mobs and the warring noble families of Rome. But Avignon lacked the aura of imperial authority that Rome had retained in spite of all the city's vicissitudes through the centuries. Without Rome, the Roman Church could not securely hold the loyalty and love of Europe's believers. Ultimately, the fabric of the entire Church was weakened.

For the time being, however, religious life turned inward, toward the national churches. In Paris, efforts were made to finish the remodeling of the cathedral, in spite of Philip the Fair's foreign wars, debasement of the currency, and heavy taxation of the clergy. Chapels were added to the choir of Notre-Dame by Pierre de Chelles and by Jean Ravy, who succeeded him in 1318. These two great architects also provided the apse with additional support by completing the flying buttresses that Pierre de Montereau had begun during the lifetime of Louis IX. Built of the hardest stone, leaping a full fifty feet in a single flight over the twin ambulatories to the top of the apse wall, these buttresses are truly wonderful achievements. The only one of the older flying buttresses remaining, the double-arched one nearest to the northern transept, emphasizes the grace and strength of the fourteenth-century work. The newer architects respected the work of their predecessors; they changed and supplemented it, but they did not tamper with its spirit.

Long before it was completed — in the first third of the fourteenth century — the cathedral of Notre-Dame de Paris had been playing a central role in the daily life of the city. Now, with its new wealth of chapels,

between fifty and a hundred masses a day could be said beneath its vaults. For there was a tremendous concentration of clerics living in the immediate vicinity of the cathedral, and many of them owed their "livings" — in the sense of prebends — to endowments for perpetual masses that went back centuries. Some of these clerics were housed in the sumptuous episcopal palace on the south side of the cathedral, some in the chapter's cloister and the various buildings for the church's administrative offices. In addition, the Île de la Cité saw a constant flow of visiting ecclesiastics from all over France, for priests considered it an honor to officiate in the great cathedral.

Paris was, in fact, assuming the character of a religious as well as a secular capital. In keeping with the growing national spirit — "nationalism" would be a misleading word for the attitudes of the fourteenth century — the French Church tended to augment its own organization. Frequent synods were held in Paris, and the meeting hall was Notre-Dame. There the assembled prelates deliberated on the pressing problems of the faith. They drew up edicts on the life of the clergy, the rules of excommunication, the maintenance of churches and cemeteries, the liturgy, and the administration of the sacraments. In ecclesiastical policy, Paris became the second capital of Christendom, and Notre-Dame often seemed more important than the Palace of the Popes at Avignon as an architectural symbol of authority.

And yet, for all the white- and red-robed prelates who bustled through the choir, Notre-Dame was very much the people's church. The pilgrimages that had been encouraged while it was still abuilding, to raise money,

persisted into later centuries. The faithful who lived in or around Paris — and this meant one-tenth the population of France — made a custom of paying an annual visit to Paris's church of Our Lady. The University of Paris, by then an institution a century old, with its own classrooms, residences, and government, did not forget its origins in the cathedral's theological schools. Once a year, students and masters paid a formal visit to the church on the Île de la Cité. Individual students came far more often to pray in the cathedral for success in their examinations and to leave testimonials to Mary when she helped them to pass. The sick came to pray for cures, and the prostitutes of the city — notably partial to Notre-Dame — flocked there, especially on Saturdays, to offer candles to the Virgin.

Innumerable processions began and ended at Notre-Dame. In times of public danger — when the Seine rose rapidly and flood threatened, during prolonged droughts, and during the pestilences that periodically ravaged city, country, and continent throughout so much of the fourteenth century — the costly shrines and reliquaries of crystal, gold, ivory, and enamel were brought out of the cathedral treasury. Chanting crowds followed the relics up and down the streets of Paris and then returned to Notre-Dame for further ceremonies.

Above all, throughout much of the fourteenth and fifteenth centuries, the people knelt countless times in Notre-Dame to pray for the success of the king's arms over the English enemy. For France and England were embroiled in that intolerable, interminable struggle that had become more a way of life than an armed conflict: the Hundred Years' War.

V

On November 9, 1422, a towering catafalque, tall as a man, with a canopy of cloth of gold on a vermilion ground and a blue border sown with gold fleurs-de-lis and rich embroidery, was carried across the Pont Notre-Dame and down the rue de la Juiverie to the cathedral of Notre-Dame. On the catafalque lay the effigy of a king, dressed in a mantle of cloth of gold trimmed with ermine and sable, the white-gloved hands holding a scepter and the rod of justice, a silver and gold crown upon the head. The people lined the streets or stood at their windows, men and women lamenting. All shops were closed, for the whole of Paris was in mourning.

Preceded by twenty-four heralds, the funeral procession passed with majestic deliberation through the streets. Behind the heralds came two hundred representatives of the poor of Paris, then the friars of the mendicant orders, the clergy of the collegiate churches, the canons of Notre-Dame and Sainte-Chapelle. All the latter walked in the right file; on the left came the students and faculty of the University of Paris. Then came the higher clergy, in black copes and white miters: the Bishop of Beauvais, the Bishop of Chartres, the abbots of Saint-Denis and Saint-Germain-des-Prés, and many others. The dignitaries of the state followed the clergy: the Provost of Paris bearing his mace, the king's chamberlains and valets, the equerries who took turns carrying the enormously heavy catafalque, the presidents of the Parlement of Paris.

Behind the bier, walking by himself in black mantle and cocked hat, came the man who had stage-managed this remarkably solemn funeral, and who more than all those other grave gentlemen represented the real

power in Paris and much of France. The people stared coldly at him, for he was an Englishman: John of Lancaster, Duke of Bedford; third son of King Henry IV of England and brother of Henry V of England, who had died three months previously; Protector and Defender of the Realm; Regent of France; and uncle to the newly crowned King of England, the infant Henry VI, who was now heir to the throne of France as well.

A dreary century of wasting struggles between England and France, of civil wars in both countries, and economic distress and recurrent plagues, had brought the two exhausted nations to this temporary union. English possession of Aquitaine and claims to Normandy, the English alliance with Flanders and the French alliance with Scotland, the intermittent naval war between French and English shipmasters — these issues provided the fuel that kept the interminable war smoldering when it was not flaming. English dynastic claims to the throne of France, stemming from marital alliances that had been arranged in order to keep the peace, offered a pretext for reviving hostilities whenever the occasion seemed favorable to either side.

At Crécy in 1346 and at Poitiers a decade later, English arms had defeated the French with terrible efficiency. England won the battles, but the victors could not hold the territory of France. In the middle of the fourteenth century the Black Death ravaged both countries. And along with the ghastly mortality — in some cities a third and more of the population died — the plague brought a sense of doom and hopelessness. Revivalist religious fervor alternated with wild superstition. The behavior of the clergy (who often, from fear of contagion, refused victims of the disease the last

Invaded Nation, Divided Faith

rites) brought the Church into disrepute. New heretical movements gathered force. The frantic search for some explanation nourished that belief in witchcraft and those actual experiments in Satanism which fascinated and horrified Europe for centuries afterward. Tremendous economic and social changes followed as population declined, labor grew scarce, and the fields went untilled. But in the lulls between resurgences of the Black Death, which became endemic after 1350, the sporadic war between England and France went on and on.

In 1415 there seemed at last some prospect that the war would end, and end in England's favor. At Agincourt an army of hungry, wet, and tired Englishmen, led by King Henry V in person met fresh French troops in a narrow defile. Though outnumbered three to one, the English slaughtered some five thousand of the chivalry of France, who were trapped by the weight of their armor, and the stupidity of their military tactics. Thereafter, the English reconquered Normandy — battering down the walls of the cities with their new-fangled artillery — and overran most of France north of the Loire. By the treaty of Troyes Henry V was recognized as heir to the French throne, and to strengthen his claim he married Catherine, the daughter of mad King Charles VI of France. Henry's death in 1422, so shortly afterward followed by that of King Charles, left the infant Henry VI to inherit both thrones.

Charles, although insane for the greater part of his reign, had been king for forty-two years. When he died, one text tells us, "there were few who remembered how in times gone by kings of France had been borne to their graves, in what order the people should be ranged, each according to his estate, for the occasion was rare and nothing was committed to writing." That, at least, was the pretext for waiting nearly three weeks between the king's death and the actual funeral; and the long delay, in turn, made it essential to place an effigy rather than the king's body upon the catafalque. But in truth the court was paralyzed; nothing could be done until the Duke of Bedford returned from Rouen, where he was staying. Bedford promptly ended all discussions. The funeral of his brother was so recent that he had the course of such ceremonies clearly in mind, and he promptly dictated the form of the arrangements.

As the cortege approached Notre-Dame, all could see the two great banners with the royal arms that hung above the portals on the outside. Inside, the nave, choir, and all the pillars were covered from top to bottom with drapes stamped with fleurs-de-lis. The lower level was lighted by two rows of torches, the gallery by a vast array of candles whose weight — one pound each — the chroniclers dutifully noted.

A chapel had been constructed in the choir, the black hangings again bearing the royal arms. In each corner of the chapel stood an enormous, twenty-five-pound candle. The Duke of Bedford took the foremost seat in the choir, behind the statue of Our Lady. The chamberlains and a contingent of the members of Parlement sat on the same side. Near the altar were the bishops of Thérouanne and Chartres, the Rector of the University, and the canons. Vigils were sung, nine psalms and nine lessons, and then the company departed. At eight the following morning a requiem mass was celebrated, and then the whole funeral pro-

cession formed anew to follow the catafalque to Saint-Denis, where the actual body of Charles VI would be buried in its lead casket. Many of those who watched the procession must have been thinking sorrowfully that from now on the English House of Lancaster would sit on the throne of France.

Such might have been the case — and who can imagine what course the history of Europe might have taken — had it not been for the brief appearance of one of the most remarkable phenomena of the waning Middle Ages. In a meteoric career that lasted only two years a fervent seventeen-year-old girl from the little town of Domrémy revived the fading fortunes of the French monarchy and created the precondition for an independent and united France.

By his skillful conduct of affairs Bedford gradually reduced French hostility to the English occupation. As regent for Henry VI, Bedford governed his half of France with diplomacy and justice, observing local customs, and keeping those French officials who were willing to serve him. He expanded his domain toward the south, which was still controlled by the Dauphin Charles. Many Frenchmen were waiting impatiently for the as yet uncrowned Charles VII to claim his inheritance. But the shambling, knock-kneed "King of Bourges," as he was called — a man ashamed of his physical deficiencies, doubtful that he was a true son of the king, and too fearful to ride a horse across a bridge — made no move to oppose the English.

At this low ebb in the fortunes of France, the Maid of Lorraine emerged from her obscure country village. It is curious to reflect that Joan of Arc, who was to become the very symbol of French patriotism, was a foreigner — for Lorraine was not then a part of France. She spoke *patois* most of the time, although she could manage correct and even eloquent French when she wished, for she was not a simple shepherdess but the daughter of a well-to-do farmer. But she and her fellow villagers believed in the cause of France and felt acute hostility toward the Burgundian allies of the English just across the River Meuse from Domrémy. Joan's hatred for the English sprang from more than romantic sympathy for poor Charles VII. English soldiers had burned her village, although her father's house, standing in the shadow of the church, was unharmed.

The miracle Joan wrought in the spirit of France, by her faith in her "voices," by her indomitable example on the battlefield, and by her martyr's death, would seem pure legend were it not amply attested to by historical documents. Joan inspired the dauphin by convincing him that he was not a bastard; she inspired the soldiers by her religious fervor combined with passionate nationalism; and she inspired the populace because she was the incarnation of their natural dislike for the foreigner. She had learned that Saint Remy, patron saint of her village church, had crowned Clovis the first King of France, and that this was the reason Reims was so closely associated with the royal line. And so, after her military victories, she dragged a reluctant Charles VII to his coronation at Reims in 1429. The king's anointment there made him legitimate in her eyes — and the common people of France held the same belief. After that coronation, the position of Charles VII was assured — and he himself lost his doubts about his own royalty.

Bedford tried to counter the prestige Charles had

won by arranging a coronation of his own. He brought the young Henry VI to Paris, but he did not dare proceed with his plan until after Joan of Arc had been captured at Compiègne. Then, after Joan had been brutally disposed of, Bedford had Henry VI crowned in Notre-Dame de Paris on December 16, 1431. There was no tradition for such crownings at Paris, and nearly four hundred years were to pass before there was another: the coronation of Napoleon as emperor. And both were the coronations of usurpers who did not reign for long. Notre-Dame was the heart of France in other respects, but the French preferred to make their kings elsewhere. Even the ceremony for Henry VI's coronation "lacked dignity," we are told.

Joan had been captured by the Burgundians, but she was turned over to the English, who determined to ruin her character. With the aid of a collaborationist French clergy, and with what seems like the passive complicity of Charles VII, they convicted her of witchcraft and heresy, and Joan was burned at the stake. Charles displayed little gratitude for her services to him; he did nothing to ransom her or to save her from her fate. Apparently Joan made Charles uncomfortable; her whole personality reminded him of the deficiencies he had not yet overcome in those years of early, unwonted, and almost unwanted victories.

But then, ingratitude was to be the pattern of Charles VII's life. He was later called Charles the Well-Served, because so many of his successes could be attributed to his good counselors. One of these was another young girl, Agnès Sorel, whom Charles evidently found more to his liking than Joan because he could take her to his bed.

Charles dubbed Agnès "Madame de Beauté" — and she seems to have deserved the title. It is a measure of changing moralities after the Black Death that she became the first officially acknowledged royal mistress at a French court — first in a long and distinguished line. A level-headed, deeply religious young woman, concerned for the condition of the poor, she gave Charles good advice and reinforced his self-esteem. But her time at his side was short; his ardor cooled after a while and he failed to protect her against the intrigues of the court, just as he had failed to protect Joan. She died young, probably of poison.

It was Agnès Sorel, apparently, who persuaded Charles to advance the career of Jacques Coeur, one of the greatest of early medieval capitalists, who for a time put the finances and administration of France on a sound basis. As master of the mint Coeur reformed the debased French currency. As a merchant, he made an enormous fortune by establishing flourishing trade relations between France and the Near East. As a diplomat, he helped put an end to a papal schism. As a general, he both financed and helped direct Charles's successful war to drive the English from northern France. With his aid, Paris was taken, and on April 13, 1436, the great bells of Notre-Dame clanged to announce the entry of French troops into the city. Thereafter, a Te Deum was sung in Notre-Dame on every first Friday after Easter for 346 years, to celebrate the deliverance of the capital from the English occupation.

Shortly after the death of his mistress, Charles VII turned against his eminent adviser. Though there was no shadow of evidence or motive for such a crime, Jacques Coeur was accused of poisoning Agnès Sorel.

Coeur's enemies or debtors were appointed his judges; he was found guilty, all his wealth was confiscated, and in addition he was fined an enormous sum. After several years of imprisonment, he escaped to Rome, where he was warmly received at the papal court and appointed captain of an expedition against the Turks. But his privations and disappointment had been too much for him; he died in 1456, soon after beginning his second career.

Charles VII survived his great minister by only five years. But if the king's conduct toward Agnès Sorel and Jacques Coeur was singularly ignoble, Charles revealed a better side to his character when he initiated the rehabilitation trial of Joan of Arc. The Bishop of Paris, Guillaume Chantier, presided over this trial, whose sessions were held in the episcopal palace, by then larger and more magnificent than Maurice de Sully's original structure. Joan's mother figured officially as the plaintiff; many witnesses who had known and fought beside Joan of Arc gave vivid testimony; and in 1456 the condemnation of 1431 was declared null and void.

The movement Joan began had established France. By the time Charles died in 1461, nothing remained of the English holdings in France but the port of Calais. There was an underlying irony in the whole career of this weakling king who succeeded, far better than his dashing and bellicose predecessors, in driving the English from the soil of France. And the irony persisted even in his burial. Again forty years had passed between the deaths of kings, but this time good records had been kept. The obsequies for Charles VII followed in the main the pattern that had been established for the funeral of Charles VI. Once more Notre-Dame was draped in hangings stamped with fleurs-de-lis, such as had been ordered by the lifelong enemy of both Charleses, the Duke of Bedford.

During the lifetime of Charles VII the word Gothic first appears in the sense of something contemptible — not, however, in France, but in Italy. The universal genius Leon Battista Alberti, poet, painter, musician, architect, and writer on architecture, used the term in the sense of "rustic" or "boorish." Alberti also commented that the pointed arch did not exist in classical antiquity — which for a man of his time and temper was equivalent to saying that it ought not to exist at all.

Alberti was expressing a new spirit, a new fascination with the vestiges, the forms, the languages, and the literatures of classical antiquity. All that had been achieved in the thousand years between A.D. 410 — when Alaric's Goths sacked Rome — and "modern" times seemed an era of darkness perhaps briefly illuminated by the age of Charlemagne. Writers had employed a "barbarous" Latin so debased from the style of Cicero that a man of taste ought not to sully his mind with reading it. Sculptors had forgotten the beautiful forms of classical statuary and created stiff, unnatural poses or horrid, misshapen creatures like the ugly gargoyles on cathedrals. Architects had lost touch with rounded forms and the harmonious geometrical proportions of classical buildings. Infected by the barbarian tastes of the Gothic conquerors of Rome, they had gone in for fantastic turrets and spires, for all kinds of protuberances and excrescences. Thinkers had indulged in fruitless scholastic speculations on the nature of God and the number of the canonical virtues instead

of studying the operations of Nature. True wisdom had once been possessed by the Greeks, Chaldeans, Hebrews, Egyptians, and Romans; it had been lost during the long dark age in between, but men could still recover it if they would make the effort.

The new Humanists, as they called themselves, began an impassioned hunt for lost works of the ancient artists, sages, and poets. Financed by the merchant princes and bankers of the burgeoning Italian city-states, they ransacked the monasteries of Europe for manuscripts, and in this way they recovered for posterity many of the priceless works of the ancient world.

The recently invented art of printing helped them to spread their learning far and wide. Within fifty years of the publication of the first printed books in the middle of the fifteenth century, an estimated 20,000,000 copies of perhaps 40,000 different books had been printed. Erasmus of Rotterdam, the intellectual leader of the Humanists, for a time earned his livelihood as a printer's proofreader and editor. He preferred the freedom of hard work to the tempting offer of King Francis I of France, who was willing to pay Erasmus an enormous salary if he would assume direction of the newly founded Royal College of France.

Friend of kings and popes, courted by all the best minds of Europe, Erasmus possessed in the sixteenth century the moral and intellectual authority that Saint Bernard had enjoyed in the twelfth. And like Saint Bernard, he tried to reform the Church from within. Although he remained a loyal if scarcely ardent Catholic, his attacks on the clergy contributed to the atmosphere in which Protestantism sprang into being and throve. His editions of the Church Fathers, and

his publication of a New Testament in the original Greek, provided the arsenal from which Martin Luther and his fellow reformers drew their weapons when they launched a frontal attack on the Roman Church.

Printing, as well as the venality of the sixteenth-century popes, had contributed largely to the scandalous increase in the sale of indulgences that Martin Luther denounced. Among the first products from Gutenberg's press had been beautifully printed indulgences; and by the first quarter of the sixteenth century these certifications for remission of sins were being turned out by the millions. Nor should we forget, since we are concerned here with the history of a cathedral, that the indulgence which brought on Luther's first dramatic act of rebellion had been issued to finance the building of Saint Peter's in Rome. This was the indulgence being distributed by Friar Tetzel when Luther challenged the whole practice by posting his Ninety-five Theses on the door of the church at Wittenberg.

The Reformation thus initiated was carried into France by the disciples of John Calvin, a former student at the Royal College. Calvin was French by birth, austerely logical by predilection, severe and moralistic because deeply convinced of man's corruptness and God's goodness. He was an effective speaker and gifted organizer, and his doctrines of predestination and lay control of the church spread rapidly among Frenchmen. The Huguenots, as the French Calvinists were called — presumably from the Swiss word *Eidgenossen,* or confederates — flourished especially in the old home of the Catharist heresy, the south of France. There the ancient antagonism to the Catholic Church had con-

Religious ferment was rampant on the Continent during the sixteenth century. In 1517 the German monk Martin Luther — seen preaching at far left — inaugurated the Reformation by posting his Ninety-five Theses condemning papal corruption. His influence spread rapidly, inspiring scenes such as the one at left in which rioters topple sacred images from a church. In England, the leader of the break with Catholicism was the king himself, Henry VIII. In the painting below, Henry rides to the Field of the Cloth of Gold, where he and Francis I of France feted one another, momentarily reviving more carefree days.

tinued to smolder like an underground fire for three centuries. It erupted violently and unpredictably.

Whenever Huguenots seized control of a town, they would drive out the bishop and strip the cathedral of its paintings and sculptures. During the disorders in Paris after the death of Francis I, they twice broke into the cathedral of Notre-Dame, smashed parts of the sanctuary screen, and knocked down the statue of the Virgin. But Paris remained resolutely Catholic throughout the disruptions of the civil and religious wars; each time the Virgin was devoutly replaced and repairs were begun on the screen.

Francis had brought the Renaissance to France; he had Leonardo da Vinci and Benvenuto Cellini in his employ for a while and tried to live with the magnificence of Italian Renaissance princes. The famous Field of the Cloth of Gold, where he and Henry VIII entertained one another and their enormous followings with tournaments and spectacles that went on for three weeks, accomplished nothing politically but provided matter for gossip for a whole generation — and cost a fortune. Francis ran through money so fast that one contemporary remarked: "He is well named after Saint Francis because he has holes in his hands."

But Francis I also left a dire heritage of hatred by his slaughter of the Vaudois Protestants at the end of his reign. And he had married his son, Henry II, to Catherine de Médicis, whose attempts to find a middle course between the struggling religious and political parties of France ended with her becoming one of the most execrated women in the country's history. Of the sons she bore Henry, three weaklings survived for a time, Francis II, Charles IX, and Henry III. During

thirty years, while each lived out his short life and reign, Catherine tried vainly to master by intrigue the tottering monarchy of a distracted realm.

It was an age of strong women who sought with varying success to rule through men. In Paris, and indeed in Notre-Dame, began the tragic career of Mary Stuart, Queen of Scots. Mary was not yet sixteen; she had been betrothed to the Dauphin Francis for ten years and had been raised in France by the family of her uncle, the powerful Duke of Guise, the great chief of the Catholic party. On April 24, 1558, the wedding of Mary and Francis was celebrated in Notre-Dame with all the éclat due to such a great union. The French regarded Mary Stuart as heiress to the throne of England as well as Scotland, for Catholics considered Elizabeth illegitimate.

In keeping with the taste of the time, what was by then regarded as a gloomy old Gothic cathedral — Notre-Dame had reached the venerable age of four hundred years — was decorated *à l'antique,* in a Renaissance conception of the splendors of imperial Rome. The society reporters of the time tell us that the Duke of Guise arrived in grand style, followed by musicians. Then came a hundred Gentlemen of the King's Household, followed by the royal princes "so richly adorned and dressed that it was a marvelous thing." The Queen of Scots wore a dress white as lilies, "so richly and sumptuously made that it would be impossible to describe." Her necklace of precious stones was as dazzling as her golden crown, set with pearls, diamonds, rubies, sapphires, and emeralds, with an enormous carbuncle in the center.

As King Henry II and the Bishop of Paris entered

the cathedral, the heralds cried three times: "Largesse!" They began scattering gold and silver coins among the crowd, evoking such a tumult that it sounded like thunder. King Henry, Queen Catherine de Médicis, the dauphin, and Mary Stuart took their places under a canopy of cloth of gold, and when they knelt their knees rested on cushions covered with the same material. The Cardinal de Bourbon pronounced the nuptials, and the Bishop of Paris celebrated the mass.

The next year the Queen of Scots had become Queen of France, for Henry II was killed in a tournament, and young Francis succeeded him. Francis II doted on his beautiful wife, and during his brief reign the Guises worked their will in France. At the castle of Amboise, where Leonardo da Vinci had died, Francis and Mary sat in the royal garden overlooking the Loire watching while some twelve hundred Huguenots were led to the scaffold for participation in a plot to undermine the power of the Guises. In vain the queen mother urged moderation. Francis would listen only to Mary, and young Queen Mary was in all things obedient to her uncle, the Duke of Guise.

Only another year passed before Notre-Dame was once more draped, this time entirely in black, for the impressive funeral of Francis II. Nine months later his widowed queen, as resolute as she was beautiful, sailed for Scotland to claim her inheritance. For the next twenty-five years, until she too ended on the scaffold, her tangled loves and intrigues helped shape the history of Scotland and England, and often influenced the politics of France. French Catholics under the Duke of Guise supported her, while the French Huguenots frequently turned to Queen Elizabeth for aid during the

many crises of the bitter religious wars in France.

Throughout those years of strife, while Elizabeth reigned in England and Mary spent much of her life a helpless captive, Catherine de Médicis attempted to govern France. Although a Catholic too, she nevertheless wanted to fend off the domination of the Guises, and so she strove to hold the balance between Huguenots and Catholics. But the factional passions were too strong for her diplomacy, and when she saw her second son, Charles IX, falling under the influence of the Huguenot Gaspard de Coligny, she repented her policy of conciliation. After Charles insisted on the marriage of his sister Marguerite to Henry of Bourbon, King of Navarre, one of the chiefs of the Huguenot party, Catherine conceived the horrible act of treachery with which her name will be forever associated.

Thousands of Huguenots had come to Paris for the wedding, and feeling was running high among the Catholics of the capital. A dais was erected on the parvis of Notre-Dame, and there the marriage ceremony was performed. Then Henry entered the cathedral with his bride, but before mass began he conspicuously withdrew to the garden of the bishop's palace. Three days of balls and tournaments followed to celebrate this first royal "mixed marriage," which was intended to unite Huguenots and Catholics.

Within a week of the wedding, Catherine had persuaded her son that a great Huguenot conspiracy was brewing and that if the Huguenots were not wiped out the cause of Catholicism in France would be lost. Unwillingly, so it is said, Charles consented to the demands of his mother and the Guises. At two o'clock in the morning on Sunday, Saint Bartholomew's Day —

At the instigation of the Catholic queen mother, Catherine de Medicis, Huguenots throughout France were slaughtered in an unprecedented massacre that began in Paris on Saint Bartholomew's Day, August 24, 1572. The helpless townspeople in the painting below die in agonized torment as royal soldiers obey their orders with a vengeance. The engraving at right depicts Henry of Navarre's triumphal entrance into Paris in 1594. Astride his horse, and surrounded by armored attendants, Henry proceeds toward the parvis of Notre-Dame.

August 24, 1572 — the dreadful work was begun.

Admiral Coligny, the gallant soldier who had led the Protestant forces to victory in many campaigns, was the first victim. A man of moderation and courage, he had stayed in Paris in spite of many warnings and had remained even after he was wounded in the arm by a would-be assassin. This time the assassins did not fail. The admiral was stabbed by a German in the employ of the Guises, and his body was thrown out the window. The Duke of Guise, who blamed the admiral for the assassination of his father by a Huguenot nine years before, wiped the blood from the face, looked at it, and said: "It is he! Courage, soldiers! We have begun well; now for the others. The king commands it." And to the tolling of the bells of Paris, the savage massacre commenced.

The Duke of Guise's soldiers, the royal Swiss guards, and the populace of Paris, mercilessly hunted down Huguenots. Homes and inns where "heretics" were staying had already been marked, and an incredible butchery then ensued. The gates of the city were closed, and for two days men, women, and children were slaughtered. The gravediggers of Paris were afterward paid for burying some 1,100 corpses in a single week; and in addition thousands of other bodies were thrown into the Seine. Only the Prince of Condé and Henry of Navarre were spared, and even they had to go through a pretense of changing their religion.

The massacre in Paris was repeated throughout the provinces of France. How many thousands of Huguenots were killed will never be known. Perhaps even more appalling than the killings was the orgy of congratulation in which Catholic Europe indulged. The horrors of Saint Bartholomew's Day and the three weeks of carnage that followed were justified on the grounds that France had been saved from Huguenot rebellion. The Catholic princes of Europe hastened to send their felicitations to Catherine de Médicis. In Rome a medal was struck to commemorate the *Ugonnotorum strages,* the massacre of the Huguenots.

In fact, the atrocity stimulated Huguenot resistance. Civil war erupted once more, and France was drowned in blood. The brutality of the struggle strengthened the party of the *politiques,* men who would nowadays be called a Third Force. The *politiques* held that France had suffered enough from religious conflict, that the state would have to hold the balance between the two parties. Henry of Navarre, who had turned Protestant again as soon as he reached safety, was at heart a *politique.* Within four years, Huguenot victories, the influence of these mediators, and above all the death of Charles IX, won back for the Huguenots the freedom and property they had lost after the massacre.

King Charles IX died only two years after the crime of Saint Bartholomew's Day. He was not yet twenty-four, and it was widely believed that his end was hastened by remorse. Henry III, the third of Catherine's sons, took his place. Henry's undisguised homosexuality and leanings toward Calvinist advisers made him widely detested. By inclination as well as necessity, he ruled for the next fifteen years through intrigue and assassination. Driven from Paris by the Guises, he lured the Duke of Guise and his brother, the Cardinal of Lorraine, to the castle at Blois and there gave them their reward for the massacre. Proudly, he announced the murders to his dying mother, Catherine; then he or-

dered the bodies burned and the ashes scattered, lest the Catholic party collect the bones of the Guises as relics. Six months later Henry III himself was stabbed to death by a fanatical Dominican friar, who thus put an end, in 1589, to the Valois dynasty. The young friar was instantly cut down by the king's guards; had he lived, he would have been appalled by the consequences of his brutal act. For the legal heir to the throne of France was none other than the heretical Henry of Navarre.

Henry IV understood that his task was to heal the wounds of division within the country. He had to fight for the succession against the Catholic party, and his most loyal supporters were of course Huguenots. For four years, therefore, he remained a Huguenot while gradually consolidating his position. But the majority of his people were Catholic, and Paris above all would not admit a Protestant king within its gates. Whether or not Henry ever said "Paris is worth a mass," he acted according to that precept. He abjured Calvinism, and in February 1594 he rode triumphantly into Paris, surrounded by his soldiers, and entered Notre-Dame to attend mass and a Te Deum. This time he did not withdraw to the bishop's garden when the mass began.

Henry's abjuration of Protestantism had naturally alarmed his former supporters. To reassure them, he issued the Edict of Nantes in 1598, guaranteeing freedom of worship for Huguenots wherever they were already established, granting them the same civil rights as Catholics, and allowing them to maintain garrisons in about a hundred fortified towns. For the time being, the Edict cooled if it did not settle the religious controversy, and Henry was able to proceed to the eco-

nomic and social reconstruction of a wrecked France. He reorganized the judicial system, stimulated manufacturing, improved the condition of the peasantry, and altogether so restored prosperity and peace that he made himself the most popular of French kings since Saint Louis.

Witty, tolerant, generous, this first king of the Bourbon line found an able and intelligent Huguenot minister in the Duke of Sully, who contrived to put order into the catastrophic finances of France. Henry made his own contribution to financial and dynastic security by divorcing Marguerite of Valois, who had given him no heirs, and marrying Marie de Médicis, the pope's niece, who brought him an enormous dowry as well as children. But the old Catholic suspicions of the Huguenots would not die, and in 1610 the well-loved king was assassinated.

At Fontainebleau in 1608 an English traveler had seen Henry IV's seven-year-old son Louis, the "Dolphin whose face was full and fat-cheeked, his hair black, his look vigorous and courageous." At the age of nine this "Dolphin" succeeded to the throne; his mother, Marie de Médicis, became regent; and the nobles, whom Henry IV had kept under control, now became strong enough to raid the royal treasury.

From prosperity France plunged to the brink of financial ruin once more, and the Estates General was summoned to vote new taxes. It met in 1614 — for the last time before the French Revolution — but did little more than present a picture of a country once more rent by internal strife and on the verge of civil war. At the age of sixteen Louis XIII tried to shake off his mother's regency and rule alone, but he soon fell un-

der the domination of Cardinal Richelieu, that most worldly of ecclesiastics. If Henry IV had laid the foundations of French absolutism, Richelieu built the superstructure. He humiliated the nobles, drove the queen mother into exile, made foreign conquests, and frustrated incessant conspiracies. Louis XIII sporadically tried to gather the reins into his own hands, but most of the time he contented himself with a passive role. In the end he became so dependent on Richelieu that he outlived his mentor by only a few months.

In 1622, two months after Richelieu received his cardinal's hat, Pope Gregory XV made Paris an archdiocese, independent of Sens at last. The bishops of Meaux, Chartres, Orléans, and Blois became suffragans of Jean François de Gondi, the first Archbishop of Paris. Gondi continued in office for thirty-two years, and was succeeded by his nephew, the Cardinal de Retz, famous for his memoirs and for his prominent part in the conspiracy of the Fronde.

Louis XIII, the son of a Huguenot, was always subject to suspicions about the genuineness of his Catholicism — suspicions that drew sustenance from the foreign policies of Richelieu, who supported the Protestant princes of Germany in their struggle with the Austro-Spanish Habsburgs. Consequently, Louis took every opportunity to stress his orthodoxy. During his reign some forty religious houses were built in Paris, and some twenty churches begun. Early in 1626 three miraculous cures before the altar of the Virgin at Notre-Dame de Paris prompted Louis and his queen, Anne of Austria, to make a gift of a new altar for the Virgin's chapel in the cathedral.

Here was a longed-for chance to embellish the "bar-

The lofty nave of Notre-Dame (left) was intended by its twelfth-century builders to glorify the Virgin. Five hundred years later, Louis XIII dedicated his entire kingdom to her. In the commemorative medal at right, the kneeling king symbolically offers the Virgin his crown.

barous" Gothic cathedral in the new baroque classi-cizing style, and the elaborate altar — with portraits of the king and queen to either side of the Virgin — so pleased the taste of the day that the queen ordered a new rood screen to harmonize with it. The screen was of wood, its large doorway framed by twisted columns, the capitals heavily gilded. To either side of the doors niches held seminude allegorical figures, which agi-tated the prudery of the chapter. (Indeed, the chapter had previously objected to the portrait of Queen Anne because the painter had boldly depicted her with ex-posed breasts.)

The new art and the free morals of the age could not be stayed. Already, the royal custom of keeping mistresses officially was widely accepted. There was little love lost between Louis XIII and Queen Anne, whom he had married when he was fourteen. Anne of Austria was in fact Spanish, of the Spanish branch of the Habsburgs, and she had spent the years at Louis's side hating her handsome husband and watching in frustration as French policy under Richelieu success-fully aimed at breaking the Habsburg ring around France. There had been no heirs to the throne, and when Anne became pregnant after twenty-three years of marriage, the event was widely regarded as a miracle. Richelieu had broken the political power of the Hugue-nots at home even while furthering the Protestant cause abroad, and miracles were becoming more common in the wake of the Catholic Counter-Reformation.

To celebrate the prospect of an heir, and to indicate once more that France was firmly in the Catholic camp — no matter how many alliances she made with Lu-theran rulers in Germany, Denmark, and Sweden —

Louis XIII decided to place all of France under the protection of the Virgin. In the Declaration of Saint Germain he proclaimed:

> We have declared and do declare that, taking the most Holy and Glorious Virgin for the Special Protector of our Kingdom, we particularly consecrate to her our Person, our State, our Crown and our Subjects, peti-tioning her to inspire holy conduct in us and to defend this Kingdom against all its enemies. . . . And in order that posterity may not fail to follow our will in this regard, as a monument and immortal token of the present consecration, we shall have rebuilt the Main Altar of the Cathedral Church of Paris, with an image of the Virgin holding in her arms the image of her Precious Son descended from the Cross; we shall be represented at the feet of both Son and Mother, offering her our Crown and our Scepter.

A handsome medal was struck commemorating this declaration; it bore a profile of Louis XIII on the obverse and on the reverse the king kneeling before the Virgin, offering his crown to her. The portraiture is remarkably clear and classical; the twisted columns so beloved of the period are again in evidence.

On September 6, 1638, Louis XIII came personally to Notre-Dame to participate in a Te Deum celebrat-ing the birth on the previous day of a male heir to the throne of France. Less than five years later this child was brought to the bedside of his father, who lay dying at the age of forty-two. "Who is it?" the king asked. And with an aplomb and self-confidence that were to remain with him throughout his life, the child replied, "Louis XIV."

The age of the Grand Monarque had begun.

VI   Notre-Dame in Eclipse

Louis XIII's vow to build a new high altar for Notre-Dame was eventually fulfilled three quarters of a century after he had made it, by the son who had scarcely known him. For Louis XIV, who had so pertly announced his imminent accession when he was not yet five years old, sat on the throne for seventy-two years — the longest reign in the history of Europe. It was also the reign during which France became the greatest power in Europe, in which French virtually replaced Latin as the language of international diplomacy, in which French culture and manners were universally admired and imitated, French wealth envied, a French colonial empire founded, the French realm enlarged, a French civil service elaborated. Under Louis XIV Descartes and Pascal dominated mathematics, philosophy, and theology; Vauban, military fortification; Turenne and Condé, military tactics; Colbert, economic theory and practice — much as the French armies dominated Europe. A host of great French writers were read not only in France but throughout the civilized world. If French painters could not compare with their Italian and Dutch contemporaries, French interior decoration, furniture, and architecture had no rivals. Every king in Europe who had the means tried to imitate the vast halls and ornate glitter of the palace at Versailles. It was only fitting that a king who so dominated his age and his country should close his reign by trying to remake in his own image the solid Gothic structure of Notre-Dame.

The great reign began inauspiciously. As so often happened when a child inherited the throne, long-repressed frustrations erupted. By custom, France barred women from the succession but allowed queen mothers to exercise regencies during the minorities of their sons. And so Anne of Austria joined the long line of female regents that stretched from Blanche of Castile through Catherine de Médicis and Marie de Médicis. Like many of her predecessors in office, she was able to control the turbulent nobles only through bribery. *"La reine est si bonne"* — "The queen is so kind" — the courtiers murmured as they lined their pockets; and meanwhile they continued to conspire against the foreign cardinal Jules Mazarin, who succeeded Richelieu. The kind queen shared her bed as well as her power with Mazarin, who manipulated the factions as skillfully as he did his royal mistress. His informers were everywhere; he anticipated the moves of his enemies, who were also everywhere; and although he could not prevent the uprising of the Fronde (named after the slingshots with which the youth of Paris attacked the royal guards), he slid, slithered, and ducked as if running the gauntlet, and emerged triumphant at the end.

The Fronde, with its multiple treasons and rapid changes of sides by the magnates of France, was half comic opera, half an earnest dress rehearsal for the Revolution 140 years later. Mazarin, desperately in need of funds for himself, his bribes, and the armies that France was maintaining during the closing days of the Thirty Years' War, had attempted to impose a tax on all goods entering Paris. The Parlement of Paris, which like French parliaments of other cities was essentially a court of law, attempted to claim the powers its English namesake was then winning. It asserted wider authority than it had and refused to accept the tax. Mazarin and Anne, infuriated, waited for an opportunity to enforce their will. With the Prince of

Condé's notable victory over the Spaniards at Lens, in northern France, the moment seemed to have come.

On August 26, 1648, this victory was celebrated by a Te Deum in Notre-Dame. Seventy-three captured flags waved over the heads of the Parisians — whose leading representatives in the Parlement were at that moment being arrested. When someone saw a councillor being dragged into a carriage, popular indignation exploded. Barricades were thrown up in the streets of Paris. Jean François Paul de Gondi, coadjutor to the Archbishop of Paris (and the future Cardinal de Retz), hastened to court and pleaded for the councillor's release. When he was rudely rebuffed, he placed himself at the head of the rebels.

The students and sons of the middle class led the way in the street fighting and in writing scorching pamphlets called *mazarinades,* which attacked the prime minister, the court, and the nobility. But the lower classes likewise enthusiastically joined the citizens' army, whose major success was the capture of the Bastille. The court fled from Paris. To Anne of Austria, to eleven-year-old Louis XIV, the world seemed to be going mad. There were revolutions in Catalonia and Portugal, and in England a king — Charles I — had actually gone to the execution block. It would have taken a hardy prophet to predict, at the midpoint of the seventeenth century, that the next fifty years would witness the triumph of absolute monarchy on a scale unprecedented in the history of Europe.

The disorders in France continued for four years. At one point the regent, king, and cardinal were all forcibly detained in Paris, and in a scene to be repeated in the later great Revolution the Paris mob broke into

the Louvre demanding proof that the king was still there. Anne was compelled to lead a delegation of Parisians into the boy-king's bedroom and to exchange friendly words with the *canaille.* Matters apparently grew even worse when the great nobles, led by the generals Condé and Turenne, took up the cause of the Fronde on their own behalf.

Mazarin, however, skillfully played on the patriotism of the bourgeoisie; he won over the Parlement by showing that the generals were making common cause with foreign enemies. Then he undermined the alliance between the Catholic Condé and the Huguenot Turenne, and took Turenne back into the royal service. Ultimately, the nobles themselves recognized that the monarchy was the sole stabilizing factor in the country, and they abandoned their opposition. But Louis XIV never forgot the humiliations he underwent during the period of the Fronde. Out of that experience sprang his lifelong distaste for the city of Paris and his determination to reduce the nobility to impotent courtiers and to keep the Parlement within its proper bounds as a legal tribunal.

The cardinal and the king emerged stronger than ever from the rebellion of the Fronde, though Louis remained under Mazarin's tutelage until the cardinal died in 1661. Then the twenty-three-year-old king announced that henceforth he would rule in his own right. His ministers smiled to themselves; surely in a week or two His Majesty would be bored and leave affairs to them. But they soon found that the king was in earnest. Moreover, he really worked at the task of governing. Although he had received a shamefully poor education, Louis had learned something from watching

Mazarin, and he was always willing to learn more. He
possessed limitless self-confidence and the patience for
close, often excessive, attention to detail. Louis rarely
read anything, but he learned from conversation and
had a retentive memory. For all his arrogance and
selfishness in personal matters, he had a keen sense of
duty, a deep conviction of his divine right to rule,
and a boundless ambition to make his country as great
as he conceived himself to be. He made cruelty a matter
of policy, but he could also be surprisingly courteous
and kind. The contradictions of the Grand Monarque
are as bewildering as the contradictions of the age in
which he lived.

In his youth Louis had as strong an appetite for
women as Henry VIII of England, and the succession
of royal mistresses was public knowledge. But he never
allowed his women to intervene in the affairs of state;
they could influence only the petty conflicts springing
from the complex etiquette of the court — where who
sat in whose presence or who handed the king his
breeches at the *levée* became the chief subjects of daily
conversation. In middle life, his amorous inclinations
subsided, and after he married his last mistress, Madame
de Maintenon, Louis remained a dutiful husband.

The king's religious bigotry was notorious. He ordered the Duke of Savoy to wipe out the Waldensians,
who had retreated into the mountains four centuries
earlier, though there could be no political threat from
these innocent and ignorant peasants. Yet he kept at
his side the Huguenot Turenne, appointing him "mar-
shal-general of the camps of the armies of the king."
Turenne was responsible for many French triumphs on
the battlefield during Louis's incessant wars. He was

a great tactician — Napoleon declared that all soldiers ought to study his campaigns as lessons in the art of warfare. Louis offered to make Turenne Constable of France if he would change his religion. Turenne refused. Toward the end of his life, however, the death of his Calvinist wife and the eloquent sermons of the great preacher Bossuet moved him to a genuine conversion. In 1668 an elaborate "abjuration of heresy" was performed in the cathedral of Notre-Dame, and Turenne was received into the Roman church at the hands of the Archbishop of Paris.

Seven years later, following Turenne's death in the battle of Sassbach, one of the pompous funerals of the age was held in Notre-Dame. The stonework of the church was entirely hidden behind festoons of drapery. A mausoleum was erected in the center of the choir — an oval tower upon a mountain, girded by four stylized palm trees on which hung trophies of the general's many battles, together with shields showing the armorial bearings of the Turenne family. Four figures representing Piety, Attachment to the King, Valor, and Wisdom supported an antique urn which was surmounted by still another figure representing Immortality. The latter trampled Death underfoot and held aloft a medallion with a portrait of the departed. The close of Louis XIV's reign saw a quick succession of state funerals, each more elaborate than the last, as illness wiped out members of the royal family. But the most overwhelming was the funeral of the great General Condé, which Madame de Sévigné termed "the most beautiful, the most magnificent, and most triumphant funeral ever held since there were mortals on this earth."

Characteristic of all this decor was the desire to do something about what was considered the ugliness of the cathedral. Molière had jibed at "the insipid taste of Gothic ornaments, those odious monsters of ignorant centuries." Blondel, the leading theorist on architecture, spoke of "that outrageous and insupportable fashion of building which our fathers long made use of under the name of Gothic architecture." Thus, the decision of Louis XIV to carry out his father's vow to build a new high altar was not only a commendable act of piety but the assertion of a new sensibility. Here was a chance to remake at least the sanctuary in a civilized style. In effect, what was done was to insert into this part of the cathedral the essentials of a "contemporary" church.

To mark it off from the rest, the floor was raised in a series of levels like a stage and paved with richly colored marble inlay in the Italian manner. The eight mighty columns that described an arc around the back of the altar were sheathed in marble, too, furnished with capitals in gilded bronze, and embellished with bronze figures and a profusion of ornaments. A niche was created to hold an impressive Descent from the Cross, one of the largest pieces of marble statuary of its day. Two of the leading sculptors, Guillaume Costeau and Antoine Coysevox, were commissioned to do the marble figures of Louis XIII and Louis XIV, who are kneeling and offering their crowns and scepters to the Virgin, as in the vision of Louis XIII. There were now two altars, one to the fore of the choir, one to the rear, faced with marble and bronze. And there were more statues of angels on richly decorated pedestals, and a great gold sun — a *gloire* — shooting its

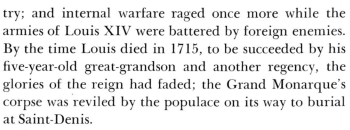

rays in all directions, and flying cherubim, and representations of the Twelve Virtues, and a marble balustrade, and a newly carved set of choir stalls, all in the style fashionable in the early eighteenth century. This redecoration took fifteen years to complete.

France grew great under Louis XIV, but his ambitious wars and magnificent palaces wasted the country. No limit was ever placed on the Sun King's appetite for grandeur — especially in the building of Versailles. In addition, vast public works were undertaken inside the capital. The demolition of what remained of medieval Paris continued. Additions were made to the enormous, still unfinished Louvre. Ramparts were leveled, squares created, and triumphal arches erected to match those of ancient Rome. Early in his reign Louis had conceived the plan of enlarging an old abbey, already serving as a refuge for disabled soldiers. This building became the huge complex of Les Invalides. Its space proved to be none too big for the veterans of Louis's numerous wars.

France was rich enough to sustain extravagant expenditures, and under the mercantilistic policies of Louis's great minister Colbert the country's wealth increased. But almost the entire burden of taxation fell upon the peasantry; the nobles were exempt, and the bourgeoisie evaded or bought exemptions. Moreover, the system of tax collection diverted the flow of revenue to middlemen, so that the tax rates had constantly to be increased and new taxes devised — which always fell upon those least able to pay. The revocation of the Edict of Nantes in 1685 and renewed persecution of the Huguenots drove thousands of the most hardworking, capable, and prosperous citizens out of the coun-

try; and internal warfare raged once more while the armies of Louis XIV were battered by foreign enemies. By the time Louis died in 1715, to be succeeded by his five-year-old great-grandson and another regency, the glories of the reign had faded; the Grand Monarque's corpse was reviled by the populace on its way to burial at Saint-Denis.

In carrying out the vow of Louis XIII, the architects had destroyed the fifteenth-century stalls and a great many of the ancient tombs within the church. Elimination of the "barbarous" Gothic continued in the eighteenth century. The saddest alteration was the removal of much of the great thirteenth-century stained glass. This was replaced by the almost clear glass known as *grisaille,* the only color being the borders of yellow fleurs-de-lis. The whole interior of the cathedral was given a coat of whitewash to hide the deplorable condition of the stones. The fruitless attempts to reconstruct the rose of the southern transept were likewise undertaken during this century.

In 1771 Soufflot breached the central portal in order to make the entrance higher and wider, so that processions carrying the enormous canopies of the day could enter more easily. In the process he destroyed much of the sculpture of the Last Judgment. During the following twenty years there were numerous efforts to repair the cathedral, most of which made matters worse. In 1780 the interior was once again whitewashed; the next year wretched repairs to the northern rose were begun. In 1787, just two years before the Revolution, Gothic gargoyles, moldings, and sculpture were systematically removed, supposedly because these were in danger of falling, actually because they offended the

In fulfilling Louis XIII's final wishes regarding the renovation of Notre-Dame, his successors did irreparable damage to the cathedral's glorious stained glass. Many small windows, among them the arched aperture at near left, were stripped of their incomparable thirteenth-century glass and fitted with a lightly tinted substitute known as grisaille. Others, such as the renowned southern rose (far left), were the victims of bungled restoration attempts. The penchant for ungainly baroque embellishment may well have reached its peak in 1746, the year the brothers Slodtz draped the entire nave (below) with black bunting and ermine swags for an elaborate state funeral.

taste of the architects. But these architects were so out of touch with the nature of the Gothic that they frequently mistook supporting members for pure ornamentation, and by removing them endangered the fabric of the cathedral.

This botchwork may be regarded as symbolic of the history of France during the eighteenth century. The reign of Louis XIV had ended in military defeat, catastrophic public debt, and death running riot: Louis's son and grandson had both died within a single year. Louis XV, who succeeded to the throne in 1715, inherited his great-grandfather's appetites, but neither his royal presence, his sense of duty, nor his discretion. Louis XIV had told his friends: "I order all of you, if you notice that any woman shows the least sign of managing me, to warn me. I shall be rid of her in twenty-four hours." Under Louis XV the mistresses, from Madame de Chateauroux and Madame de Pompadour to Madame Du Barry, virtually ruled France. All attempts to shore up the Ancien Régime were as unavailing as the inept repairs to Notre-Dame. When Louis XV died of smallpox in 1774 and the news was brought to his twenty-year-old grandson, Louis, and his wife, Marie Antoinette, they burst into tears and fell to their knees, crying out: "God guide and protect us. We are too young to govern." They might well despair, for they had inherited a riddled and bankrupt state.

On February 9, 1779, Notre-Dame was the scene of a mass wedding that for a time enormously increased the popularity of the new king and queen. To celebrate the birth of a daughter to Marie Antoinette, the royal pair bore the expenses for the weddings of a hundred girls and young men of the people. In addition to

trousseaux, the king and queen provided money for the young couples to set up their households and dowries of five hundred livres for each of the girls.

This action was rather characteristic. Louis XVI was a man of simple tastes, personally kindhearted and virtuous, in striking contrast to his profligate predecessors. He was even a Freemason and a reader of the Encyclopédistes. As for his wife, the pretty, pampered Austrian princess was a disciple of the late Jean Jacques Rousseau. At her model farm in the park of Versailles Marie Antoinette and her court ladies played at the simple life. Louis, too, preferred hunting or his hobby of locksmithing to forcing through the fundamental reforms then generally known to be necessary. Whatever measures he did take turned out to be unfortunate. The privileged classes stubbornly resisted giving up any of their privileges or allowing the Third Estate an equal voice in public affairs. It was thus inevitable that the assembly of the Estates General, called at last by an unwilling king, should have reached an impasse.

When, in those July days of 1789, the common people of Paris emerged from their wretched quarters to listen to the inflammatory speeches of such youthful radicals as Camille Desmoulins and Georges Danton, they were hardly showing solidarity with the delegates of the Third Estate at Versailles who were defying the king's order to disband. Rather, the people poured into the streets from impatience with promises made and never kept, from indignation at the luxuries of the nobility, and from fear — which was to be the motive force for the excesses of the years to come. For word spread that there would be a Saint Bartholomew's Day massacre of liberals. Rumors flew that the Swiss and German troops in the capital would be set upon the populace. The mob coursed through Paris, seizing arms. When it stormed the Bastille, it was attacking a symbol more than an actuality. The grim old fort, once part of the city's defenses, was already slated for demolition. In its place was to stand a statue of the enlightened and kindly Louis XVI, who was already doing away with past wrongs.

The Bastille, of course, was intimately associated with repressions and persecutions. Thousands of Huguenots, political troublemakers, pamphleteers, and others guilty of spreading seditious doctrines had been imprisoned there. There were also memories of the Fronde. In 1789 the Bastille fell easily. After the first few days of riot and bloodshed, the king took a conciliatory tone and promised the people a constitution. To celebrate the restoration of peace, a Te Deum was sung in the cathedral of Notre-Dame.

At its outset, the Revolution had scarcely any anticlerical cast. In fact, *les bons curés,* the lesser clergy, were hailed as friends of the common people. With their help, the Church was to be cleansed of its corruptions and a better social order created. In those few weeks of strong emotion when all classes seemed united in recognition of the need for sacrifice, the Archbishop of Paris, Monseigneur de Juigny, set a personal example by donating 20,000 livres for the unemployed of the Saint-Antoine district. The canons of Notre-Dame made a gift of 12,000 livres. The people turned to their Church to sanctify their movement and asked to have the banners of their newly formed National Guard kept inside the cathedral. There was again a solemn ceremony in Notre-Dame, with the archbishop

blessing the banners. Further ceremonies of this sort were attended by the king and queen, and every effort was made to place the Church on the side of peaceful reforms.

But by October of 1789 the National Assembly, looking for suitable quarters, had installed itself inside the archiepiscopal palace. Monseigneur de Juigny began to feel uneasy and asked for a passport to leave the city and take the waters at Aix-les-Bains. Conditions were still stable in the south. The archbishop's departure was the signal for a general flight of the higher clergy. Within a few more weeks, a decree had been passed declaring all possessions of the Church the property of the nation.

The articles of precious metals in the cathedral's treasury were the first objects of this edict. Inventories were drawn up and receipts issued as reliquaries and chalices were delivered to the mint. But once the church had been stripped of its most conspicuous riches, an attack began on its larger holdings and prerogatives. The Chapter of Notre-Dame was dissolved, and the canons were forbidden to enter the cathedral. In November 1790 they celebrated their last mass. Religious establishments of every sort were banned and their buildings seized. The clergy were to be servants of the people, receiving fixed salaries, and they were required to sign a pledge of loyalty to the law, the king, and the nation.

About half the clerics accepted these conditions; they made up the so-called constitutional clergy. In March 1791 they met in the cathedral to elect an archbishop — to be known, since memories of the old hierarchy were to be suppressed, as the Metropolitan of the Seine.

The structure of the entire French Church was reorganized, the number of dioceses greatly reduced, and Notre-Dame designated as simply one parish church among others. It was now to serve for civil ceremonies as well as religious ones. Thus the anniversary celebration of the fall of the Bastille was held in the cathedral, with martial trumpet blasts and cymbals imitating the roar of cannon, while the chorus sang, "Down with the bastion of slavery." The performance, however, concluded with the traditional Te Deum.

Even such compromises could not quiet the growing spirit of anticlericalism. Among the flood of pamphlets and broadsides issued at the time were some that specialized in the most savage attacks on religion and the Church. This propaganda accorded with the general temper of militancy and panic. The new republic was barely proclaimed when it was fighting for its life against German regiments reinforced by troops of émigré nobles. In haste, a mass army was being formed. Arms, uniforms, and food were desperately needed, but the coffers of the new government were empty. Again the answer to the problem lay in the churches. Articles of bronze, tombs, monuments, choir grilles were carted off to be melted into cannon. Since those churches still authorized for worship were permitted only one bell, an inventory was made of the size and weight of the bells of Notre-Dame.

Each bell had a popular name and a well-known history. In the north tower hung Guillaume, a gift of Bishop Guillaume of Auvergne, dating back to the thirteenth century; Gabriel, a gift of Louis XI in 1477; Pugnese, Pasquier, Thibault, Jean, Claude, Nicholas, and Françoise. The south tower held Marie, a fifteenth-

century bell, and Jacqueline — who had been there since 1400, although she had had to be recast in 1681 and then underwent a change of sex, being renamed Emmanuel. Weighing 25,000 pounds, this deepest-voiced of all the bells was called the *gros bourdon*.

These bells were lowered from their towers, but except for Marie they were somehow never taken to the foundry. Forces were at work to countervail the destructive temper of the moment. For even while extremists called for the elimination of all vestiges of superstition, a prudent and art-loving man named Alexandre Lenoir, himself a painter, conceived the project of saving the imperiled treasures. Some powerful politicians backed the plan. The abbey of the Petits Augustins was given to Lenoir for a storehouse. Methodically, he gathered there the vast number of art objects stranded in the disused churches of the city. Paintings, statues, tapestries, and general furnishings were carefully listed and classified by period. In one case Lenoir personally fended off a band of citizens bent on smashing the royal sepulchers at Saint-Denis. Some tombs had already been destroyed and the remains of kings thrown into a mass grave. But those tombs that Lenoir protected were removed to the Petits Augustins, which was designated a Museum for National Monuments. When, some ten years later, Notre-Dame was once more restored to dignity, the revived chapter had only to look in the Petits Augustins to find what was needed to clothe the cathedral's nakedness.

The attack on the tombs of Saint-Denis was part of the antimonarchical frenzy that seized the city in 1793. This was the year of the Terror, when the prisons were filled as never before, not only with hated aristocrats but with a host of ordinary citizens whose zeal had been questioned. All moderates were traitors.

For the past few years King Louis XVI had been unwillingly held in Paris. He had granted a constitution and had even given his blessing to the creation of the civil clergy, though halfheartedly. He had seemed only dimly aware of the dangers around him. But letters of the queen were intercepted and an ill-conceived flight by the whole royal family was foiled. The king was brought to trial and condemned in January 1793; the next day he was taken to the scaffold. In October Queen Marie Antoinette, derisively identified in the documents as the Widow Capet, was also tried and executed. Every day wagonloads of prisoners rolled through the Paris streets toward the Place de la Révolution, formerly the Place Louis XV. There stood the guillotine, that comparatively humane mechanism for wholesale beheadings.

Inspired by the wild rhetoric against royalty and everything connected with it, the Paris Commune decided that the Gallery of Kings, which spanned the entire west façade of Notre-Dame, could no longer be tolerated, and a group of citizens was sent to remove the offending figures. The statues were roped and tugged down to the pavement. Their broken heads were distributed among the various communes around Paris like trophies, but their shattered bodies lay where they had fallen. The painter Jacques Louis David, who had made a name for himself as a revolutionary, proposed that the debris be used for a monument to the new age. "Let the effigies which royalty and superstition conceived and deified for fourteen hundred years be heaped up into a pedestal on which would be seated

In 1793, the year of the Terror, an upsurge of antimonarchism led to the jailing and eventual execution of thousands of French aristocrats. At first the imprisoned royal family (strolling in the garden of their prison at far left) seemed safe, but on January 21, 1793, Madame Guillotine claimed her most eminent victim (left). Eight months later, Louis's surprisingly self-possessed queen followed her husband to the block. The sketch at right by Jacques Louis David, court painter to Louis XVI, depicts "the Widow Capet" on her final journey.

a gigantic figure representing the French people." A competition was announced for such a monument, but nothing more came of the matter. The stone remained on the parvis for three years, although complaints were repeatedly made that the rubble was a gathering place for refuse and an obstruction to traffic. Eventually the headless trunks of several of the biblical kings were removed to the city coal yard and used as posts. There they were found and identified almost fifty years later.

The Commune also had hired masons to go about the building systematically removing every trace of monarchy and feudalism. Thus every crown or diadem was chiseled off the statues, as were the blazons ornamenting the archiepiscopal palace and the sacristy. The marble facings were pried from altars and chapels, and even representations of the Three Magi were destroyed — because they were Oriental kings.

The wave of anticlericalism continued to rise. Soon it was being said that the constitutional clergy were no better than the older variety. Gobel, the Metropolitan of the Seine who had received his office from the people, was called before the Commune. Of his own accord he stripped himself of his insignia of priesthood, his letters of election, his crucifix, his ring, and placed on his head the red bonnet that had become the symbol of patriotism. On the same day the Commune prohibited any further religious observances and decided that the church of Notre-Dame should be officially converted into a Temple of Reason.

The transformation called for an appropriate ceremony, and one was quickly whipped together. The Paris Opera was currently presenting a modish *Homage to Liberty* by Gossec. Freshened with a few new choruses, this would do splendidly for the occasion. The Opera also obligingly lent its sets. In the forepart of the choir, screening the high altar, a mountain was set up, crowned by a pagan temple. An enthusiastic parade made up of members of the Convention and the entire opera troupe of dancers, singers, and musicians entered the cathedral. A lovely young star of the moment, wearing a white tunic, blue mantle, and red bonnet was brought in on a litter and installed within the temple. The spectacle was performed, the brand-new "Marseillaise" sung, and a young firebrand of the Commune gave an impassioned speech proclaiming that in the contest between Liberty and Reason, Reason was sovereign.

Some two thousand churches throughout France were promptly renamed temples of Reason. Christianity was officially overthrown, and a flood of new calendars, almanacs, and catechisms of revolutionary maxims appeared. All this sanctioned a new wave of looting of the churches. Bands of atheist masqueraders dressed in ecclesiastical vestments and carrying crucifixes and censers went through the streets dancing and singing.

But the Church had not died, nor the desire for its offices. An underground Church was organized, and a number of clandestine chapels were soon in operation, almost all of them in the streets surrounding Notre-Dame. But the most famous of such chapels was hidden in the top floor of a building close to the Conciergerie and the headquarters of the Tribunal. There a Parisian couple, the Bergerons, ran a small metalworking shop. Obtaining a contract to produce muskets for the revolutionary army, they hired two new assistants, who were in fact secret priests. On days when the mass was being said, Madame Bergeron would notify communicants by hanging a bouquet of flowers from the shop sign. At last the chapel was discovered, and the conspirators were arrested. All would have been sentenced to death but for a new turn of events.

Robespierre, charismatic leader of the Jacobin faction, now made use of the religious issue in his power struggle with the more extreme members of the Convention. A decree was passed affirming that the French people recognized the existence of a Supreme Being and the Immortality of the Soul. Those who taught otherwise were branded counterrevolutionaries. The victims of this policy reversal were not only the rabid antireligious forces, but also leading members of the erstwhile constitutional clergy. Thus the deposed Metropolitan Gobel went to his death for his part in discrediting the Church. The recently created Temple of Reason was renamed the Temple to the Supreme Being and was so proclaimed by a vast wooden signboard hung over the central portal. An official republican prayer to the Supreme Being was given wide circulation. But the new cult never had much appeal, and with the fall of Robespierre was more or less laid aside.

As the eighteenth century drew to a close, Notre-Dame reached the lowest ebb of its fortunes. It stood disused, along with all the other churches of France. Extremists called for its demolition, with the stone to be sold for building material. In the meantime, its chapels were put up for sale, and some were actually bought, although the purchasers were apt to complain that the space was still encumbered by marble and bits of sculpture. The cathedral nave was used to store wine casks for the people's army.

By 1795 it had become clear that the attempt to refashion national feeling and reeducate the masses was largely a failure. There was widespread longing for the familiar religion. The exiled clergy were trickling back into France. Since the state now recognized freedom of worship, a small group called the Société Catholique petitioned for the use of the cathedral. Permission was given, though the clergy were strictly forbidden to ask payment for their traditional services at baptisms, weddings, and funerals.

The reconstituted Chapter of Notre-Dame was so poor that in those early days the gift of a broom with which to commence the vast task of cleaning the cathedral was considered significant enough to be noted in the records. Moreover, the church had to be shared with other religious groups; the Catholics were restricted to the north transept. The revolutionary spirit had left its mark even on the clerics, for in a council held in 1797 the demand was raised that bishops be elected rather than appointed and that French rather than Latin be used in the liturgy. The government, which had permitted the council, had hoped for far more fundamental results — the legalization of divorce, the marriage of priests, and the elimination of confession. But in such matters the Church showed itself deeply conservative.

So, indeed, did the French nation. After ten years of upheaval, anarchy, perpetual war, and economic hardship, it craved a stable government. A plebiscite brought an overwhelming endorsement for young Napoleon Bonaparte, who had led French troops to impressive victories. Himself a Deist, like Robespierre, he felt that religion was indispensable to a well-ordered

society. After two years of negotiations with Pope Pius VII, he prepared to restore the Roman Catholic Church to its old dignity, if not to its old power.

The date set for the celebration of the Concordat was Easter Day, 1802. The prefect of the police made a hasty report on the condition of the cathedral. He found the inside fairly clean except for the chapels, which were boarded over with rough planks and had been robbed of flooring. These would have to be masked with tapestries, which fortunately were readily available at the Museum of National Monuments. There was even a suitable monstrance still at the mint. Desecrated, denuded, the cathedral was to be revivified and once more arrayed for a solemn Te Deum.

The *bourdon,* long absent from its loft, was hoisted back into its place. As the first rays of the April sun began to bathe the towers of Notre-Dame, the strong low notes of the bell rang out. Instantly, all the inhabitants of the nearby streets came to the windows. People on the streets embraced each other and wept. The consuls set out from the Tuileries, along with the ministers, councillors of state, and the members of the diplomatic corps seated in the old ornate royal carriages. Crowds lined the streets to look at the unwonted display. The first consul, Napoleon, in red uniform, was wildly applauded. The corps of soldiers that surrounded him, however, indulged themselves in shockingly antireligious remarks. The new Archbishop of Paris greeted the consuls at the west portal with the ceremonial used for royalty. They were accompanied to a dais set up facing the one on which the pope's emissary sat. Solemn addresses hailed the reestablishment of peace between France and her European ene-

mies, a peace sealed by the restoration of religion.

Nevertheless, a certain cynicism was in the air. Emerging into the sunlit parvis filled with Parisians who had crowded about the cathedral in solid ranks, the first consul asked one of his generals what he had thought of the ceremony. The reply he made was quoted widely throughout Napoleon's entourage. "A fine show," the general said. "All that was lacking were the million or so men killed in order to destroy the thing which you have just reinstituted."

In August of that same year another plebiscite overwhelmingly confirmed the first consul's popularity. He was given the consulship for life, with the right to choose his successor. Two years later an unprecedented ceremony took place in Notre-Dame. Napoleon took the crown from the hands of Pius VII and crowned himself Emperor of the French. Monarchy was back, though under another name and with a different complexion. The old social order had been utterly smashed by the violence of the Revolution, but Napoleon fabricated a new one, which retained many of the reforms of republicanism, though within an authoritarian and centralized framework. His troops continued to win extraordinary victories and were greeted everywhere as liberators, freeing the people from outworn feudal regimes. Napoleon set his brothers and closest associates on the thrones of conquered kingdoms. France was truly an empire now, controlling the whole of Western Europe, and the coastline from Antwerp as far south as Genoa.

Napoleon's marriage to Joséphine, which dated from the time he was a mere officer, was without issue, and he had prudently left himself an opening for divorce.

Napoleon's evident determination and undeniable charisma — both suggested in the bas-relief study at left — help explain his meteoric rise to power. Only a man of such dynamism and self-assurance would have dared to assume the title Emperor of France a mere twelve years after the monarchy had been so overwhelmingly rejected. One of David's preliminary sketches (right above) for his panoramic coronation scene shows Napoleon placing the crown upon his own head, while a reproving Pius VII looks on. Another sketch (below), depicting the emperor's first wife, Joséphine, kneeling at her husband's feet to receive her own diadem, was incorporated in the final canvas (overleaf).

His second marriage, to the eighteen-year-old Archduchess Maria Louisa of Austria, perhaps marked the peak of his fortunes. The populace was treated to an elaborate show of fireworks above the cathedral of Notre-Dame, and a year later the cathedral was the scene of a magnificent baptism. The child's godfather was none other than Emperor Francis I of Austria, Maria Louisa's father, who was represented by one of his sons; the godmother was Napoleon's mother. An uncle of Napoleon, the Cardinal-Archbishop of Lyons, administered the sacraments. When the ritual was over, Napoleon took the baby from the arms of his attendants, kissed him heartily three times, and bestowed on him the title of King of Rome. The realm the child would have inherited was almost that of an emperor of the Romans.

In fact, he inherited nothing, and spent most of his short life at his grandfather's palace of Schoenbrunn in Vienna. He died at the age of twenty-one, thus sparing Europe what might have been a political embarrassment. For within a few years after his birth his father's star had waned. The record of fantastic victories turned into a series of defeats, and the Emperor of the French became General Bonaparte, a lonely prisoner of the English on a desolate island in the middle of the South Atlantic Ocean.

VII   A Treasure Preserved

With the restoration of the Bourbons in 1814, the marble statues of Louis XIII and Louis XIV could once more enrich the sanctuary of Notre-Dame. The theatrical Descent from the Cross by Costeau had already been returned, on Napoleon's orders, to its place behind the high altar. But the other two figures of the ensemble, the kneeling kings, had been tactfully kept in the Museum of National Monuments until the time was ripe for their reappearance. Tact was in fact the keynote of the restored monarchy. The new king, Louis XVIII, was already sixty years old, afflicted with gout, and chastened by his long exile. He offered the country a constitution modeled closely on English lines and promised to recognize the results of the Revolution.

At the moment such common sense was precious. France had paid dearly for the years of Napoleonic glory. Her manpower had been exhausted by a quarter century of continual levies, so that the new monarchy's reforms in the conscription system were especially welcome. Louis XVIII managed to mitigate the harshness of the peace treaties. He also faced the long-term task of maintaining a balance between the two distinct and irreconcilable elements of French society — the émigrés and conservative interests on the one hand, the republicans and Bonapartists on the other.

Gradually, however, the government shifted to the right — freedoms were abridged, the press muzzled, the propertied class blatantly favored by changes in suffrage. When Charles X succeeded his brother in 1824, he made no secret of his impatience with constitutional processes. A series of confrontations between the king and the Chamber of Deputies ended with Charles X dissolving that body early in 1830. His troops were totally unprepared for the riots that erupted in Paris. Barricades sprang up and the king, who remembered 1789, thought it best to abdicate.

At the very outset of the rioting an assault was made on the archiepiscopal headquarters, Maurice de Sully's old palace, which flanked the cathedral on the south. A mob broke in and with lively memories of revolutionary tradition began to pillage and destroy whatever ecclesiastical goods they could find. A second attack on the palace, this time accompanied by arson, took place the following year. It would seem that the building, like the late unlamented Bastille, had a symbolic meaning for any insurrection. The cost of repairs would be great, and it was decided to raze the palace.

The site so long occupied by the archiepiscopal palace was converted to a broad promenade along the Seine. This was a democratic bit of civic improvement, in keeping with the character of the new head of state. Louis Philippe, the former Duke of Orléans, had been called in by the moderates after the abdication of Charles X. In the early stages of the Revolution, Louis Philippe had been a fervent advocate of republicanism, and now he studiously avoided the monarchical manners and reactionary policies that had been the downfall of his predecessor.

The cathedral, hemmed in from the beginning by a huddle of other buildings, more and more was standing in the clear. Everyone could now see how poor its condition was. Gothic structures had been little prized in the past several centuries — indeed, some ten medieval churches on the Île de la Cité alone had been demolished in various building programs, without the least regret on the score of their antiquity or artistic

value. But in 1830 a new feeling for the monuments of the past was arising. This was part of the romantic movement then sweeping Europe. Vast changes in the social fabric, whose extent could not yet be seen and whose implications could not be fathomed, produced a countercurrent: a passion for the strange, the faraway, the fantastic, the exalted, for richer forms of life than the banal present seemed to allow. Suddenly a building like Notre-Dame, so long taken for granted if not detested as an embodiment of superstition, was seen in a new light.

A rising young writer named Victor Hugo set the tone for this revaluation. In his *Notre-Dame de Paris*, published in 1831, he glorified architecture as living history; to Hugo a building was "a book in stone" — Gothic cathedrals in general and Notre-Dame in particular. Turning upon the eighteenth century, he denounced its refinements as silly fashion. He listed the indignities that had been wreaked on the cathedral of Paris in the name of so-called taste: its richly colored windows gone, its interior whitewashed, its flèche ripped off, the shape of the central portal mutilated, its chapels choked with showy rubbish, its choir floored with gaudy marble, its sanctuary cluttered with histrionic statuary.

Hugo's novel strongly influenced another young Parisian of talent, only seventeen at the time but already devoting himself to architecture. This was Eugène Emmanuel Viollet-le-Duc. The name was to become almost synonymous with restoration. While still in his early twenties, Viollet-le-Duc was appointed to the newly established commission for the preservation of historic monuments. For there was a movement afoot, thanks largely to Hugo's novel, to save the buildings that represented the country's great past.

Prosper Mérimée, a man of letters best known to us as the author of the tale of Carmen, headed the commission. He took Viollet-le-Duc on a strenuous tour of the south, where they inspected a vast number of buildings, many dating from the eleventh century, which were in desperate disrepair. Soon Viollet-le-Duc was given charge of difficult projects. His ardor and competence were extraordinary, his capacity for work prodigious. The experience he accumulated from working on these projects gave him a staggering knowledge of Gothic and Romanesque building techniques. He could say at once what strategies were safe and what measures would be fatal to the intricate medieval balances. He drew up reliable estimates of costs and schedules. He organized building crews, trained craftsmen, promoted the growth of workshops — all this for as many as twenty projects at a time. He traveled continually, checking on reconstructions in progress and advising on those being considered. In 1845 he was appointed architect for the restoration of Notre-Dame de Paris. He was to be occupied with that task for the next twenty years.

Viollet-le-Duc had developed a philosophy of restoration. He was to state it again and again in his many writings, and above all in his vast study of French architecture, cast in the form of a dictionary that ran to ten volumes. But he expressed his principles early and clearly in his proposals for Notre-Dame:

In a project of this sort, one cannot proceed with enough prudence and discretion. A restoration can do more harm to a monument than the ravages of the

centuries and the fury of rioters. For time and revolution destroy but add nothing. A restoration, on the other hand, by adding new forms, can erase a host of details which are all the more interesting for being worn and rare. It is hard to say which is more dangerous — the indifference which lets buildings fall into total ruin or the ignorant zeal which shears away, adds on, carries to completion, and ends by transforming an ancient building into a new one, devoid of the slightest historical interest.

Yet he was not a purist. He appreciated the singularity of each building, which arose precisely from the span of time and range of styles it embodied. He was seeking an unspecific yet tangible quality of authenticity. To him the Gothic exemplified logic, honesty, lucidity, and function, and he preached these virtues for contemporary building too. Contrary to a popular misconception, which has equated his work with the archaizing pasticherie of the beaux arts tradition, Viollet-le-Duc should be considered one of the fathers of modernism. In addition to stressing the interdependence of form and function, he took great interest in the birth of such new architectural creations as railroad stations and market halls, in the possibilities of new materials such as cast iron, and even in the future of prefabrication.

Although he may first have fallen in love with the Gothic on romantic grounds, he came to admire it for its serviceable qualities. "Here are monuments which have lasted for six or seven hundred years, in spite of a destructive climate, in spite of three centuries of abandonment, in spite of fires and revolutions. Yet they are still in daily use, prove themselves convenient,

and need nothing but a little repairing, often no more than ordinary maintenance."

Viollet-le-Duc was keenly aware of the limits of restoration. The naïve spirit that had guided the original sculptor's chisel was dead and could not be willed into being again. Instead of creating new ornaments, he leaned heavily on archaeology and based his reconstructions on precedent. Thus he re-created the windows of Notre-Dame by copying other stained glass which had escaped destruction. It was he who enlisted the new techniques of chemistry for an analysis of the secrets of thirteenth-century glassmaking. To replace the sculptures of Notre-Dame smashed during the Revolution, he could draw on pictorial records and careful studies of the figures at Chartres, Reims, and Amiens. He designed the delicate wooden flèche to crown the crossing of the transept, the hinges of the great doors, the gargoyles of the rooftops. He had the inside of the cathedral scoured of its old whitewash and the outside treated with a silicone process to protect it from the atmospheric pollutants that were already a problem in nineteenth-century Paris. In addition, he built the sacristy adjoining the south side, needed for the cathedral's religious functions since it had lost its former annexes.

In this one portion of the building he was "Gothicizing," and the result has a charm all its own for our century. He also allowed himself such scholarly liberties as restoring some of the windows of the clerestory back to their twelfth-century form: smaller than the later windows and paired with blind roses. Since he filled these windows with clear rather than colored glass, they gave the interior a bit more light, welcome

Only seventeen when he sketched the sack of the archiepiscopal palace (far left) behind Notre-Dame in 1831 — and only three years older when Monvoisin executed his portrait (near left) — Eugène Emmanuel Viollet-le-Duc was destined to oversee the triumphant restoration of the cathedral of Paris. During the two decades he devoted to "Gothicizing" Notre-Dame, Viollet-le-Duc supervised the demolition of many of the crumbling structures (right) that hemmed in the cathedral — a task that continued after the architect's death in 1879.

to our modern taste. They also make an interesting historical point. He had endless decisions to make, for the cathedral incorporated a great many styles, not one of which could be considered definitive. He himself was biased toward a certain ascetic bareness, particularly where the chapels were concerned, and he has been somewhat criticized for this. But he relented in regard to the high altar built to fulfill the vow of Louis XIII. "It would be a shame to destroy a thing of such luxurious and tasteful workmanship and put in its place something of which we have only a few vague descriptions."

Restoring Notre-Dame was an enormous task. Viollet-le-Duc repaired the structure literally from the foundations to the tiling of the roofs. As he explained in his report, it was only in taking the work in hand that he saw how grave the cathedral's troubles were, the essential nature of what had to be done, and the danger of half measures. His diagnoses and remedies have proved their soundness. Notre-Dame stands substantially as he left it in 1864. Although he ran through more than one allocation, new funds were always voted for him. Building in France no longer depended on the whim of kings but on sober-minded deputies — yet they proved remarkably generous toward the cause of restoration.

Nevertheless, the country was undergoing severe economic strains. The crisis of 1848, marked by a stock exchange crash, unemployment, hunger, and workers' uprisings bloodily suppressed, brought to the fore an unlikely figure. This was Charles Louis Napoleon Bonaparte, third son of Napoleon's brother Louis. In the turbulence that swept away the citizen-king Louis Philippe, he came forward as the heir to Napoleon, representing order, authority, religion, and concern for popular welfare. For a few years Louis Napoleon was President of the Republic. As such, he systematically suppressed all opposition forces and used the machinery of government to eliminate constitutional checks on his power. By 1852 he had the title he had long coveted: emperor.

The following year the cathedral of Notre-Dame, though not too far along in its refurbishment, saw the last of France's royal weddings. Napoleon III's bride was a titled Spanish girl, Eugénie de Montijo. Her striking beauty, her feeling for elegance, and her charm were to leave their stamp on the era. The outward brilliance of the Second Empire was to a large extent identified with Eugénie.

Viollet-le-Duc was commissioned to plan the wedding decorations for the cathedral. His design was a triumph of showmanship, and in its superabundance the very epitome of the regime's style. A pavilion was erected in front of the western façade, its panels painted in the manner of tapestries with representations of the saints and ancient kings of France. Vast figures of Charlemagne and Napoleon were fixed to the two main piers of the façade. The balustrade above the Gallery of Kings was decked with eagles and garlands. Nine green banners embroidered with Napoleonic bees and the imperial insignia waved above that. The higher levels of the façade were lost behind the flags of the eighty-six departments of France, more green streamers decorated with bees, vast standards of eagles, canopies of cloth of gold, and — topping each tower — an enormous tricolor flag.

For a while the country seemed prosperous and all went well for the imperial couple. A son was born to them and was baptized in the cathedral in the presence of no fewer than eighty-five high church dignitaries. Viollet-le-Duc was asked to design a great font for the ceremony, something in Byzantine style to be made out of Sèvres porcelain. He answered dryly that there was a copper vessel in the Louvre which had been used for the baptism of Saint Louis's children and should do perfectly well in this case. The suggestion was accepted, although in other respects there was no stinting of expense. Four new bells were installed in the towers and rung for the first time on this fourteenth of June 1856. The day before, Viollet-le-Duc was asked to make a personal search of the cathedral cellars — the architect knew them so well — as a security check.

Acts of terrorism had become common all through Europe, and a deep nervousness had begun to pervade the Second Empire. Louis Napoleon saw his popularity waning and attempted to win it back by making long-promised concessions to constitutional freedom. Then in a desperate desire to show strength, he provoked a war with Prussia in 1870.

Viollet-le-Duc was climbing in the Alps when news of the declaration of war reached him. His forebodings were expressed in a letter to his son: "Even if this war will not be a long one, it cannot be other than terrible." Although already fifty-six, he returned quickly to Paris and threw himself into the improvised defense effort there. The news from the front was bad, and soon it became worse. In a month the French forces were outflanked and large numbers taken prisoner, including the emperor himself.

With the Prussians on French soil, the patriotism of Paris rose to great heights. "We are in a pretty mess," Viollet-le-Duc wrote. But he praised the spirit of his outfit, made up of architects and workers in the building trades, almost all of whom he knew. With the Prussians on their way to encircle the city, he and his men were dispatched to Saint-Denis to take hasty measures to protect the edifice. He had scaffolding set up and sandbags piled, but the heavy Prussian bombardment severely damaged the abbey church. Some of the oldest stained glass in France was smashed.

War plays tricks on concepts of morality. In Paris, too, such tricks were being played. Cut off from food and fuel, with all normal functioning halted, the city abounded in terrible sights. Typhus broke out. There were many deaths from general privation. The poor, with nothing to sell or pawn, had the worst of it, but apparently their will to resist continued strong. In the rest of France there was one party that favored making peace, another for holding out against the harsh Prussian terms. A monarchist assembly had been elected, but it inspired little confidence. The National Guard, holding Paris against the encircling Prussians, was largely made up of the working class. When the legal government finally capitulated — Prussia's price was an indemnity of five billion francs, the cession of Alsace and Lorraine, and a long period of occupation — these contingents refused to give up their arms. Faced with revolution, the government fled to Versailles. The insurgents ran up the red flag over the Hôtel de Ville and proclaimed a people's government, the Commune.

Karl Marx, writing an account of the experiment only a few days after it was over, described the Com-

mune as a self-controlled, courageous venture run on the highest moral principles, and able — in the ten weeks at its disposal — to create a host of viable institutions. He saw Louis Napoleon's war and all that followed as a complicated plot on the part of the ruling classes to crush the rising power of the workers. The rest of France, he maintained, would soon have risen and made the revolution general. These interpretations were consonant with his larger theories on the historical inevitability of revolution. Whatever the case, in the last days of May 1871 the Versailles troops broke into the city. They had to win it street by street.

In the cathedral of Notre-Dame there is a black marble plaque commemorating sixty-three hostages shot by the Commune, among them the archbishop and five other ecclesiastics. The plaque tells only one side of the story. It would be only fair to tell the other side. The Communards had repeatedly asked for the release of their leaders. The hostages were being held as guarantees for the lives of these leaders, and the shootings took place only when the Bloody Week — as the days of May 21 to 28 were henceforth known — began. The government forces remained confident of eventual victory and obdurately refused to exchange prisoners. When the city fell and the government troops moved in to restore order, they rounded up all who could be suspected of taking part in the defense of the Commune. At least 20,000 persons, including women and mere boys, were mowed down by the *mitrailleuse,* the primitive machine-gun introduced into the French army just before the war. These victims of martial law were executed without even the pretense of a trial. There were also many more "legal" victims. For years

afterward trials continued and sentences of death or transportation to the colonies were meted out to the survivors of the massacre.

"I passed my day looking at Paris burn. It is a dead, destroyed, and annihilated city," the novelist Ludovic Halévy wrote of May 24, 1871. But seventeen days later, he reconsidered. "It is still the most beautiful city in Europe, and the most brilliant, and the most gay."

With so many painters setting up easels in the open air — according to the decree of Impressionism — it was inevitable that the cathedral should become a favorite subject of artists in the succeeding Third Republic. Much painted, much sketched, much etched and, with increasing interest in the camera, much photographed, Notre-Dame became an ever more familiar image to those who might not actually set eyes upon her. To local inhabitants she was more visible than before, as several more buildings around her were razed. Admirers of the medieval might criticize the change and point out that widening the vista detracted from the effect of the façade. But there was surely something to be said for the sunny park, the bright parterres, and the softening line of trees that took the place of the Hôtel Dieu, that ancient, insalubrious hospital, and the equally obsolete foundling home.

This new fringe of green about the gray old edifice, where children played and lovers met, where the old enjoyed the sun and tourists collected their strength, represented still another face that Paris disclosed to the twentieth century. Paris was the City of Light, of heightened sensibility, of seasoned beauty, of humane tolerance and worldly wisdom, of faith and skepticism, of artistic audacity, and of intellectual rigor. It was

dense with tradition yet receptive to the new. No wonder Paris was the mecca for aspiring artists from all of France, all of Europe, all the world. Everyone who came, whether to visit or to stay, paid his respects to the cathedral. Notre-Dame was the soul of the city.

The uses of the cathedral had changed somewhat; it had a new part to play in the life of the nation. For in the twentieth century the nature of ceremony had altered. There were still great formal rites set in Notre-Dame, but these were no longer hierarchic, revolving about the fortunes of royalty, their weddings, baptisms, and funerals. The Third Republic, born with such pangs, proved remarkably durable. The ceremonies of a republic are apt to be lacking in color, but perhaps make up for this by wider and more genuine participation. Their real theme is the survival of the nation.

The ceremonies for the beatification of Joan of Arc were no exception to this rule. These took place in Notre-Dame in 1909 and evoked an outpouring of emotion all over France. Not only did this inspired, fearless, and unconventional girl correspond to a new ideal of femininity emerging at this time, but she was also the Maid of Lorraine. Forty years had passed since the short, disastrous war in which that province had been forfeited, but the loss still rankled. Joan had rallied the French to expel the foreign invader and recapture lost territories. It was timely indeed that she was now numbered among the blessed.

By that year the enemy was no longer the English, but those offensively successful Germans. Their disparate states were unified into an empire whose interests crossed with those of France in more than one sector. The Kaiser rattled his saber in a manner that

other European nations found hard to bear. Alliances formed. England, France, and Russia discovered a common bond, while on the other side were ranged Germany, Austria-Hungary, and that once formidable but now crumbling Moslem power, the Ottoman Empire.

The Great War came in 1914. The German general staff had envisaged it as another quick thrust. They attacked through Belgium and almost reached Paris, but the resolute stand of British, Belgian, and French troops checked their impetus. There were fresh advances and breakthroughs, then stalemate. This was an unprecedented form of warfare with new rules and new weapons. Tanks were used, as were long-range artillery and the small, fragile airplanes that opened possibilities for destruction so far undreamed of. Science provided another innovation: poison gas.

Strangely enough, all sides had gone to the battlefield in a mood of patriotic exaltation and readiness for sacrifice. But the slaughter on both sides was ghastly; the euphoria wore off as the ordeal dragged on. Russia fell away, victim of defeat and internal revolution. In 1917 a fresh and jaunty army of Americans arrived.

All through the war, prayers had been said in the cathedral for France and her armies. Once more the ancient relics, whose efficacy would seem to have dwindled in modern times, were brought out and carried in procession down the aisles of Notre-Dame. Paris was spared the worst blows of the war, although the first small shells fell upon her as early as September 1914. In October of that same year one bomb penetrated the roof of Notre-Dame over the north transept, causing some damage. Other great Gothic monuments did not get off so lightly. Reims cathedral, where

French kings since Clovis had been crowned, was reduced to near ruin.

To hail the armistice of November 1918 there was a great Te Deum in Notre-Dame. The cathedral was filled to bursting. The decorations were all flags, the important personages generals, and the altar draped in the tricolor. The priest who said mass came from Alsace, once more a part of France. The score had been righted. This time it was the Germans who saw their empire dismembered. Moreover, they had to pay heavy indemnities for war guilt and surrender the iron-rich Saar to French occupation; they were also denied the right to an army. But the price had been staggering on both sides. This came to light over the next two decades in the insecurity of the social order, in economic collapse, and in the emergence of pathological creeds among the vanquished.

In both France and Germany commanding figures of the previous era passed away. In 1929 Notre-Dame was draped in black for the funeral of Marshal Foch, the Allied supreme commander of World War I. There was a somber ceremony before the casket was placed on a horse-drawn gun carriage waiting on the parvis before the cathedral. The cortege consisted of other eminent and aging generals who followed on foot as the procession made its way to the Arc de Triomphe, where the casket was set beside the tomb of the Unknown Soldier, to lie in state before burial at the Invalides. Thus public ritual paid homage to the innumerable *poilus* on whose sacrifices the reputations of the great ultimately rested.

This emphasis was natural for France, where the principles of Rousseau's *Social Contract* had become

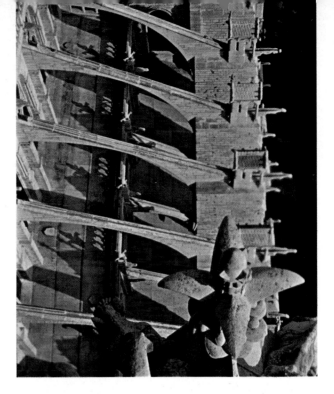

The massive bulk of the twin towers of Notre-Dame — seen at left from the southeast — is relieved by the presence of decorative finials and crockets. At right is an unusual view from above of the cathedral's famed flying buttresses.

assimilated into the national character. It was somewhat different in Germany. There General von Hindenburg, the German counterpart of Foch in the Great War, had been installed as president since 1925. Hindenburg, too, stood for the soldierly virtues. He was an authoritarian figure, still an honorable one, hewn on majestic nineteenth-century lines. His death in 1934 opened the way to absolute power on the part of an authoritarian figure of quite another sort: Adolf Hitler. A thwarted self-taught architect, a lowly corporal during the war who in the difficult postwar years joined the flotsam and jetsam of the big cities, Hitler conceived a mission for himself, came forth as a leader, and built up a heterogeneous party. He understood the grievances of the Germans and their crying need for simple answers and large promises. Germany's new chancellor unilaterally abrogated the humiliating peace terms of the treaty of Versailles, built an army, moved troops into prohibited areas, made outrageous demands — and found that they were granted. In France, all this was chiefly seen as the stirrings of the hated Boche. France strengthened her military defenses. The Maginot Line was considered impregnable.

When, after a deceptive lull, the Germans attacked France in May 1940, they again relied on the impetus of surprise. They parachuted troops behind the fortified lines and, coming through the Low Countries, outflanked the Maginot Line. They could also count on secret allies in the invaded regions. But even more significant than outright treachery was the general mood of fatalism in France. Many responsible people, including large portions of the officer corps, saw little hope in holding off this onslaught. The previous war

was too recent, its toll too well remembered. Within five weeks German troops were occupying Paris.

Hitler himself came to see his prize. He made a sightseeing tour, surely one of the most bizarre ever undertaken. It began at five-thirty in the morning and was over by nine. Hitler knew what he wanted to see: the Opéra, the Trocadero, the Eiffel Tower, the Arc de Triomphe, and the Invalides, where he stood for a long time by the tomb of Napoleon. He admired the Pantheon and had himself driven to Montmartre to see the church of Sacré-Coeur. Notre-Dame was not on his itinerary.

That same evening, back in his command post, Hitler gave orders reactivating his ambitious plans for the rebuilding of Berlin. "Wasn't Paris beautiful?" he said. "But Berlin must be made far more beautiful. In the past I have often considered whether we would not have to destroy Paris. But when we are finished in Berlin, Paris will be only a shadow. So why should we destroy it?"

France, divided into the occupied territory and the so-called Free Zone, lived for the next four years at the mercy of such caprices. In the first days of the war, measures had been taken to protect the cathedral. The rose windows were removed, the portals blocked with sandbags. After the Germans had entered the city, the bells remained silent. On the first anniversary of the unhappy armistice, a special votive lamp was set at the feet of the statue of Our Lady and kept burning day and night — a tradition going back to the Middle Ages.

Life in Paris was subdued. The German grip on the city was strong. Arrests and summary executions were frequent. But beneath the gray surface of submission,

The liberation of Paris from the Nazis was celebrated in a solemn ceremony at Notre-Dame on August 26, 1944. At right the hero of the day, Charles de Gaulle, greets General Leclerc, commander of the Second French Armored Division, in front of the cathedral.

of universal shortages and widespread fear, a spirit of opposition was gathering. An underground network developed, organized along tight conspiratorial lines. Activists carried out a campaign of harassment. Production was sabotaged. German patrols were ambushed, German soldiers shot under cover of darkness. Intelligence was gathered and transmitted, downed airmen and commandos sheltered, underground leaflets and newspapers distributed. The V for Victory sign, painted on walls, or two fingers surreptitiously lifted, kept alive the knowledge that a Resistance existed, and this knowledge strengthened the will to resist.

Young men faced with conscription into German labor brigades disappeared in the night. They went to the south and joined guerrilla bands operating in the rough terrain known as the *maquis*. Soon the name was being applied to the Resistance forces themselves. Armed with stolen weapons and with matériel dropped by British planes, they trained for the eventual rising. Others managed to get to England, crossing the Channel in small boats or taking the arduous route over the Pyrenees and escaping through Spain and Portugal. In England they joined the Free French forces headed by General Charles de Gaulle.

Until the general assumed this role, he had been a little-known figure. He had behind him the fairly standard career of a professional officer — service in World War I, a spell of teaching military history at Saint-Cyr, a post in the War Office, assignments in French Africa, command of an armored division on the Belgian front in 1940. He also had to his credit a remarkable but little-heeded book entitled *The Army of the Future*. De Gaulle had been named Undersecretary

of Defense in an ephemeral cabinet put together a few days after the surrender. When this fell, to be replaced by the more compliant government under the aged Marshal Pétain, de Gaulle went to England and lost no time announcing the existence of the Free French forces.

He had no easy time of it in England. The British and Americans were not disposed to take him as seriously as he expected. Concerned exclusively with military victory, they also had no sympathy for the political considerations with which de Gaulle seemed unnecessarily preoccupied. But he tenaciously upheld his claims and wrested support for his forces. Contingents of the Free French helped rout Rommel's army in the desert war and landed with the Allies in Italy. When the moment came for the full-scale invasion, de Gaulle was determined that the Free French should have a conspicuous role in the liberation of Paris.

Although few knew it, the city was in terrible jeopardy. The Germans had already been given orders for its destruction — orders that came directly from Hitler's headquarters. A special squad had been sent to Paris to prepare all the bridges for demolition. A master plan was drawn up for wrecking factories and power plants. All communications were to be shattered, and for symbolic purposes the historic monuments would be blown up. There were enough explosives on hand for the work. Dynamite was placed at the Eiffel Tower, the Invalides, and the Chamber of Deputies. Three tons of TNT were placed in the crypt of Notre-Dame.

Near the cathedral is the massive Prefecture of Police, and so the area around Notre-Dame became the very center of the crisis on August 19, 1944. After the Allied landing in Normandy, the Germans had taken the precaution of disarming the police. Now, with other civic employees, the entire Paris police force went on strike. A secret nest of Resistance fighters, the police responded to the first call for the uprising and seized their own headquarters. Almost at once, the long-planned insurrection broke out all over the city. Barricades were thrown up and street fighting began. Besieged inside the Prefecture, the Resistance forces hurled Molotov cocktails at the German tanks closing in on the building.

Meanwhile, couriers slipped through the German lines to reach the Allied armies, still a hundred miles away, and implore them to speed to Paris. Their strategy had called for bypassing Paris altogether in their eastward drive. But plans were revised, at least to the extent of sending the Second French Armored Division toward the capital. These troops made slow progress and took heavy losses, for the German defenses were still formidable. Once inside the city, there was more fighting to be done — clumsy, murderous combat between tanks and unexpected death from snipers' bullets. But on the night of August 24 the *bourdon* of Notre-Dame, mute for four years, gave the signal for a general tolling of the bells of Paris. The ringing of the church bells convinced the Germans that their cause was lost.

There was to be a Te Deum in the cathedral on August 26, 1944 — the first day the city was truly in French hands. General de Gaulle, on foot, his scanty forces following informally behind him, led a victory parade from the Arc de Triomphe to Notre-Dame. In thus exposing himself to enormous risk, either from enemy air attack, from German snipers, or from his political foes, the general demonstrated again that indifference to consequences that was to become his special mark.

As he was about to enter Notre-Dame, rifle fire broke out, at first somewhere on the parvis, then inside the cathedral itself. The congregation, reflexes sharpened by four years' experience with war, hugged the floor. But de Gaulle moved imperturbably down the aisle to his seat in the transept. His example recalled others to a sense of proper bearing, and the ceremony began. Outside, the French forces were firing at the rooftops around the cathedral, against the presumptive snipers. A few suspects were taken into custody, but the mystery of who had done the firing was never solved.

After official peace, there were many political battles whose ultimate effect was to paralyze the state. Indochina flung off French rule, and the African territorial possessions, which had shown moving loyalty to France during the war, now asked for their reward in the form of independence. The most painful struggle took place in Algeria, legally a Department of France, with a sizable French population. There the French army obstinately took its final stand, under the slogan of *Algérie française* to counter the slogan of *Algérie libre*. The war there was particularly ugly, marked by terrorism and torture. It spread to France, especially to Paris, where bombings and assassinations became commonplace. There seemed no way out of the impasse. In 1958 Charles de Gaulle, who had withdrawn from public life, made his return. But to universal astonishment, de Gaulle, who seemed to have taken power to execute the will of the army, liquidated the war and let

Algeria go her own way. Only then was the country able to begin the immense tasks of reconstruction and modernization that had so long been delayed.

Charles de Gaulle headed the government for a decade, under a new constitution that greatly increased the power of the executive. Like Napoleon and Louis Napoleon, he made effective use of the plebiscite. Direct elections gave him overwhelming endorsement. He was sometimes likened, in his manners and policy, to a king. But he did not manifest the monarchical passion for palatial building. Instead, he fostered a program of public housing and highway construction and undertook as well the dramatic cleansing of the buildings of Paris.

Dictatorial but never a dictator, de Gaulle stepped down when the French people repudiated him in the elections of 1969. A year later, he died. In deliberate rejection of any conception of himself as a sovereign, Charles de Gaulle had left directions that his funeral was to be one of extreme simplicity. It took place at Colombey-Les-Deux-Eglises, the village in the Marne countryside where the de Gaulles had made their home since the 1930's. But the nation could not let the occasion go by without paying honor to the general. However much hostility had gathered around him in his years as president, no one could deny his stature. In proof of the worldwide respect he had earned, leaders from more than eighty nations came at short notice to attend the high requiem mass inside Notre-Dame.

Only a limited number of the general public had been admitted into the cathedral, but the public address system relayed the proceedings to the parvis. There some 70,000 persons waited, observing silence as had been requested. This being Anno Domini 1970, many had come with their transistor radios and could hear every word of the liturgy. Maurice de Sully, who eight hundred years earlier had conceived the cathedral on a grand scale so that it could accommodate the multitudes, would have found this perfectly in order.

After the ceremony, many of those who remembered de Gaulle as the hero of the Liberation made their way around to the rear of the cathedral. There, behind the apse, recent history meets ancient tradition. At the very end of the Île de la Cité, the waters of the Seine lapping against its walls, is the Monument to the Deportation. Dedicated to the 200,000 Frenchmen who died in German concentration camps, the monument is a crypt of concrete, like a wartime bunker, bomb shelter, or prison. Barred corridors heighten the impression of a prison house. Scratched on the walls, like the messages of the condemned in cells, are quotations from contemporary writers — Camus, Sartre, and other voices of the war years. This memorial to the martyred of World War II stands, like Notre-Dame herself, upon ground hallowed for many centuries. For here, in medieval times, was the priory of Saint-Denis-du-Pas, erected on the very spot where, according to legend, Saint Denis had been tortured before his execution.

Among the inscriptions on the wall of the crypt is one urging the modern pilgrim: "Forgive but do not forget."

Adorning the flèche of Notre-Dame is this statue of Saint Thomas with the facial features of Viollet-le-Duc.

NOTRE-DAME
IN LITERATURE

*Outraged and appalled by the dilapidated condition of the famed cathedral of
Paris in the mid-nineteenth century, France's intellectual elite galvanized public
opinion in support of restoration. A committee was formed, petitions were circu-
lated, funds were solicited, and a competition for the best plan was held. Eugène
Emmanuel Viollet-le-Duc, a leading architect and a fervent advocate of the contemporary Gothic revival, was awarded the commission. He began work in 1845
but the extensive restorations were not completed until 1864. In his* Discourses
on Architecture, *first published in 1860, Viollet-le-Duc praised the innovative
twelfth-century architects who conceived and built the magnificent façade of
Notre-Dame de Paris.*

Every one knows the front of Notre Dame de Paris; few perhaps realise the
amount of knowledge, taste, study, care, resolution, and experience implied
by the erection of that colossal pile within the space of at most ten or twelve
years. Still it is an unfinished work; the two towers were to have been
terminated by spires in stone, which would have completed and rendered
intelligible the admirably designed lower masses. Here we have indeed Art,
and Art of the noblest order. . . .

. . . First observe — what is of rare occurrence in buildings, particularly
when they attain very considerable dimensions — that the architect has managed to divide his front by grand horizontal lines, which, without cutting it
up into sections, form so many resting-places for the eye; that these divisions
are made by an accomplished artist, inasmuch as they present spaces that
are unequal, sometimes plain, sometimes ornamented, varied in their details,
and yet presenting perfect unity in the entire effect. We have not here, as is
so frequently to be seen in Roman, Byzantine, or modern buildings, the
piling up of features that seem introduced at hap-hazard, and that might be
changed, modified, or omitted. . . .

Above [the] basement, which, despite the profusion of sculpture spread
beneath the arches, preserves an aspect of gravity and strength, there extends
across the whole breadth of the front a gallery — a portico composed of hol-
lowed lintels, supported on monolithic shafts surmounted by large capitals;
in each opening is placed a colossal statue of a king. The architect, without
interrupting his portico, took care to render apparent the projection of the
buttresses; this cincture, which is of great severity in design and execution,
and is low in proportion to the height of the front, has the effect of its actual
dimensions restored by being surmounted by a balustrade which recalls the
size of the human figure. Above, the buttresses continue upwards with
offsets; but the three divisions of the front are set back to a considerable
depth to leave a broad terrace over the Gallery of the Kings and to aid in
giving this gallery great importance as a decorative line. . . .

. . . if from the examination of the general features we proceed to the
details of the building, every one who understands construction will be
amazed when he sees what numberless precautions are resorted to in the
execution, — how the prudence of the practical builder is combined with
the daring of the artist full of power and inventive imagination; while in
examining the mouldings and the sculpture we remark the use of reliable
methods, a scrupulous adherence to principles, a perfect appreciation of
effect, a style unequalled in purity by modern art, an execution at the same
time delicate and bold, quite free from exaggeration, and owing its merit
to the study and love of form. . . .

The front of Notre Dame also renders conspicuous an excellence belonging exclusively to French architects at the time when France possessed an architecture of its own; that of variety in unity. At first sight the portals appear symmetrical; nevertheless the love of variety is evident; thus the doorway on the left is unlike that on the right. The north tower (that of the left) is sensibly larger than the south. On that side the arcading of the great gallery is more severe and solid than that of the other; whence we may conclude that — according to a custom generally followed — the two stone pieces would present dissimilarities in the details, though designed to present two equiponderant masses. We know how imperatively variety is required by our western genius. It is evident here as in other edifices built up at once in the same period, that the architect could not resolve to produce the same detail twice: in erecting two towers he gave a different drawing for each; and the increase of work he thereby imposed on himself was of no account with him in comparison with the *ennui* he would have experienced in letting his workmen execute two colossal towers exactly alike. Many find fault with these dissimilarities that contravene absolute symmetry; but it cannot be denied that in this craving for variety there is manifested an intellectual effort — a constant seeking for the better, — an emulation, shall I say, which is in accordance with our Western character.

EUGÈNE EMMANUEL VIOLLET-LE-DUC
Discourses on Architecture, 1860

In 1902 Hilaire Belloc — essayist, poet, historian, biographer, and novelist — wrote his famous panegyric to medieval Paris. The British author's devotion to Notre-Dame de Paris is matched only by his ire over the damage the cathedral suffered during the eighteenth century.

A drawing by Viollet-le-Duc of a gargoyle-adorned buttress from one of Notre-Dame's two towers

Notre Dame was built for a little Gothic capital, and a huge metropolis has outgrown her. The town was once, so to speak, the fringe of her garment; now she is but the centre of a circle miles around. . . . To a man who loves and knows the city, there soon comes a desire to communicate constantly with the memories of the Cathedral. And this desire, if he is wise, grows into a habit of coming close against the towers at evening, or of waiting under the great height of the nave for the voices of the Middle Ages.

Notre Dame thus lost in distance, central and remote, is like a lady grown old in a great house, about whose age new phrases and strange habits have arisen, who is surrounded with the youth of her own lineage, and yet is content to hear and understand without replying to their speech. She is silent in the midst of energy, and forgotten in the many activities of the household, yet she is the centre of the estate. . . .

The building of Notre Dame may be taken as a centre round which to group every characteristic of [the twelfth-century] renascence, which I have called a revolution. I have already insisted on the novelty of the Gothic spirit; I would now insist upon its daring. There was in all Paris nothing larger than buildings of from fifty to sixty yards in length, from thirty to forty feet in height. The Palace occupied a great area, but it was rather a group of buildings than one. Square towers here and there marked the churches; they were . . . of little height. But a man coming in from the countrysides would have seen, when Notre Dame was building, something typical on the material side of what the mind of the twelfth century had been. For the first time in centuries upon centuries that creative passion for vastness, whose exaggeration is the enormous, but whose absence is the sure mark of pettiness and decline, had found expression. High above the broken line of the little flat grey town, one could see a great phalanx of scaffolding, up and thick like the spears of a company, and filled in with a mist of building and the distant noise of workmen. . . . Three times, four times the height of the tall things of the town, occupying in its bulk a notable division of the whole island, it would have made such a man think that for the future Paris would not hold a cathedral, but rather that the cathedral would make little Paris its neighbourhood. . . .

It was natural that the eighteenth century should have seen little in the Gothic glories of the thirteenth. There lay between the opening of our period and the last of the Gothic two hundred years . . . and these two hundred years were completely ignorant of the spirit which had built Notre Dame. The first of these centuries had indeed retained the old gables and deep lanes of medieval Paris . . . but the second . . . rebuilt Paris so completely that it destroyed even the outward example of a thing whose idea had long disappeared. Therefore the reign of Louis XIV had treated the Cathedral carelessly; had put in, just before the king's death, that huge, ugly high altar, and had destroyed the revered flooring of tombs to make way for the chess-board pattern of black and white that still displeases us. But throughout its action it left the shell and mass of Notre Dame the same. With the reign of Louis XV a very much worse spirit came upon the architects, for they were no longer content to neglect the old work, they were bent upon improving it. . . .

In the first place, they destroyed the old windows. It is written somewhere that the destruction began with the desire to let a shaft of white light come down upon the new high altar; even this insufficient excuse will hardly hold, for all the glass seems to have been taken away bodily and at one time, in 1741. We lost in that act the fulness and the spirit of Notre Dame, and the loss can never be made good. . . .

[Another] example of the evil done to Notre Dame was the action of Soufflot. I do not mean that heavy, great sacristy that he built, and that many men can still remember; I mean his curious restoration of the central door. Here was the chief glory of the West front. . . . Its carvings . . . were designed to symbolize the kernel of Christianity, and to make, as it were, a continual Credo for the people who passed beneath. . . . This door especially laid stress upon the end of man (which it showed in the Last Judgment carefully carved on the tympanum), and it had, on either side of the doorway, the twelve apostles listening to the teaching of Our Lord, whose statue stood in the central pier. . . . So, if the door was to have any meaning at all, the statue of Our Lord was its natural centre, the apostles whom He was teaching made the bulk of the design; and then, as a result and pendant to this, came the ogival tympanum above, with that subject of the Last Judgment which is the favourite theme of medieval Paris. The canopy carried over the Sacrament during processions was, in the Middle Ages in France (and is still in most countries), a flexible cloth, with four poles to support it. This, when a procession passed through a door, could be partly folded together if it was too wide to go through at its full stretch. Now it so happened that the canopy in the Church of France had been, of late times, made with a stiff framework;

there was therefore a certain inconvenience and difficulty in passing through the main door on feast days, because the central pier divided it into two narrow portions. With this little pretext, the canons did not hesitate to ruin the principal door of their church. . . .

Since the main object was to widen the door, [Soufflot's] first act was to throw down the central pier, and to destroy the teaching Christ, for which, we may say, the whole porch existed. But even with this he was not content; for, looking at the heavy, triangular tympanum overhanging this broadened space, he thought to himself that it looked top-heavy, and might even fall, now that it lacked its old support. He therefore, very quietly and without comment, cut through the relief and the carving, brought his chisel just where a fine sweeping curve might be traced, dividing kings in the middle, cutting saints slantwise and removing angels, till he had opened a small ogive of his own within the greater one. Then he finished off the whole with a neat moulding. . . .

This hideous thing remained throughout the first part of our century, till Montalembert, in a fine speech, opened the reform, and saw the restoration of the Cathedral begun; and though, in that restoration, most of what was done was in reparation of what the Revolution destroyed, yet it is well to remember that the energy and the great schemes of the generation to which Montalembert and Viollet le Duc belonged were due to the Revolutionary movement, and that the sack and ruin of 1793 had been long prepared by the apathy and ignorance and forgetfulness of the generation preceding it. If Soufflot and the canons could see no beauty in, and could destroy the statuary of Notre Dame, it is not wonderful that the populace should deliberately throw down the memorials of a spirit of which they knew nothing, save that its heirs were then fighting the nation.

HILAIRE BELLOC
Paris, 1902

Three sketches by Auguste Rodin of French ecclesiastical architecture

In the early years of the twentieth century Auguste Rodin, France's preeminent modern sculptor, was inspired by his periodic visits to the cathedrals scattered across the countryside. His profoundly personal notes, published in 1914, constitute a great artist's unique testament to the glory of French Gothic architecture, "the marvel of our marvels."

No one defends our Cathedrals.

The burden of old age crushes them, and under the pretext of curing them, of "restoring" what he should only uphold, the architect changes their features.

Crowds stop in silence before the Cathedrals, incapable of understanding the splendor of these architectural immensities, yet instinctively admiring them. Oh, the mute admiration of these crowds! I want to cry out to them that they are not mistaken; yes, our French Cathedrals are very beautiful! But their beauty is not easy to understand. Let us study them together; understanding will come to you as it has come to me. . . .

They still possess, despite all things and all persons, so much beauty, our old living stones! None has succeeded in killing them, and it is our duty to gather together and defend these relics.

Before I myself disappear, I wish at least to have told my admiration for them. I wish to pay them a debt of gratitude, I, who owe them so much happiness! I wish to honor these stones, so lovingly transformed into masterpieces by humble and wise artisans; these moldings admirably molded like the lips of a young woman; these beautiful lingering shadows where softness sleeps at the heart of power; these delicate and vigorous ribs springing up toward the vault and bending down upon the intersection of a flower; these rose windows whose magnificence was inspired by the setting sun or by the dawn. . . .

The art of the Middle Ages, in its ornamentation as well as in its constructions, derives from nature. It is therefore always to nature that one must go for an understanding of that art.

See Reims: in its tapestries we find the same color, leaves, and flowers as in its capitals. This is true of all the Cathedrals.

Then let us give ourselves the joy of studying these flowers in nature, that we may have a just notion of the resources which the decorator of living stones required of them. He penetrated the life of flowers by contemplating their forms, by analyzing their joys and their sorrows, their virtues and their weaknesses. These are our sorrows and our virtues.

So flowers have given the Cathedral.

To be convinced, go into the country and open your eyes.

At each step you will have a lesson in architecture. Men of yore looked before us and understood. They sought the plant in the stone and now we find their immortal stones in the eternal flowers. And (is this not the greatest homage they could have hoped for?) nature, although certainly without taking account of our dates, ceaselessly speaks to us of the 12th century, of the 15th, of the 14th, of the 18th. . . .

For me, these beautiful studies in the open air are beneficial. My room hurts me as shoes a size too small would hurt my feet. And how much more the city, the new city! It is in the fresh air of the fields and the woods, I must repeat, that I have learned all that I know.

As if thrown all at once into this immense garden in the beautiful sunshine, I feel myself live through my eyes a new, more intense, and unknown life. But so much splendor makes me dizzy. These flowers that a horticulturist grows for the seeds in massive squares filled with plants all alike, these juxtaposed layers of color, create an impression of stained glass and make me live with them.

It is too radiant. My powers are insufficient. I cannot endure the sudden burst of this beauty, of this motionless beauty! . . .

This eye of the anemone is angry and bloody. I know nothing more heart gripping than this flower. The one I am looking at is at the critical age; it is covered with fine wrinkles; its petals are as if disjointed; it is going to fall. The Persian vase in which I have placed it, blue, white, and cream, makes for it a worthy tomb. Its sisters in full bloom are designs for rose windows.

This large flower, of the violet color that I love in certain stained-glass windows of Notre Dame, touches me like a memory, especially now that we are returning to God, this flower and I. Its sad heart, where a black bud is forming, is also encircled by a black crown which the petals exaggerate, and these violet petals make the window seem to stand before the light. This flower is a widow.

AUGUSTE RODIN
Cathedrals of France, 1914

PROCESSIONS AND PAGEANTS

Thomas Coryat, a "buffoon," or jester, at the court of King James I of England, embarked on a walking tour of the Continent in 1608. On one of his many stops he visited Notre-Dame de Paris. His quaint account of a feast day at the cathedral reveals both his Protestant distaste for sumptuous display and his grudging fascination with "Papist" extravagance.

About nine of the clock . . . in the morning, I went to the Cathedral Church which is dedicated to our Lady . . . to observe the strange ceremonies of [Corpus Christi] day, which for novelty sake, but not for any harty devotion . . . I was contented to behold, as being the first that ever I saw of that kinde, and I hartily wish they may be the last. No sooner did I enter into the Church but a great company of Clergy men came forth singing, and so continued all the time of the procession, till they returned unto the Church againe, some by couples, and some single. They walked partly in coapes [copes], whereof some were exceeding rich, being (in my estimation) worth at the least a hundred markes a peece; and partly in surplices. Also in the same traine there were many couples of little singing choristers, many of them not above eight or nine years old, and few above a dozen: which prety innocent punies were so egregiously deformed by those that had authority over them, that they could not choose but move great commiseration in any relenting spectator. For they had not a quarter so much haire left upon their heads as they brought with them into the world, out of their mothers wombs, being so clean shaved away round their whole heads that a man could perceive no more then the very rootes. A spectacle very pittifull (me thinks) to behold, though Papists esteeme it holy. The last man of the whole traine was the Bishop of Paris, a proper and comly man as any I saw in all the city, of some five and thirty years old. He walked not sub dio, that is under the open aire, as the rest did. But he had a rich cannopy carried over him, supported with many little pillers on both sides. This did the Priests carry: he himselfe was that day in his sumptuous Pontificalities, wearing religious ornaments of great price, like a second Aaron, with his Episcopall staffe in his hand, bending round at the toppe, called by us English men a Croisier, and his Miter on his head of cloth of silver, with two long labels hanging downe behind his neck. As for the streets of Paris they were more sumptuously adorned that day then any other day of the whole yeare, every street of speciall note being on both sides thereof, from the pentices of their houses to the lower end of the wall hanged with rich cloth of arras, and the costliest tapistry that they could provide. The shewes of our Lady street being so hyperbolical in pomp that day, that it exceeded the rest by many degrees. And for the greater addition of ornament to this feast of God, they garnished many of their streets with rich cupboords of plate as ever I saw in all my life. For they exposed upon their publique tables exceeding costly goblets, and what not tending to pompe, that is called by the name of plate. Upon the middest of their tables stood their golden Crucifixes, with divers other gorgeous Images. . . . Wherefore the foresaid sacred company, perambulating about some of the principall streets of Paris, especially our Lady street, were entertained with most divine honours. For whereas the Bishop carried the Sacrament, even his consecrated wafer cake, betwixt the Images of two golden Angels, whensoever he passed by any company, all the spectators prostrated themselves most humbly upon their knees, and elevated their handes with all possible reverence and religious behaviour, attributing as much divine adoration to the little wafer

The bishop leads a procession in honor of the reliquaries of Geneviève, patron saint of Paris.

cake, which they call the Sacrament of the Altar, as they could doe to Jesus Christ himselfe, if he were bodily present with them. If any Godly Protestant that hateth this superstition, should happen to be amongst them when they kneele, and forbeare to worship the Sacrament as they doe, perhaps he may be presently stabbed or otherwise most shamefully abused, if there should be notice taken of him. After they had spent almost two houres in these pompous (I will not say theatricall) shewes, they returned again to our Lady Church, where was performed very long and tedious devotion, for the space of two houres, with much excellent singing, and two or three solemne Masses, acted by the Bishops owne person.

THOMAS CORYAT
Coryat's Crudities, 1611

In 1793 the Committee of Public Safety abolished the worship of God in France. Nine years later the first consul, Napoleon Bonaparte, presided over the reestablishment of the Roman Catholic faith. J. G. Lemaistre, one of the first Englishmen to arrive in Paris following the temporary termination of hostilities between Great Britain and France, was an eyewitness to that historic ceremony, held at Notre-Dame on Easter Sunday 1802.

To day will probably be long remembered in the annals of France, on account of the promulgation of the law for the reestablishment of religion; on account of the definitive treaty of peace with England, the ratifications of which were exchanged this morning at the Thuilleries; and of the "Te Deum" sung at *Notre Dame,* in honour of these united events.

I wished very much to be present at a ceremony, which was rendered so particularly interesting by the number of curious concurring circumstances, too obvious to be detailed. Having no ticket, I went to the church at six o'clock in the morning, hoping to make my way, among the crowd, into those places, which were not appropriated to the constituted authorities. The doors were not open; and about a hundred persons, who were already arrived, stood enclosed in a kind of barrier, which seemed to have been put up for the purpose of preventing too great a press at the first opening of the gates. I placed myself against this bar, and hoped to gain admittance in the second division. I was soon followed and surrounded by a considerable crowd; and, after we had all remained about two hours in this uncomfortable state, a detachment of soldiers arrived, and attempted instantly to clear a passage. We were already so squeezed together, that it was impossible to make room for the military, without either losing our places, or incurring the danger of suffocation. When the soldiers perceived that, notwithstanding the blows which they dealt around them without ceremony, the people did not immediately make way, they lost all patience; and, not content with fixing their bayonets, called out for a detachment of horse. The brandishing of the one, and the fear of the other, soon dispersed the mob; but not till some had been wounded, and several severely bruised.

I could not help reflecting, with some degree of indignation, on this singular scene. In England, under a monarchical form of government, the military are not allowed to interfere, but in cases of positive danger, or actual insurrection; and even then under the orders of a civil magistrate. In France, where the system is called "republican," and every man is supposed to constitute a part of the sovereignty, the body of the people, coming quietly to see the first solemn service of that religion, which is said to be restored in compliance with their wishes, are driven with blows and military violence from the doors of that church, in which peace, liberty, equality, and good order, are about to be celebrated. . . .

It is needless for me to say, that I soon relinquished all hope of getting into the church, and thought myself happy in being able to make my escape unhurt from the claws of these heroes.

In going away, I perceived at the window of an adjoining hospital, nearly opposite the church, some ladies of my acquaintance, who were so obliging as to offer me a place near them, from which I might see the procession.

I had scarcely taken this situation, when a ticket for one of the privileged places in the church was given me by a person, who was unwilling to risk the difficulties, with which the approach to the doors seemed attended. After being sent about to different gates, I at last found admittance at one. When I reached the gallery, it was so completely full, that I found myself compelled to take refuge in the orchestra. From this situation I was again driven by the soldiers; and in despair I returned to the gallery, where, standing on the back of a tottering chair, and with at least twenty rows of spectators before me, I caught, not without some danger, a very imperfect glimpse of this splendid ceremony. . . .

The procession began with a numerous escort of different regiments. Among these were particularly remarked "les guides," a corps of handsome young men, clad in hussar dresses, and mounted on beautiful horses, who excited universal admiration. Next to them came the *"gens d'armes,"* or *"regiment d'élites,"* lately raised. They are men of a very respectable appearance, in blue uniforms, faced with yellow, whence long epaulets are suspended. These, as well as the buttons, are of silver, as is the lace of their hats. Their horses are black. The consular guards, and several regiments of the line, completed the military cavalcade. The ministers of state, and the "corps diplomatique," came next, and formed a long line of carriages. . . . A small corps of *Mamalukes* in their egyptian *costume,* some of whom led unmounted arabians, and a few aides-de-camp, immediately preceded the carriage, in which sat Bonaparte, accompanied by the other two consuls. His coach, new on the occasion, was simply elegant, and drawn by eight very fine horses richly caparisoned. His servants appeared in green coats and red waistcoats, on all the seams of which were rows of broad gold lace. The consuls were received at the door of the church by the archbishop of Paris, who placed over their head a *dais* (or canopy).

Bonaparte, with [the other consuls] *Cambaceres* on his right, and *le Brun* on his left hand, was conducted in this manner to a throne erected near the altar, under which their three chairs were placed. A similar throne appeared opposite, in which sat the cardinal legate.

The bishops bowed first to the altar, secondly to the consuls, and lastly to the cardinal. This was remarked by the public; as, under the monarchy, the representative of the pope was permitted to receive this homage before the sovereign of the country.

The oath settled by the *concordat* having been taken by the clergy, high mass was instantly said.

At the conclusion of this ceremony, M. *de Boisgelin,* formerly archbishop of Aix, lately named archbishop of Thoulouse, ascended the pulpit and

A ORA PRO NOBIS

Parisians honor Sainte Geneviève.

delivered a discourse appropriate to the occasion. I regretted much, that the distance at which I was placed was so great, that it was impossible for me to hear the venerable preacher, who excited no little curiosity, from the singularity of his situation. He is the same man, who, at the *"sacre,"* or coronation, of Lewis XVI, preached in the same pulpit, before that unfortunate monarch. . . .

It was the custom formerly on these occasions, for the bishop, in beginning his discourse, to address himself to the king. A similar form was observed to day, and the expression of *"sire"* was exchanged for that of *"citoyen premier consul."* After the sermon, "Te Deum" was chanted. All the band of the opera house was employed, and *Lais* and *madame Bolla* supplied the vocal parts. The effect was fine, yet, comparatively, very inferiour to our musical meetings in Westminster abbey. . . .

The church was immensely full. The aisle was filled with the military, the different uniforms of which had a splendid effect. Behind the consuls sat the ambassadors, the ministers, and the generals. In a box above, at the entrance of the chapel, was placed madame Bonaparte, accompanied by her daughter and some other ladies. On the other side was a similar box, appropriate to the use of the ladies of the "corps diplomatique."

The two galleries or choirs, which surround the church, were divided into an orchestra for the music, seats for the different constituted authorities, and places for such individuals as were favoured with tickets. In the latter were of course seen all the persons at Paris most distinguished for situation, talent, or beauty. . . . The procession returned with the same ceremony as that in which it arrived; and all the streets of Paris were lined with spectators.

A discharge of sixty cannon was heard at the departure of the first consul from the Thuilleries; and his arrival at the church, and his return to the palace, were announced in the same manner. . . .

. . . Bonaparte was much applauded by the populace, in going to *Notre Dame*; and . . . *madame* received the same compliment, though she went there without any parade, in a plain handsome carriage, and seemed to decline, rather than to court, the notice of the public.

J. G. LEMAISTRE
A Rough Sketch of Modern Paris, 1802

SKEPTICAL
REPORTS

Frances Trollope, the mother of Victorian novelist Anthony Trollope, established her reputation as a formidable social commentator with the publication in 1832 of Domestic Manners of the Americans, *a disparaging account of her three years' sojourn in Cincinnati, Ohio. In 1835 Mrs. Trollope studied the manners of the Parisians while attending a sermon given by the controversial Dominican monk Jean Baptiste Henri Lacordaire at Notre-Dame.*

The great reputation of [this] preacher induced us on Sunday to endure two hours more of tedious waiting before the mass which preceded the sermon began. It is only thus that a chair can be hoped for when the Abbé Lacordaire mounts the pulpit of Notre Dame. The penalty is really heavy; but having heard this celebrated person described as one who "appeared sent by Heaven to restore France to Christianity" — as "a hypocrite that set Tartuffe immeasurably in the background" — as "a man whose talent surpassed that of any preacher since Bossuet" — and as "a charlatan who ought to

The Archbishop of Paris blesses the faithful in Notre-Dame.

harangue from a tub, instead of from the *chaire de Notre Dame de Paris*," — I determined upon at least seeing and hearing him, however little I might be able to decide on which of the two sides of the prodigious chasm that yawned between his friends and enemies the truth was most likely to be found. There were, however, several circumstances which lessened the tedium of this long interval: I might go farther, and confess that this period was by no means the least profitable portion of the four hours which we passed in the church.

On entering, we found the whole of the enormous nave railed in, as it had been on Easter Sunday . . . upon applying at the entrance to this enclosure, we were told that no ladies could be admitted to that part of the church — but that the side aisles were fully furnished with chairs, and afforded excellent places.

This arrangement astonished me in many ways: — first, as being so perfectly un-national; for go where you will in France, you find the best places reserved for the women, — at least, this was the first instance in which I ever found it otherwise. Next, it astonished me, because at every church I had entered, the congregations, though always crowded, had been composed of at least twelve women to one man. When, therefore, I looked over the barrier upon the close-packed, well-adjusted rows of seats prepared to receive fifteen hundred persons, I thought that unless all the priests in Paris came in person to do honour to their eloquent confrère, it was very unlikely that this uncivil arrangement should be found necessary. There was no time, however, to waste in conjecture; the crowd already came rushing in at every door, and we hastened to secure the best places that the side aisles afforded. We obtained seats between the pillars immediately opposite to the pulpit, and felt well enough contented, having little doubt that a voice which had made itself heard so well must have power to reach even to the side aisles of Notre Dame.

The first consolation which I found for my long waiting, after placing myself in that attitude of little ease which the straight-backed chair allowed, was from the recollection that the interval was to be passed within the venerable walls of Notre Dame. It is a glorious old church, and though not comparable in any way to Westminster Abbey, or to Antwerp, or Strasburg, or Cologne, or indeed to many others which I might name, has enough to occupy the eye very satisfactorily for a considerable time. The three elegant rose-windows, throwing in their coloured light from north, west, and south, are of themselves a very pretty study for half an hour or so; and besides, they brought back, notwithstanding their miniature diameter of forty feet, the remembrance of the magnificent circular western window of Strasburg — the recollection of which was almost enough to while away another long interval. . . .

I had another source of amusement, and by no means a trifling one, in watching the influx of company. The whole building soon contained as many human beings as could be crammed into it; and the seats, which we thought, as we took them, were very so-so places indeed, became accommodations for which to be most heartily thankful. Not a pillar but supported the backs of as many men as could stand round it; and not a jutting ornament, the balustrade of a side altar, or any other "point of 'vantage," but looked as if a swarm of bees were beginning to hang upon it.

But the sight which drew my attention most was that displayed by the exclusive central aisle. When told that it was reserved for gentlemen, I imagined of course that I should see it filled by a collection of staid-looking, middle-aged, Catholic citizens, who were drawn together from all parts of the town, and perhaps the country too, for the purpose of hearing the celebrated preacher: but, to my great astonishment, instead of this I saw pouring in by dozens at a time, gay, gallant, smart-looking young men, such indeed as I had rarely seen in Paris on any other religious occasion. Amongst these was a sprinkling of older men; but the great majority were decidedly under thirty....

... the organ pealed, the fine chant of the voices was heard above it, and in a few minutes we saw the archbishop and his splendid train escorting the Host to its ark upon the altar.

During the interval between the conclusion of the mass and the arrival of the Abbé Lacordaire in the pulpit, my sceptical neighbour ... addressed me.

"Are you prepared to be very much enchanted by what you are going to hear?" said he.

"I hardly know what to expect," I replied....

"You will find that he has a prodigious flow of words, much vehement gesticulation, and a very impassioned manner. This is quite sufficient to establish his reputation for eloquence among *les jeunes gens*."

"But I presume you do not yourself subscribe to the sentence pronounced by these young critics?"

"Yes I do, — as far, at least, as to acknowledge that this man has not attained his reputation without having displayed great ability. But though all the talent of Paris has long consented to receive its crown of laurels from the hands of her young men, it would be hardly reasonable to expect that their judgment should be as profound as their power is great."

"Your obedience to this beardless synod is certainly very extraordinary," said I: "I cannot understand it."

"I suppose not," said he, laughing; "it is quite a Paris fashion; but we all seem contented that it should be so. If a new play appears, its fate must be decided by *les jeunes gens*; if a picture is exhibited, its rank amidst the works of modern art can only be settled by them: does a dancer, a singer, an actor, or a preacher appear — a new member in the tribune, or a new prince upon the throne, — it is still *les jeunes gens* who must pass judgment on them all; and this judgment is quoted with a degree of deference utterly inconceivable to a stranger."

... I glanced my eye towards the pulpit, but it was still empty; and on looking round me, I perceived that all eyes were turned in the direction of a small door in the north aisle, almost immediately behind us. "Il est entré là!" said a young woman near us, in a tone that seemed to indicate a feeling deeper than respect, and, in truth, not far removed from adoration. Her eyes were still earnestly fixed upon the door, and continued to be so, as well as those of many others, till it reopened and a slight young man in the dress of a priest prepared for the *chaire* [pulpit] appeared at it. A verger made way for him through the crowd, which, thick and closely wedged as it was, fell back on each side of him, as he proceeded to the pulpit, with much more docility than I ever saw produced by the clearing a passage through the intervention of a troop of horse.

Silence the most profound accompanied his progress; I never witnessed more striking demonstrations of respect: and yet it is said that three-fourths

The 1864 consecration of the newly restored Notre-Dame

of Paris believe this man to be a hypocrite. . . .

It is easier to describe to you everything which preceded the sermon, than the sermon itself. This was such a rush of words, such a burst and pouring out of passionate declamation, that even before I had heard enough to judge of the matter, I felt disposed to prejudge the preacher, and to suspect that his discourse would have more of the flourish and furbelow of human rhetoric than of the simplicity of divine truth in it.

His violent action, too, disgusted me exceedingly. The rapid and incessant movement of his hands, sometimes of one, sometimes of both, more resembled that of the wings of a humming-bird than anything else I can remember. . . .

. . . I cannot remember having ever heard a preacher I less liked, reverenced, and admired, than this new Parisian saint. . . .

In describing the two hours' prologue to the mass, I forgot to mention that many young men — not in the reserved places of the centre aisle, but sitting near us, beguiled the tedious interval by reading. Some of the volumes they held had the appearance of novels from a circulating library, and others were evidently collections of songs, probably less spiritual than *spirituels.*

The whole exhibition certainly showed me a new page in the history of *Paris as it is,* and I therefore do not regret the four hours it cost me: but once is enough.

FRANCES TROLLOPE
Paris and the Parisians in 1835, 1836

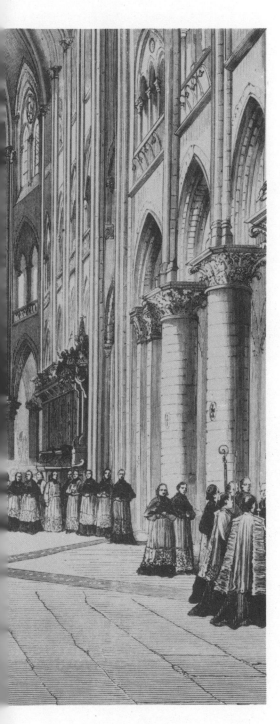

Samuel Langhorne Clemens — better known by his pen name, Mark Twain — gently spoofed the sentimental travel books of the nineteenth century in The Innocents Abroad, *based on a series of letters he wrote in 1869 as a roving European correspondent. While in France, America's foremost storyteller and humorist made an obligatory stop at Notre-Dame de Paris.*

We went to see the Cathedral of Notre Dame. — We had heard of it before. It surprises me, sometimes, to think how much we *do* know, and how intelligent we are. We recognised the brown old Gothic pile in a moment; it was like the pictures. We stood at a little distance and changed from one point of observation to another, and gazed long at its lofty square towers and its rich front, clustered thick with stony, mutilated saints who had been looking calmly down from their perches for ages. The Patriarch of Jerusalem stood under them in the old days of chivalry and romance, and preached the third Crusade, more than six hundred years ago; and since that day they have stood there and looked quietly down upon the most thrilling scenes, the grandest pageants, the most extraordinary spectacles that have grieved or delighted Paris. These battered and broken-nosed old fellows saw many and many a cavalcade of mail-clad knights come marching home from the Holy Land; they heard the bells above them toll the signal for the St. Bartholomew's Massacre, and they saw the slaughter that followed; later, they saw the Reign of Terror, the carnage of the Revolution, the overthrow of a king, the coronation of two Napoleons, the christening of the young prince that lords it over a regiment of servants in the Tuileries to-day — and they may possibly continue to stand there until they see the Napoleon dynasty swept away and the banners of a great Republic floating above its ruins. I wish

149

these old parties could speak. They could tell a tale worth the listening to.

They say that a pagan temple stood where Notre Dame now stands, in the old Roman days, eighteen or twenty centuries ago — remains of it are still preserved in Paris; and that a Christian church took its place about A.D. 300; another took the place of that in A.D. 500; and that the foundations of the present Cathedral were laid about A.D. 1100. The ground ought to be measurably sacred by this time, one would think. One portion of this noble old edifice is suggestive of the quaint fashions of ancient times. It was built by Jean Sans-Peur, Duke of Burgundy, to set his conscience at rest — he had assassinated the Duke of Orleans. Alas! those good old times are gone, when a murderer could wipe the stain from his name and soothe his troubles to sleep simply by getting out his bricks and mortar and building an addition to a church. . . .

We loitered through the grand aisles for an hour or two, staring up at the rich stained glass windows embellished with blue and yellow and crimson saints and martyrs, and trying to admire the numberless great pictures in the chapels, and then we were admitted to the sacristy and shown the magnificent robes which the Pope wore when he crowned Napoleon I.; a waggon-load of solid gold and silver utensils used in the great public processions and ceremonies of the Church; some nails of the true cross, a fragment of the cross itself, a part of the crown of thorns. We had already seen a large piece of the true cross in a church in the Azores, but no nails. They showed us likewise the bloody robe which that Archbishop of Paris wore who exposed his sacred person and braved the wrath of the insurgents of 1848, to mount the barricades and hold aloft the olive branch of peace in the hope of stopping the slaughter. His noble effort cost him his life. He was shot dead. They showed us a cast of his face, taken after death, the bullet that killed him, and the two vertebrae in which it lodged. These people have a somewhat singular taste in the matter of relics. Ferguson told us that the silver cross which the good Archbishop wore at his girdle was seized and thrown into the Seine, where it lay embedded in the mud for fifteen years, and then an angel appeared to a priest and told him where to dive for it; he *did* dive for it and got it, and now it is there on exhibition at Notre Dame, to be inspected by anybody who feels an interest in inanimate objects of miraculous intervention.

SAMUEL LANGHORNE CLEMENS
The Innocents Abroad, 1869

AN INSPIRATION FOR NATIVE SONS

The novel Gargantua — *a bawdy and boisterous satire of French society written by the sixteenth-century humanist François Rabelais — recounts the extraordinary adventures of an amiable family of giants. In this excerpt from Book I,* Gargantua *steals the bells of Notre-Dame and meets a pedantic theologian.*

Gargantua considered the great bells in the Towers of Notre Dame and made them ring out most harmoniously. The music suggested to him that they might sound very sweet tinkling on his mare's neck when he sent her back to his father laden with Brie cheese and fresh herring. So he promptly picked up the bells of the Cathedral and carried them home. . . .

The whole city was in an uproar, for Parisians, as you know, are ever prone to insurrection. Indeed, foreigners marvel at the patience of French

Rabelais's gentle giant, Gargantua, towers over the cathedral of Paris.

kings who, faced with troubles arising daily out of the mob's violence, will not justifiedly stamp them out at their source. . . .

You will readily believe that the place where all these people stormed and rioted was the royal Hotel de Nesle, then the seat of the University Court, but now no longer the site of the Oracle of Lutetia. Here the whole grievance of the stolen bells was discussed and deplored. After extensive argumentation *pro* and *con,* they moved . . . to empower the oldest and most authoritative member of the faculty to apprize Gargantua of the dreadful damage they suffered through the loss of these bells. Despite certain objections that this mission could be better fulfilled by an orator than by a divine, our Master Janotus de Bragmardo, Doctor of Theology, was delegated.

Master Janotus, with a haircut like that affected by Julius Caesar, settled the traditional doctoral hood over his cootlike head. Next, he antidoted his stomach against possible contamination, with cakes baked in the most secular ovens, and holy water from his excellently stocked cellar. Then, he proceeded to Gargantua's. Before him crawled three black beadles; behind him he dragged five or six servile and artless Masters of Arts. . . .

. . . Gargantua, learning what had happened, called aside his tutor Ponocrates, his steward Philotomus — the name means a lover of carving — his esquire Gymnastes ("teacher of esthetics") and Eudemon. A summary conference was held instanter to plan their reply and subsequent actions. It was unanimously agreed to take the learned doctors to the conservatory or wine room and there make them drink uproariously. Thus this wheezing old dryasdust would be denied the vainglory of supposing the bells had been restored at his request, for, while he tippled, they would summon the Provost of the City, the Rector of the University and the Vicar-General to the Bishop of Paris. To these officers they would hand over the bells ere ever the old sophister had delivered his message. . . .

Which is exactly what happened. The authorities arrived, our theologian was ushered into the official meeting, and having hawked and spluttered, began as follows.

"Ahem, hem, hem! *B'na dies,* Sir, g'day to you, *b'nadies vobis* and g'day to you, gentlemen. It were but right that you should return our bells, for we are in sore need of them! Hem, ahem, ughsh! Many a time we have heretofore refused good money for them from the citizens of London (near Cahors) and of Bordeaux (in the land of Brie). These aspired to purchase our bells for the substantific quality of their elementary complexion which is intronificated in the terrestrality of their quidditative nature to extraneize the tempests and hurricanes that fall upon our vines. . . .

"If you restore them to us at my request, I shall gain one and one-quarter yards of sausage by it. And a fine pair of breeches, too, which will do my legs a lot of good — or, if I don't, then they'll have broken their promise! . . .

"O Sir, *Domine, restor bellsimus nobis,* give us back our bells! Truly, *est bonum urbis,* it is for the good of the city. Every one here uses them. If your mare enjoys them, so does our faculty. . . .

"*Omnis bella bellabilis, in bellerio bellando, bellans bellativo bellare bellantes. Parisius habet bellas. Ergo Gluc.* Every bellable bell, to be belled in the belfry, belling by the bellative, makes the bellers bell bellfully! In Paris there are bells. Q.E.D. . . ."

FRANÇOIS RABELAIS
Gargantua, 1535

Hugo's "hunchback of Notre-Dame" frightens a would-be assailant.

152

In his introduction to Notre-Dame de Paris, *Victor Hugo exhorted the reader: "Let us, if possible, inspire the nation with the love of national architecture. That, the author declares, is one of the principal objects of this book; that, one of the principal objects of his life." Hugo's epic novel is, of course, far more than a polemic: it is the poignant story of the tragic hunchback, Quasimodo.*

Now, in 1482, Quasimodo had grown up. He had been made, some years previous, bell-ringer of Notre-Dame, thanks to his adopted father, Claude Frollo. . . . In time, a peculiar bond of intimacy grew up between the ringer and the church. Cut off forever from the world by the double fatality of his unknown birth and his deformity, confined from infancy in this doubly insuperable circle, the poor wretch became used to seeing nothing of the world outside the religious walls which had received him into their shadow. Notre-Dame had been to him by turns, as he grew and developed, egg, nest, home, country, universe.

And it is certain that there was a sort of mysterious and pre-existing harmony between this creature and the structure. When, still a child, he dragged himself tortuously and jerkingly along beneath its gloomy arches, he seemed, with his human face and animal-like limbs, to be some reptile native to that damp dark pavement upon which the Roman capitals cast so many grotesque shadows.

Later on, the first time that he mechanically grasped the bell-rope in the tower, and clung to it, and set the bell ringing, he seemed to Claude, his adopted father, like a child whose tongue is loosed, and who begins to talk.

It was thus, little by little, growing ever after the pattern of the cathedral, living there, sleeping there, seldom leaving its precincts, forever subject to its mysterious influence, he came to look like it, to be imbedded in it, to form, as it were, an integral part of it. His sharp angles (if we may be pardoned the simile) fitted into the re-entering angles of the building, and he seemed not only to inhabit it, but to be its natural tenant. He might almost be said to have assumed its form, as the snail assumes the form of its shell. It was his dwelling, his hole, his wrapper. There was so deep an instinct of sympathy between him and the old church, there were so many magnetic affinities between them, that he in some sort clung to it, as the tortoise to its shell. The rugged cathedral was his shell. . . .

. . . This dwelling was his own. It contained no deeps which Quasimodo had not penetrated, no heights which he had not scaled. He often climbed the façade several stories high by the mere aid of projecting bits of sculpture. The towers upon the outer face of which he was frequently seen crawling like a lizard gliding over a perpendicular wall — those twin giants, so lofty, so threatening, so terrible — had no vertigoes, no terrors, no giddiness for him. They were so docile to his hand, so easily climbed, that he might be said to have tamed them. . . .

Moreover, not only his body but also his spirit seemed to be moulded by the cathedral. What was the state of that soul? What bent had it assumed, what form had it taken under its knotty covering in this wild life? It would be hard to tell. Quasimodo was born blind of one eye, humpbacked, lame. It was only by great patience and great painstaking that Claude Frollo had succeeded in teaching him to speak. But a fatality followed the poor foundling. Bell-ringer of Notre-Dame at the age of fourteen, a new infirmity soon put the finishing touch to his misfortunes; the bells had broken the drum of his ears: he became deaf. . . .

. . . he never turned his face to the world of men save with regret; his cathedral was enough for him. It was peopled with marble figures, kings, saints, and bishops who at least did not laugh at him, and never looked upon him otherwise than with peace and good-will. The other statues, those of monsters and demons, did not hate Quasimodo; he looked too much like them for that. They rather mocked at other men. The saints were his friends, and blessed him. The monsters were his friends, and protected him. . . .

And the cathedral was not only company for him, it was the universe; nay, more, it was Nature itself. He never dreamed that there were other hedgerows than the stained-glass windows in perpetual bloom; other shade than that of the stone foliage always budding, loaded with birds in the thickets of Saxon capitals; other mountains than the colossal towers of the church; or other oceans than Paris roaring at their feet.

But that which he loved more than all else in the motherly building, that which awakened his soul and bade it spread its poor stunted wings folded in such misery where it dwelt in darkness, that which sometimes actually made him happy, was the bells. He loved them, he caressed them, he talked to them, he understood them. From the chime in the steeple over the transept to the big bell above the door, he had a tender feeling for them all. The belfry of the transept and the two towers were to him like three great cages, in which the birds, trained by him, sang for him alone; and yet it was these very bells which made him deaf. . . .

It is impossible to give any idea of his joy on those days when full peals were rung. When the archdeacon dismissed him with the word "Go," he ran up the winding staircase more rapidly than any one else could have gone down. He reached the aerial chamber of the big bell, breathless; he gazed at it an instant with love and devotion, then spoke to it gently, and patted it, as you would a good horse about to take a long journey. He condoled with it on the hard work before it. After these initiatory caresses he called to his assistants, stationed on a lower story of the tower, to begin. They then hung upon the ropes, the windlass creaked, and the enormous mass of metal moved slowly. Quasimodo, panting with excitement, followed it with his eye. The first stroke of the clapper upon its brazen wall made the beam on which he stood quiver. Quasimodo vibrated with the bell. "Here we go! There we go!" he shouted with a mad burst of laughter. But the motion of the great bell grew faster and faster, and as it traversed an ever-increasing space, his eye grew bigger and bigger, more and more glittering and phosphorescent. At last the full peal began; the whole tower shook: beams, leads, broad stones, all rumbled together, from the piles of the foundation to the trefoils at the top. Then Quasimodo's rapture knew no bounds: he came and went; he trembled and shook from head to foot with the tower. The bell, let loose, and frantic with liberty, turned its jaws of bronze to either wall of the tower in turn, — jaws from which issued that whirlwind whose roar men heard for four leagues around. Quasimodo placed himself before those gaping jaws; he rose and fell with the swaying of the bell, inhaled its tremendous breath, gazed now at the abyss swarming with people like ants, two hundred feet below him, and now at the huge copper clapper which from second to second bellowed in his ear. That was the only speech which he could hear, the only sound that broke the universal silence reigning around him. He basked in it as a bird in the sunshine. All at once the frenzy of the bell seized him; his

look became strange; he waited for the passing of the bell as a spider lies in wait for a fly, and flung himself upon it. Then, suspended above the gulf, launched upon the tremendous vibration of the bell, he grasped the brazen monster by its ears, clasped it with his knees, spurred it with his heels, doubling the fury of the peal with the whole force and weight of his body. As the tower shook, he shouted and gnashed his teeth, his red hair stood erect, his chest labored like a blacksmith's bellows, his eye flashed fire, the monstrous steed neighed and panted under him; and then the big bell of Notre-Dame and Quasimodo ceased to exist: they became a dream, a whirlwind, a tempest; vertigo astride of uproar; a spirit clinging to a winged crupper; a strange centaur, half man, half bell. . . .

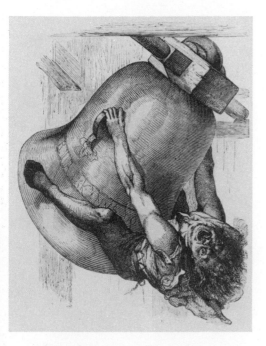

At left, a fanciful gargoyle observes the city; above, Quasimodo swings joyfully on Notre-Dame's huge bell.

The presence of this extraordinary being pervaded the whole cathedral with a peculiar breath of life. It seemed, at least in the opinion of the grossly superstitious mob, as if mysterious emanations issued from him, animating every stone in Notre-Dame and making the very entrails of the old church throb and palpitate. His mere presence there was enough to lead the vulgar to fancy that the countless statues in the galleries and over the doors moved and breathed. And in very truth the cathedral seemed a creature docile and obedient to his hand: it awaited his pleasure to lift up its mighty voice; it was possessed and filled with Quasimodo as with a familiar spirit. He might be said to make the vast edifice breathe. He was indeed omnipresent in it, he multiplied himself at every point of the structure. Sometimes the terrified spectator saw an odd dwarf on the extreme pinnacle of one of the towers, climbing, creeping, writhing, crawling on all fours, descending head-first into the abyss, leaping from one projection to another, and diving deep into the maw of some sculptured gorgon: it was Quasimodo hunting for daws' nests. Sometimes a visitor stumbled over a sort of living nightmare, crouching and scowling in a dark corner of the church: it was Quasimodo absorbed in thought. Sometimes an enormous head and a bundle of ill-adjusted limbs might be seen swaying frantically to and fro from a rope's end under a belfry: it was Quasimodo ringing the Vespers of the Angelus. Often by night a hideous form was seen wandering along the frail delicately-wrought railing which crowns the towers and runs around the top of the chancel: it was still the hunchback of Notre-Dame. Then, so the neighbors said, the whole church took on a fantastic, supernatural, horrible air, — eyes and mouths opened wide here and there; the dogs and dragons and griffins of stone which watch day and night, with outstretched necks and gaping jaws, around the monstrous cathedral, barked loudly. And if it were a Christmas night, while the big bell, which seemed uttering its death-rattle, called the faithful to attend the solemn midnight mass, the gloomy façade assumed such an aspect that it seemed as if the great door were devouring the crowd while the rose-window looked on. And all this was due to Quasimodo. Egypt would have taken him for the god of the temple; the Middle Ages held him to be its demon: he was its soul.

So much so that to those who know that Quasimodo once existed, Notre-Dame is now deserted, inanimate, dead. They feel that something has gone from it. That immense body is empty; it is a skeleton; the spirit has left it, the abode remains, and that is all. It is like a skull; the sockets of the eyes are still there, but sight is gone.

VICTOR HUGO
Notre-Dame de Paris, 1831

Based on the legend of the sinner condemned to wander aimlessly through eternity,
The Wandering Jew, *written by the nineteenth-century French novelist Eugène Sue, is a complex melodrama of greed, prejudice, and treachery. In this scene the famed cathedral of Paris becomes the setting for a macabre masquerade.*

Of all the quarters of Paris that which, during the period of the increase of the cholera, offered what was, perhaps, the most fearful spectacle, was the *Quartier de la Cité;* and, in the Cité, the façade of Notre-Dame was almost every day the theatre of terrible scenes, as the majority of the sick of the neighboring streets, whom they were conveying to the Hôtel Dieu, were brought to this spot.

The cholera had not one physiognomy — it had a thousand. Thus, . . . several events in which the horrible mingled with the strange took place in the front of Notre-Dame. . . .

On the black and cracked wall of the arcade might be read a placard recently put up. . . .

"Vengeance! vengeance! The people who are conveyed to the hospitals are poisoned there, because they find the numbers of sick too many. Every night boats filled with dead carcasses go down the Seine! Vengeance and death to the murderers of the people! . . ."

The sun was beginning to set, and threw his golden beams on the black sculpture of the portal of Notre-Dame and the imposing mass of its two towers, which rose in the midst of a perfectly blue sky. . . .

. . . there were heard the noisy sounds of joyous music, and repeated cries, as it advanced, of *"The cholera masquerade!"*

These words bespoke one of those episodes, half buffoon, half terrible, yet scarcely credible, which marked the progress of this scourge.

In truth, if contemporary testimony was not completely accordant with the details of the public papers on the subject of this masquerade, we should say, that instead of an actual fact, it was the invention of some demented brain. *The masquerade of the cholera* came into the square of Notre-Dame. . . .

The masquerade was composed of a four-wheeled car, escorted by men and women on horseback; cavaliers and amazons wore fancy costumes. . . .

There had been a rumor that a masquerade had been organized with the intention of *bullying* . . . the *Cholera,* and, by a merry display, raise the spirits of the frightened populace; and thus artists, young men of fashion, students, clerks, etc., had answered the appeal, and, although up to this period unknown to each other, they *fraternized* immediately. Many of them, to complete the fête, brought their lady-loves. A subscription had covered the expenses of the fête, and on the morning, after a splendid breakfast at the further end of Paris, the joyous group had started bravely on their way to conclude the day by a dinner in the square of Notre-Dame.

We said *bravely,* because it required in the young females a singular strength of mind, an unusual firmness of character, in order thus to traverse this great city, plunged in consternation and amazement, to cross at every turn litters charged with the dying, and vehicles loaded with the dead, in order to attack, by the strangest pleasantry, the scourge that was decimating Paris.

EUGÈNE SUE
The Wandering Jew, 1845

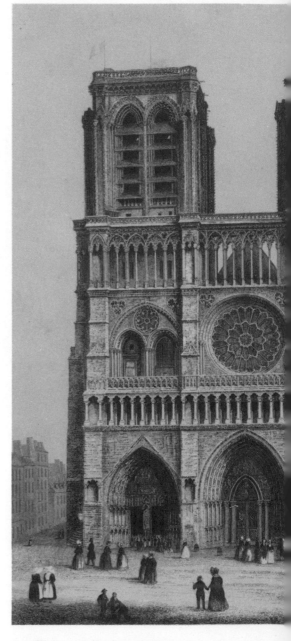

Soufflot's mutilation of Notre-Dame's central portal is visible in this nineteenth-century engraving.

"CATHEDRAL LIKE A ROCK"

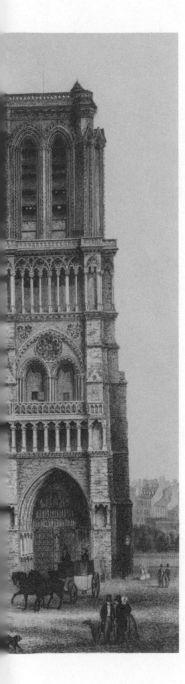

Henry James's 1903 novel The Ambassadors *portrays the moral dilemma of a middle-aged American in Paris. Torn between his mission as an "ambassador" — to rescue his fiancée's son from the clutches of Mme. de Vionnet, a sophisticated Frenchwoman — and his growing realization that life may be more meaningful in Europe, Lambert Strether seeks solace within Notre-Dame de Paris.*

It was not the first time Strether had sat alone in the great dim church — still less was it the first of his giving himself up, so far as conditions permitted, to its beneficent action on his nerves. He had been to Notre Dame with [several friends], and had found the place, even in company, such a refuge from the obsession of his problem that, with renewed pressure from that source, he had not unnaturally recurred to a remedy that seemed so, for the moment, to meet the case. He was conscious enough that it was only for the moment, but good moments — if he could call them good — still had their value for a man who, by this time, struck himself as living almost disgracefully from hand to mouth. Having so well learnt the way, he had lately made the pilgrimage more than once by himself — had quite stolen off, taking an unnoticed chance and making no point of speaking of the adventure when restored to his friends. . . .

. . . [The] impulse that had now carried him across to Notre Dame [was] the impulse to let things be, to give them time to justify themselves or at least to pass. He was aware of having no errand in such a place but the desire not to be, for the hour, in certain other places; a sense of safety, of simplification, which, each time he yielded to it, he amused himself by thinking of as a private concession to cowardice. The great church had no altar for his worship, no direct voice for his soul; but it was none the less soothing even to sanctity; for he could feel while there what he couldn't elsewhere, that he was a plain tired man taking the holiday he had earned. He was tired, but he wasn't plain — that was the pity and the trouble of it; he was able, however, to drop his problem at the door very much as if it had been the copper piece that he deposited, on the threshold, in the receptacle of the inveterate blind beggar. He trod the long, dim nave, sat in the splendid choir, paused before the clustered chapels of the east end, and the mighty monument laid upon him its spell. He might have been a student under the charm of a museum — which was exactly what, in a foreign town, in the afternoon of life, he would have liked to be free to be. . . .

. . . He had the habit, in these contemplations, of watching a fellow-visitant, here and there, from a respectable distance, remarking some note of behavior, of penitence, of prostration, of the absolved, relieved state; this was the manner in which his vague tenderness took its course, the degree of demonstration to which, naturally, it had to confine itself. It had not indeed so felt its responsibility as when, on this occasion, he suddenly measured the suggestive effect of a lady whose supreme stillness, in the shade of one of the chapels, he had two or three times noticed as he made, and made once more, his slow circuit. She was not prostrate — not in any degree bowed, but she was strangely fixed, and her prolonged immobility showed her, while he passed and paused, as wholly given up to the need, whatever it was, that had brought her there. She only sat and gazed before her, as he himself often sat; but she had placed herself, as he never did, within the focus of the shrine, and she had lost herself, he could easily see, as he would only have liked to do. She was not a wandering alien, keeping back more than she gave, but one of the familiar, the intimate, the fortunate, for whom these dealings had a method and a meaning. She reminded our friend — since it was the way of nine-tenths of his current impressions to act as recalls of things imagined — of some fine, firm, concentrated heroine of an old story, something he had heard, read, something that, had he had a hand for drama, he might himself have written, renewing her courage, renewing her clearness, in splendidly-protected meditation. Her back, as she sat, was turned to him, but his impression absolutely required that she should be young and interesting, and she carried her head, moreover, even in the sacred shade, with a discernible faith in herself, a kind of implied conviction of consistency, security, impunity. But what had such a woman come for if she hadn't come to pray? Strether's reading of such matters was, it must be owned, confused; but he wondered if her attitude were some congruous fruit of absolution, of "indulgence." He knew but dimly what indulgence, in such a place, might mean; yet he had, as with a soft sweep, a vision of how it might indeed add to the zest of active rites. All this was a good deal to have been denoted by a mere lurking figure who was nothing to him; but, the last thing before leaving the church, he had the surprise of a still deeper quickening.

He had dropped upon a seat half-way down the nave and, again in the museum mood, was trying with head thrown back and eyes aloft, to reconstitute a past, to reduce it in fact to the convenient terms of Victor Hugo, whom, a few days before, giving the rein for once in a way to the joy of life, he had purchased in seventy bound volumes, a miracle of cheapness, parted with, he was assured by the shopman, at the price of the red-and-gold alone. . . . Turning, he saw that a lady stood there as for a greeting, and he sprang up as he next perceived that the lady was Mme. de Vionnet, who appeared to have recognized him as she passed near him on her way to the door. She checked, quickly and gayly, a certain confusion in him, came to meet it, turned it back, by an art of her own; the confusion threatened him as he knew her for the person he had lately been observing. She was the lurking figure of the dim chapel; she had occupied him more than she guessed; but it came to him in time, luckily, that he needn't tell her and that no harm, after all, had been done. She herself, for that matter, straightway showed that she felt their encounter as the happiest of accidents — had for him a "You come here too?" that despoiled surprise of every awkwardness.

"I come often," she said; "I love this place; but I'm terrible, in general, for churches. The old women who live in them all know me; in fact I'm already myself one of the old women. It's like that, at all events, that I foresee I shall end." Looking about for a chair, so that he instantly pulled one nearer, she sat down with him again to the sound of an "Oh, I like so much your also being fond — !"

He confessed the extent of his feeling, though she left the object vague; and he was struck with the tact, the taste of her vagueness, which simply took for granted in him a sense of beautiful things. . . .

. . . They talked, in low, easy tones and with lifted, lingering looks, about the great monument and its history and its beauty — all of which, Mme. de Vionnet professed, came to her most in the other, the outer view. "We'll presently, after we go," she said, "walk round it again if you like. I'm not in a particular hurry, and it will be pleasant to look at it again with you."

HENRY JAMES
The Ambassadors, 1903

The gloomy gallery of Notre-Dame.

The appeal of Notre-Dame de Paris — a medieval Gothic cathedral devoted to Roman Catholic worship — transcends the limits of time and culture. Kotaro Takamura, a twentieth-century Japanese sculptor and poet, has written a lyrical tribute to France's most famous cathedral.

Another squall!
Looking up at you, the collar of the overcoat
Lifted against the slanting rain — It is I,
He who makes it a rule to come at least once each day —
The Japanese.

This morning
A terrible storm, increasing since daybreak,
Now rages in the four corners of Paris.
I cannot distinguish east from west,
Nor even which way the storm is moving, as it runs amok, here in the
      Ile de France . . .
But here I am again,
Oh Notre-Dame of Paris!
Soaked with rain,
Just to gaze at you, to touch you,
To steal a kiss from you, your flesh of stone. . . .

Oh Notre-Dame, Notre-Dame!
Cathedral like a rock, a mountain, an eagle, a squatting lion —
A hidden rock in a mist,
The bulwark of Paris,
Pelted by blinding rain,
Buffeted head-on by the beating wind,
You rise up before me, oh my Notre-Dame of Paris!
It is I, who look up at you,
The Japanese.
My heart thrills at the sight of you;
Before the semblance of heroic tragedy,
This youthful heart, come from a strange and different land,
      is over-full —
It throbs irrationally, trembles in time with the screaming air.

Another squall!
How they rage, the four elements, striving to efface you, to turn
      you back to nothingness!
Rain splashes in smoke and phosphorescence;
The scaly spotted cloud grazes against your peaks;
The entwining cyclone seeks to snatch in its claw just one of your belfry
      pillars;
Beyond count, tiny bright fluttering elves collide, burst and stream on
      the tracery of the rose-windows . . .
The gargoyles, glimpsed through the splashes high on the edge of the
      building —
They alone bear the brunt of the fluttering mob of elves,
Lifting their paws and craning their necks,

With bared teeth, voiding the fiery stream of wind and rain . . .
Rows of curious stone saints nod to each other, with odd gestures,
Huge buttresses on the sides lay bare their arms as ever,
And the storm beats on those slanting arcs with all its force!
The peal of the organ on the day of Mass!
What has become of the cock on the thin high steeple?
Fluttering curtains of water are falling on all sides now —
And you stand in the middle of it all. . . .

The rain-beaten Cathedral!
After a pause, another squall, in *allegro* —
Down swings the baton in a sudden flash,
And all the instruments of heaven are in commotion —
All round, the chaotic revolutions of a rhapsody . . .
And in the midst of it, oh Cathedral, towering in sheer silence,
Watching intently over the roofs of storm-ridden Paris!
Do not take it amiss
That someone stands here now,
A hand against your corner-stone,
A fevered cheek against your flesh —
It is I, drunk with beauty,
The Japanese!

KOTARO TAKAMURA
The Rain-beaten Cathedral, 1921

Notre-Dame's location, on the Île de la Cité, heightens its impact.

REFERENCE

Chronology of French History

1558	**Wedding of Mary Stuart and the Dauphin Francis**
1562–98	Religious wars waged against French Huguenots
1572	**Henry of Navarre's marriage to Marguerite of Valois the occasion of the massacre of St. Bartholomew's Day**
1593	Henry of Navarre abjures Protestantism
1598	Edict of Nantes grants political equality and limited freedom of worship to Huguenots
1610	Accession of Louis XIII
1614	Last meeting of Estates General before Revolution
1625	**Marriage of Henrietta Maria of France to King Charles I of England**
1631–48	French participation in Thirty Years' War
1638	**Louis XIII vows to rebuild main altar; Te Deum chanted at birth of future Louis XIV**
1643	**Te Deum chanted for coronation of Louis XIV**
1648–53	Revolt of the Fronde
1661	Louis XIV assumes absolute personal rule
1675	**Funeral of Vicomte de Turenne**
1685	Revocation of the Edict of Nantes
1699	**Work begun on rebuilding the main altar**
1711	**Workmen discover remains of Gallo-Roman votive pillars**
1713	Treaty of Utrecht confirms permanent separation of crowns of France and Spain
1715	Accession of Louis XV
1726	**New roofing installed; northern rose remodeled**
1728	**Interior of cathedral whitewashed**
1741	**Stained-glass windows removed**
1756–63	Seven Years' War
1771	**Soufflot, architect of the Pantheon, enlarges central portal of cathedral**
1774	Accession of Louis XVI
1779	**Louis XVI and Marie Antoinette organize a mass marriage for 100 poor maidens**
1781	**Western rose window repaired**
1789	Storming of the Bastille; Declaration of the Rights of Man proclaimed
1793	Execution of Louis XVI; beginning of Reign of Terror
1793	**Citizens remove statues from the Gallery of Kings**
1794	**Notre-Dame renamed the Temple of Reason; festival of the Goddess of Reason celebrated**
1801	Napoleon signs Concordat with papacy
1802	**First Roman Catholic service held since 1793**
1804	**Napoleon crowns himself emperor at Notre-Dame**
1811	**Baptism of Napoleon's heir as the King of Rome**
1815	Battle of Waterloo
1830	Revolution of 1830; Louis Philippe elected king
1845	**Viollet-le-Duc undertakes extensive restorations**
1848	Abdication of Louis Philippe; Louis Napoleon named president of the new republic
1852	**Coronation of Louis Napoleon as Napoleon III**
1853	**Marriage of Napoleon III to Spanish Princess Eugénie de Montijo**
1864	**Restorations completed; cathedral officially reconsecrated in elaborate ceremony**
1870–71	Franco-Prussian War; Napoleon III capitulates; Third Republic proclaimed
1871	**Notre-Dame set on fire during Paris Commune**
1878	**Demolition of Hôtel Dieu relieves congestion around cathedral**
1894–1906	The Dreyfus Affair
1905	Official separation of Church and State
1909	**Beatification of Joan of Arc celebrated**
1914–18	World War I
1918	**Armistice Te Deum sung**
1920	Joan of Arc canonized
1936	First Popular Front ministry under Léon Blum
1939–45	World War II
1940	German forces occupy Paris; fall of France
1944	**Liberation of Paris; Te Deum sung in presence of General de Gaulle to celebrate capitulation of German troops**
1945–46	De Gaulle serves as interim president
1957	France joins the European Economic Community
1958–59	De Gaulle — recalled during crisis over Algeria — named premier, then president, of Fifth Republic
1963	**Restorations of interior undertaken**
1968	**Cleaning of exterior begun**
1969	De Gaulle resigns; Pompidou elected president
1970	**State funeral for Charles de Gaulle**

Gothic Cathedrals of France

An abiding faith in God, an increase in the wealth of urban centers, and an evolving sophistication of building techniques combined, in the mid-twelfth century, to create a new architectural style that swept rapidly across Europe. Within less than three hundred years, eighty Gothic cathedrals were erected in France alone. Of these, perhaps a dozen stand out from the rest for magnificence and originality.

The new mode — initiated by Abbot Suger in about 1137 at Saint-Denis — inspired an extraordinary surge of dedication and talent as successive bishops and their communities embarked on the Cathedral Crusade. The rebuilt abbey church of Saint-Denis outside Paris formed the prototype of the Gothic. Saint-Denis's emphasis on the transcendental nature of light and the glory of stained glass became the lodestar for innovative advances in size, structure, and ornamentation. The technical devices that were employed in building the great cathedrals — the pointed arch, ribbed vault, and flying buttress — no more define the Gothic than an alphabet defines a language. They were primarily the means by which an aesthetic based on luminosity and verticality could be implemented.

The first Gothic cathedral was built at *Sens,* seventy-five miles southwest of Paris. Under the guidance of Archbishop Henry Sanglier, a friend of Abbot Suger, the original Romanesque plan of 1130 was abandoned in favor of a structure that would incorporate ribbed vaulting throughout. The choir, begun about 1145, was completed in 1163 — the year that ground was broken for Notre-Dame de Paris.

Sens cathedral consists of five main divisions — three square bays in the nave and two in the choir, topped by six-part vaults sprung from pier clusters. The tripartite nave elevation of arcade, triforium, and clerestory may have prompted the advanced design of Chartres

fifty years later. Early in the thirteenth century, the clerestory windows at Sens were enlarged to admit more light, and flying buttresses were installed.

Staunch partisans of Thomas Becket, Henry Sanglier and his successor played host to the exiled English archbishop during his four-year stay at Sens. A vivid stained-glass window in the ambulatory depicts scenes from the martyr's life.

Among the church dignitaries present at the consecration of Saint-Denis in 1144 was Bishop Baudouin II of *Noyon.* Using Suger's choir as a model, he began to rebuild his cathedral in 1150. By 1185 the choir was completed. Work on the nave bays continued until 1205, and the western façade was not finished until 1235. As with other Early Gothic cathedrals, both rounded and pointed arches were used. The original sexpartite vaults of the nave — resting on alternating single and compound pillars — collapsed during a fire in 1293 and were replaced by more conventional quadripartite vaults. Flying buttresses were also added at that time to the nave and choir.

Although the height of Notre-Dame de Noyon is seven feet less than that of Sens, its narrower width contributes to a

greater sense of unbounded spaciousness. The addition of a fourth story to the nave heightens this impression.

The rounded transept arms, built between 1170 and 1185, are the cathedral's most distinctive feature; unfortunately, their magnificent stained-glass windows are no longer in place.

In 1153, three years after ground was broken at Noyon, Bishop Thibaut inaugurated a new cathedral dedicated to the Virgin at *Senlis.* The smallest of French cathedrals — only sixty-nine feet high — it was consecrated in 1191. In the thirteenth century a spire and transept arms were added. In 1504 a severe fire destroyed the upper levels of the choir and transept; as a result, so much of the original structure was rebuilt that only the lovely apse and western façade are examples of pure Early Gothic.

The thirteenth-century architect Villard de Honnecourt declared that the towers of Notre-Dame de *Laon* were the finest he had ever seen. Seven towers were planned but only five were actually built — two on the western façade, one on each transept arm, and a lantern tower above the crossing. The elaborate, traceried western towers are adorned with sixteen carved oxen — said to honor the animals that hauled the building blocks up the steep hill. Succeeding generations echoed Villard's opinion and broadened it to include the entire façade. A masterpiece of comprehensive design, its two levels of porches, gables, turrets, tympana, sculpture, and central rose set the standard for many later cathedrals.

Begun in 1160 by Bishop Gauthier de Montagne, the choir of Laon was completed fourteen years later. By 1190 the transept and five bays of the nave had been erected. In 1205 the final bays of the nave and the western façade were in place. In that year the choir was remodeled, lengthened to encompass ten bays, and given an unusual flat-ended apse. The extreme length of the choir,

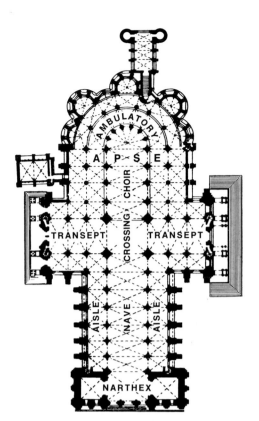

Ground plan of Chartres

the quadripartite elevation, the seventy-eight-foot-high vaults, and the open lantern tower give the interior of Laon a glowing, airy quality.

Throughout the Middle Ages, the efforts of the cathedral builders were intermittently confounded by the devastating scourge of fire. One such conflagration in 1194 gutted Notre-Dame de *Chartres*; only the Early Gothic crypt built by Bishop Fulbert and the towers, three lancet windows, and the Royal Portal of the western façade survived. The town of Chartres — for centuries the traditional center of the cult of the Virgin —

responded to this disaster by rebuilding its cathedral in the unprecedented span of twenty-seven years.

The unknown master of Chartres synthesized the structural solutions of previous masters to create a new and innovative harmony. For the first time, flying buttresses were designed as an integral part of an entire cathedral. Elimination of the gallery vastly simplified the elevation and made possible the installation of two lancets surmounted by a rose in the forty-five-foot-high clerestory — which matches the height of the nave arcade. The uniform quadripartite vaults — resting on slim piers with four attached colonnettes — are sprung from a point midway in the clerestory and climb to a height 120 feet above the pavement. The plan of the choir, with its double ambulatory and seven radiating chapels of unequal size, was determined by the presence of the old crypt below.

The incomparable stained-glass windows that illuminate the austere interior of Chartres are its main ornament. Chartres alone has retained all of its incredibly beautiful thirteenth-century glass. Forty-four feet in diameter, the western rose depicting the Last Judgment is the most famous — but the transept roses and the hundred-odd other windows all contribute to the jewel-like radiance of the cathedral's interior.

The richness of the windows is only rivaled by the abundance of the exterior sculpture. The profusion of 10,000 figures in the triple porches of each transept and in the portals of the western façade is a striking testament to the artistry and genius of the medieval sculptor. Dominating the lofty western façade are the asymmetrical spires of its towers: the severe south steeple, 147 feet high, was completed in the twelfth century; the much taller north spire, built between 1507 and 1513, is a marvel of High Gothic enthusiasm.

The rebuilding of the cathedral of *Bourges* was initiated by Archbishop

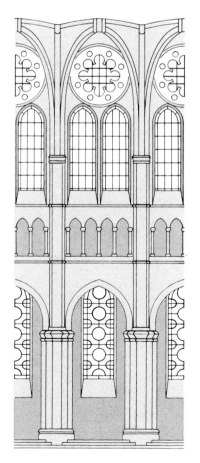

Chartres's nave elevation: arcade, triforium, clerestory

Henry de Sully in 1195, the year after Chartres was begun. The choir was finished in 1214, the nave and façade around 1255. Unlike most High Gothic cathedrals, which took their plan from Chartres, Bourges represents a unique departure. By raising the nave arcade — the pier shafts are fifty-four feet high — and reducing the height of the triforium and clerestory, the Bourges master created a church whose lofty proportions are overwhelming. The inner of the two aisles that flank the nave rises to the astounding height of sixty-nine feet — and has its own tripartite elevation. The cathedral shimmers with rainbow-hued light. Bourges' collection of thirteenth-century glass is second only to that of Chartres in quantity and quality.

The massiveness of the cathedral's exterior is accentuated by the absence of a projecting transept. Piercing the broad expanse of the façade are five richly carved portals that exactly reflect the plan of the nave interior.

The plan of the cathedral of *Soissons* shows the unmistakable influence of Chartres. There is the same tripartite elevation, consisting of nearly equal arcade and clerestory levels divided by an arcaded triforium. Begun in 1197, the choir was completed by 1212; the nave by 1225; and the façade by 1250. In the fourteenth century a northern transept arm was added to balance the lovely Early Gothic southern transept, which was built in the 1170's. This charming wing — with its apsidal termination, four-story elevation, and off-center chancel — was miraculously spared during the World War I bombardment that reduced the nave to a near-ruin.

The Romanesque cathedral of *Rouen* was destroyed by fire in 1200; reconstruction along Gothic lines was immediately begun by architect Jean d'Andely. The basic form was completed by 1250 although the southern transept façade was not begun until 1280. Rouen is remarkable for its three beautiful towers and its ornate sixteenth-century façade. Lightning destroyed its central

spire in 1822, and an incongruous cast-iron replacement was installed by 1876. The cathedral suffered serious damage during World War II. In anticipation of the Nazi advance, the outstanding fifteenth-century rose window was removed; the opening is still boarded over.

Notre-Dame de *Reims,* begun in 1210, occupies the site of several earlier cathedrals. As the traditional coronation

site of France's kings, Reims was conceived on a majestic scale. The choir and transept were completed in 1241; the nave and the western façade, to the level of the rose, by 1290. In 1427 — two years before the historic coronation of Charles VII — the last tower of the façade was finally erected.

Although based on the tripartite mode of verticality established at Chartres, Reims has a much longer nave and the inner walls seem even more transparent. Bar tracery appears in the stained-glass windows for the first time. Each column in the sharply pointed nave arcade is adorned with a floral capital that leads the eye effortlessly toward the graceful choir with its single ambulatory and five radiating chapels.

The regal western façade is the stage for five hundred animated figures of saints, angels, kings, and patriarchs. Although severely damaged during World Wars I and II, the cathedral of Reims has been fully restored.

Notre-Dame d'*Amiens* was begun in 1220. Contrary to customary procedure, the nave was completed first, by about 1235. The fire that had consumed the earlier church on the site had spared the old choir; the vaults of the new choir were finally sprung by about 1260.

The largest Gothic cathedral in France, with an area of 9,000 square yards, Amiens is a classic example of High Gothic at its climax. Basing his plan on the Chartrian scheme, Amiens's architect Robert de Luzarches introduced certain modifications appropriate to the huge scale of the cathedral. As at Chartres, the choir consists of four bays flanked by double aisles. Radiating off the single ambulatory are six uniform chapels and one deeper chapel. Wide transept arms stress the Latin-cross shape of the cathedral.

The Gothic tendency to "dissolve" the walls of the nave into a multiplicity of window surfaces and soaring lines reaches its peak at Amiens. The sixty-foot-high nave arcade almost equals the combined height of the triforium and clerestory. And the arched arcade of the triforium is linked visually and structurally to the glazed clerestory by a series of slim colonnettes — creating an unbroken line of dramatic ascent.

The imposing façade of Amiens is dominated by the high placement of its sixteenth-century rose window. The massive twin towers that were completed in the late fourteenth century are logically integrated into the whole. Three deep portals, richly carved in relief, correspond to the three aisles of the nave.

Above an open gallery is the traditional array of kings.

Beset by structural problems and natural disasters, the cathedral of *Beauvais* was never completed. The truncated half-church consists of only a choir and transept. The ambitious choir, begun in

1225, was completed in 1272. One hundred and fifty-seven feet above the pavement, the choir vaults are the highest in the world. But in 1284 they collapsed, destroying portions of the choir and apse. Reconstruction proceeded over the next forty years and additional stout piers were installed for increased strength. Work was suspended until the sixteenth century when the transept arms were built. Undaunted by centuries of bad luck, the architects constructed a five-hundred-foot-high openwork spire above the crossing in 1569. Four years later it fell and was never rebuilt.

The unique façade of the cathedral of *Strasbourg* was begun in 1277 and com-

pleted in the mid-fourteenth century. A huge recessed portal is surmounted by two stories of openwork gables and arcades. The northern tower terminates in an awe-inspiring steeple, 466 feet high, that gives the façade a lopsided majesty. Within, the wide and somber nave is adorned with a series of masterful statues of patriarchs and emperors.

Selected Bibliography

Adams, Henry. *Mont Saint-Michel and Chartres*. Boston: Houghton Mifflin Co., 1933.

Bloch, Marc. *Feudal Society*. Translated by L. A. Manyon. 2 vols. Chicago: University of Chicago Press, 1964.

Bottineau, Yves. *Notre-Dame de Paris and the Sainte-Chapelle*. Translated by Lovett F. Edwards. New York: Rand McNally and Co., 1967.

Branner, Robert. *Gothic Architecture*. New York: George Braziller, 1961.

Evans, Joan, ed. *The Flowering of the Middle Ages*. New York: McGraw-Hill Book Co., 1966.

Fletcher, Banister. *A History of Architecture*. 17th ed., rev. New York: Charles Scribner's Sons, 1967.

Frankl, Paul. *The Gothic*. Princeton: Princeton University Press, 1960.

Gimpel, Jean. *The Cathedral Builders*. New York: Grove Press, 1961.

Jantzen, Hans. *High Gothic*. Translated by James Palmer. New York: Pantheon Books, 1962.

Postgate, R. W. *Revolution from 1789 to 1906*. New York: Harper & Row, 1962.

Roubier, Jean. *Notre-Dame de Paris*. Paris: M.-J. Challamel, 1954.

Simson, Otto von. *The Gothic Cathedral*. New York: Pantheon Books, 1956.

Stoddard, Whitney S. *Monastery and Cathedral in France*. Middletown, Conn.: Wesleyan University Press, 1966.

Temko, Allan. *Notre-Dame of Paris*. New York: The Viking Press, 1959.

Acknowledgments and Picture Credits

The Editors make grateful acknowledgment for the use of excerpted material from the following works:

Cathedrals of France by Auguste Rodin. Translated by Elizabeth Chase Geissbuhler. Copyright 1965 by Elizabeth Chase Geissbuhler. The excerpt appearing on pages 141-42 is reproduced by permission of Beacon Press and Hamlyn Publishing Group Ltd.

Gargantua and Pantagruel by François Rabelais. The extract on pages 151-52 is from The Heritage Press edition, translated by Jacques LeClercq, reproduced by permission of The George Macy Companies, Inc., copyright 1936, renewed 1964.

Paris by Hilaire Belloc. Copyright 1902 by Methuen & Co. Ltd. The excerpt appearing on pages 139-41 is reproduced by permission of A. D. Peters & Co.

Parisian Points of View by Ludovic Halévy. The quotation from the novel appears on page 127. New York: Harper and Brothers, 1894.

"The Rain-beaten Cathedral" by Kotaro Takamura. The selection appearing on pages 159-60 is reproduced by permission of John Murray Ltd.

The Editors would like to express their particular appreciation to the Musée Notre-Dame in Paris for its generous cooperation, to Robert Branner of Columbia University for his critical comments on the text, to Kate Lewin in Paris for her invaluable assistance in obtaining pictorial material, and to Adam Woolfitt in London for his creative photography. In addition the Editors would like to thank the following organizations and individuals:

Centre de Recherches sur les Monuments Historiques — Mme. Legendre
Marilyn Flaig, New York
Pierre Joly — Musée Notre-Dame

The title or description of each picture appears after the page number (boldface), followed by its location. Photographic credits appear in parentheses. The following abbreviations are used:

AN,P	— Archives Nationales, Paris	BL	— Boudot-Lamotte
AP,P	— Archives Photographiques, Paris	MMA	— Metropolitan Museum of Art
BN,P	— Bibliothèque Nationale, Paris	MND(D)	— Musée Notre-Dame (Dorka)

ENDPAPERS Anonymous colored engraving of Notre-Dame, 19th century. Musée Carnavalet (Dorka) HALF TITLE Symbol designed by Jay J. Smith Studio FRONTISPIECE Exterior of southeast side of the apse (Adam Woolfitt) **9** Silver and gilded copper reliquary of the right arm of St. Louis, 14th century. Château de Castelnau-de-Bretenoux, Prudhomat (Dorka) **10** Engraving of the western façade with superimposed spires, from *Discourses on Architecture* by Eugène Emmanuel Viollet-le-Duc, 1889 **12-13** Illumination of Louis II, Duke of Anjou, arriving in Paris, from *Chroniques de Froissart de Louis Bruges*. BN,P, Ms. Fr. 2645, fol 321v

CHAPTER I **14** Gargoyles on the tower (Culver Pictures) **16-17** Notre-Dame from the south at dawn (Adam Woolfitt) **18-19** Three reliefs from a Gallo-Roman votive pillar. Musée de Cluny **20** Illumination of St. Denis preaching in Paris, from *La Vie de Mgr. St. Denis*, 14th century. BN,P, Ms. Fr. 2091, fol 111 **21** Statue of St. Denis, from the Portal of the Virgin (Adam Woolfitt)

22 Illumination of the baptism of Clovis, from *Vie de St. Denys*, 13th century. BN,P, Nouvelles Acquisitions 1098, fol 50 24 Wooden head of a lion, from the Oseburg Find, *c.* 800. Universitetets Oldsaksamling, Oslo 25 Wooden head of a man, from the Oseburg Find, *c.* 800. Universitetets Oldsaksamling, Oslo 26 Illumination of a miracle of the Virgin. BN,P, Ms. Fr. 9198, fol 54 (Giraudon) 29 The nave of the cathedral of Vézelay, 1120-35 (Giraudon)

CHAPTER II 31 Gargoyles on the tower (Adam Woolfitt) 32 top, Serpentine "Paten of St. Denis," 9th century. Louvre; bottom, Illumination of the Bishop of Paris blessing the people at the Fair of Lendit, from *Pontificale Senonense*, 14th century. BN,P, Ms. Lat. 962, fol 264 33 Silver reliquary bust of St. Denis, 14th century. Cathedral Treasury of St. Denis (Adam Woolfitt) 34 Illumination of the letter "I", from St. Gregory's *Moralia in Job*, *c.* 1111. Bibliothèque Publique de Dijon, Ms. 173, fol 41r 35 Illumination of Dagobert overseeing the building of St.-Denis in the 7th century, from *Les Grandes Chroniques de France*, 15th century. BN,P, Ms. Fr. 2609, fol 60v 37 top, The choir and north transept of St.-Denis, 13th century; bottom, The ambulatory of the choir at St.-Denis, 12th century (both, Jean Roubier) 38 Leaf of a diptych *The Mass of St. Giles*, by the Master of St. Giles, 1495. By Courtesy of the Trustees of the National Gallery, London 39 top, Stained glass of Abbot Suger at the feet of the Virgin, from St.-Denis, *c.* 1140 (Jean Roubier); bottom, Illumination of St. Bernard and the Devil. BN,P, Ms. Lat. 10532, fol 330 41 Sardonyx and gold chalice made for Abbot Suger, *c.* 1140. Widener Collection, National Gallery of Art, Washington 42 Two reliefs of student life, from Portal of St. Stephen at Notre-Dame (Jean Roubier) 43 The great seal of Maurice de Sully, *c.* 1170. AN,P 44-45 The tympanum of the Portal of St. Anne. BL 46 Drawing of the spire of Laon cathedral by Villard de Honnecourt, 1225-50. BN,P, Ms. Fr. 19093, fol 10 49 Illumination of *Building the Tower of Babel,* from a Flemish book of hours, 15th century. British Museum, Ms. Add. 35313, fol 34r

CHAPTER III 51 Gargoyles on the tower (Culver Pictures) 52 Illumination of the letter "D", from the *Missal of Jouvenal des Ursins, c.* 1450. Bibliothèque de L'Arsenal (Giraudon) 53 Illumination of the building of twelve churches in honor of the twelve apostles, from *Girart de Roussilon und seine Frau Errichten*, 1448. Oesterreichische Nationalbibliothek, Vienna, Cod 2549, fol 164 54 top, Columns in the ambulatory of the choir of Notre-Dame; bottom, Columns in the south lateral nave (both, Commissariat Général au Tourisme) 56 Illumination of Philip Augustus and Richard Coeur de Lion, from *Histoire de la Terre d'Outremer* by Guillaume de Tyr, 13th-14th centuries. BN,P, Ms. Fr. 24209, fol 272v 57 Statute of a king, possibly Philip Augustus, at Reims cathedral. AP,P 58-59 Illumination of Richard Coeur de Lion tilting with Saladin, from the *Luttrel Psalter, c.* 1340. British Museum, Ms. Add 42130, fol 82 59 Illumination of Richard Coeur de Lion viewing the massacre of the Saracen hostages, from *Passages faiz oultre mer par les François contre les Turcqs*, 1490. BN,P, Ms. Fr. 5594, fol 213 61 The nave of Notre-Dame (Commissariat Général au Tourisme) 62 Illumination of building the Temple of Solomon, from *Le Livre des Anciennetez des Juifs selon la Sentence de Josephe*, by Jean Fouquet, *c.* 1470. BN,P, Ms. Fr. 247, fol 163r 64 Wash drawing of the western façade of Notre-Dame by Viollet-le-Duc, 1848. AP,P 66 top, Tympanum of the Portal of the Last Judgment; bottom, left and right, Details of scenes in Hell and weighing of souls from Portal of the Last Judgment; 67 top, Portal of the Virgin; bottom left, Iron grillwork from door of the Portal of the Virgin; bottom right, Gallery of Kings on the western façade (66-67: All, Adam Woolfitt)

CHAPTER IV 68 Gargoyles on the tower (Adam Woolfitt) 70 Stone and polychrome tomb figure of Eleanor of Aquitaine, 1204-10. Abbey Church, Fontevrault (Brenwasser) 71 Stone bas-relief of the siege of Toulouse, 13th century. Basilique St.-Nazaire, Carcassonne (Dorka) 72 The western façade (Adam Woolfitt) 73 Exterior of the southern rose window (Adam Woolfitt) 74-75 Flying buttresses (both, Adam Woolfitt) 76 The north rose window, built by Jean de Chelles, *c.* 1250. (Adam Woolfitt) 77 The south rose window, restored by Viollet-le-Duc. (Adam Woolfitt) 78-79 Five pages from the sketchbook of Villard de Honnecourt, 1225-50. All: BN,P, Ms. Fr. 19093, fols from left, 1, 19v, 22v, 24v, 17 80 top, Illumination of St. Louis and the bishops, from *Le Grand Coutumier de Normandie*, *c.* 1340. Musée du Petit Palais, Paris (Dorka); bottom, Illumination of the crusades of St. Louis, 15th century. MMA, Gift of J. Pierpont Morgan, 1917 82 Relief of the flight from Egypt, from the Portal of the Cloister (Adam Woolfitt) 83 left, Statue of the Virgin and Child in Notre-Dame, 13th century; right, Relief of the Coronation of the Virgin from the Red Portal, *c.* 1270 (Adam Woolfitt) 84 Polychrome statue of St. Louis, 1306-15. Église de Mainneville (Dorka) 86 Polychrome sculpture of the three wise men and Virgin and Child, from the choir of Notre-Dame by Jean Ravy and Jean le Bouteiller, 14th century (Adam Woolfitt) 87 Silver and gilded copper reliquary of the Shrine of St. Taurin, 1240-55. Église St.-Taurin, Évreux (Dorka)

CHAPTER V 88 Gargoyles on the tower (Adam Woolfitt) 90 Illumination of the funeral of Charles VI, from *Chroniques de Charles VII*, 15th century. BN,P, Ms. Fr. 2691, fol 11r 91 Portrait of Charles VII by Jean Fouquet. Louvre 92 Sketch of Joan of Arc, from a page of the *Register of the Council of Parlement of Paris*, 1429. AN,P (Giraudon) 94 left, Illumination of Martin Luther preaching, 16th century. British Museum, Ms. Add. 4727, fol 2; right, Engraving of rioters in a church, from *Engravings of Scenes from the History of France and the Netherlands* by Franz Hogenberg, 1559–82. Spencer Collection, New York Public Library **95** Detail of an anonymous painting of *The Field of the Cloth of Gold*, 16th century. Her Majesty the Queen. Copyright Reserved **96** Medal commemorating the marriage of Francis II and Mary Stuart by Guillaume Martin, 1558. MMA, Anonymous Gift, 1907 **98** Painting of the *Massacre of the Innocents* by François Dubois, 16th century. Musée Cantonal des Beaux Arts, Lausanne (André Held) **99** Engraving of Henry IV entering Paris by Leclerc after Bollery. BN,P **100** left, Engraving of the second of the three miracles of the Virgin, 1626. Collection Joly (Dorka); right, Engraving of the Te Deum for the victory at Avain, 1635. BN,P **101** Drawing of the arrival at Notre-Dame of the flags taken at Rhinfeld, 1638. Cabinet des Estampes, BN,P **102** Interior of Notre-Dame showing the elevation (Adam Woolfitt) **103** Medal commemorating the Declaration of St. Germain, February 10, 1638, by I. Bernard. Collection Joly (Dorka)

CHAPTER VI **105** Gargoyles on the tower (Adam Woolfitt) **106** top, Marble statue of Louis XIII in Notre-Dame; bottom, Marble statue of Louis XIV in Notre-Dame; both by Antoine Coysevox (both, Adam Wollfitt) **107** left, Pen drawing of the major altar of Louis XIII by Jules Hardouin-Mansard, 1699. AN,P (Dorka); right, Anonymous painting of north crosspiece of Notre-Dame at the end of the 18th century. MND(D) **108** left, Engraving of the southern rose window by Aveline, 1727. MND (D); right, Watercolor of a high window of the nave by Pierre and Jean le Vieil, 1756. AN,P (Dorka) **109** Engraving of the funeral of Philip V, King of Spain, by C. N. Cochin, 1746. MND (D) **110-11** Engraving of the reception of Marie Antoinette at Notre-Dame after the birth of Louis Joseph Xavier François by Née after Moitte, 1782. MND (D) **112** Engraving of the confession of Favras before Notre-Dame by Berthault, 1790. Musée Carnavalet, Paris (Dorka) **113** Engraving of the taking of the Bastille by Janinet, 1789. Collection Roger Castaing (Dorka) **114** left, Engraving of Louis XVI and his family in the prison garden (Bulloz); right, Engraving of the beheading of Louis XVI, from *La Revolution Française* by Berthault, 1793. Cabinet des Estampes, BN,P **115** Sketch of Marie Antoinette by Jacques Louis David, 1793. Louvre (Bulloz) **117** Engraving of the entrance of First Consul Napoleon Bonaparte to Notre-Dame, Easter 1802. Collection Roger Castaing (Dorka) **118** Medal of Napoleon by David d'Angers. MMA, Rogers Fund, 1908 **119** top and bottom, Preliminary sketches of Napoleon and Joséphine for *Le Sacre* by Jacques Louis David, 1805-7. Louvre (Bulloz) **120-21** *Le Sacre*, by Jacques Louis David, 1805–7. Louvre

CHAPTER VII **123** Gargoyles on the tower (Culver Pictures) **124** left, Sketch of the sack of the archiepiscopal palace by Viollet-le-Duc, 1831; right, Portrait of Viollet-le-Duc by Monvoison, 1834. AP,P **125** Watercolor of the demolition around Notre-Dame, 19th century. Collection Joly (Dorka) **126** Watercolor of the reliquary for the Crown of Thorns by Viollet-le-Duc. AP,P **127** Sketch of the choir grilles by Viollet-le-Duc. AP,P **128** The spire by Viollet-le-Duc, 1860 (Adam Woolfitt) **129** The portals of the western façade sandbagged in 1918 (Roger Viollet) **130** The towers from the southeast (Adam Woolfitt) **131** The buttresses from the roof (Adam Woolfitt) **132** De Gaulle and Leclerc at Notre-Dame, August 26, 1944. MND (L.A.P.I.) **135** Notre-Dame at twilight from the east. (Adam Woolfitt)

NOTRE-DAME IN LITERATURE **136** Statue of St. Thomas with the features of Viollet-le-Duc on the spire at Notre-Dame by Geoffroy-Dechaume (Adam Woolfitt) **139** Drawing of the buttress of the tower by Viollet-le-Duc. BL **140-41** Three sketches of church architecture by Auguste Rodin, 1914 (New York Public Library) **142-43** Anonymous engraving of a procession for Sainte Geneviève, 1652. BN,P(D) **144-45** Engraving of a procession for Sainte Geneviève by Blanchard, 1693. BN,P(D) **146-47** Anonymous engraving of the Archbishop of Paris blessing the faithful, 1865. *Monde Illustré*, April 22, 1865 (Dorka) **148-49** Engraving of the consecration at Notre-Dame by F. Thorigay, from *Monde Illustré*, June 11, 1864. BN,P (D) **150** Engraving of Gargantua by Gustave Doré, from *Gargantua* by François Rabelais (The Granger Collection) **152-53** Engraving from Victor Hugo's *Notre-Dame de Paris*, 1882 (Dorka) **154** Engraving of a gargoyle overlooking Paris by Charles Meryon. MMA, H.O. Havemeyer Collection, 1929 **155** Engraving by Steinheil Laisne from Victor Hugo's *Notre-Dame de Paris* (Dorka) **156-57** Engraving of the western façade, from *Collection de Vues de Paris*, 1845-51. George Eastman House **158-59** Engraving of the gallery by Charles Meryon. MMA, Harris Brisbane Dick Fund, 1917 **160** Engraving of Notre-Dame and the Île de la Cité by Charles Meryon. MMA, H.O. Havemeyer Collection, 1929

REFERENCE **164** The nave of the cathedral of Sens. BL **165** top left, The cathedral of Laon (French Government Tourist Office); bottom left, The Royal Portal at the cathedral of Chartres. BL; top and bottom right, drawings by Francis & Shaw, Inc. **166** left, The elevation at the cathedral of Bourges; center, The cathedral of Rouen. Both, BL; right, The western rose window at the cathedral of Reims (French Government Tourist Office) **167** top center, The cathedral of Amiens (French Government Tourist Office); bottom center, The cathedral of Beauvais from the air (Alain Perceval); right, The cathedral of Strasbourg (French Government Tourist Office)

Index

Notre-Dame de Paris is the first venture in joint authorship by Richard and Clara Winston, both noted writers. Mr. Winston has written two biographies, *Charlemagne: From the Hammer to the Cross* and *Thomas Becket,* and is currently completing a volume on Thomas Mann. Mrs. Winston is a novelist with several works to her credit, including *The Closest Kin There Is*. Both Richard and Clara Winston have been recipients of Guggenheim fellowships. Together, the Winstons have translated more than 100 volumes, most recently *Inside the Third Reich* by Albert Speer.

Notre-Dame de Paris is a new volume in the Newsweek Book Division's series of illustrated histories, *Wonders of Man*. Each volume, focusing on a well-known historical monument, is divided into three major sections: a lively and informative history of the monument by a distinguished and authoritative writer, profusely illustrated in color and black and white; a selection of literary excerpts about the monument; and a comprehensive reference section. Other titles in the series include: *The Colosseum, Tower of London, Statue of Liberty, The Pyramids and Sphinx, El Escorial, The Kremlin, Hagia Sophia, The Forbidden City,* and *Versailles*.